CREATIVE POLITICS

Joe Allman
University of Oregon

CREATIVE POLITICS

Goodyear Publishing Company, Inc.
Pacific Palisades, California

Current printing (last digit):
10 9 8 7 6 5 4 3 2 1

ISBN: 0-87620-200-8

Library of Congress Catalog Card Number: 71-179010

Y-2008-4

Printed in the United States of America

CONTENTS

Preface   **ix**

PART I   **GROUND FOR STUDYING POLITICS**   **1**

    Chapter 1   **Problems, People and Politics**   **3**

    Introduction: The Problem and Some
Solutions   3

    About My Values: The Good Life, Good
Society and Creative Politics   9

    Social Control in Human
Organization   13

v

Chapter 2   **Science and the Study of Politics**   19

Some Background on the Discipline of
Political Science   19

What is Science?   22

Behavioral Political Analysis   34

Limitations of the Behavioral Approach   36

Chapter 3   **Evaluating the Study of Politics**   39

An Introduction to a Critical Appraisal   39

What Political Scientists Study and
Teach   40

How Political Scientists Study Problems   44

Evaluating the Scope and Methods of
Political Analysis: Some Sources of
Skepticism   51

PART II   A WAY OF LOOKING AT POLITICS   59

Chapter 4   **Politics in Conflict, Consensus, and Change**   61

Concepts Relevant to Political
Behavior   63

Concepts Relevant to Political Thinking   66

Specifying the Ingredients of Politics   69

A Sketch of the Theory   75

Chapter 5   **Using the Theory to Cope with a Real
Problem**   79

The University as an Example of the
Model and Theory   82

Using the Theory for Diagnosis of and
Prescriptions for the Problem   91

PART III   UNDERSTANDING CHANGE **97**

Chapter 6   Understanding Social Change **99**

The Sources of Social Change   100

Some Things We Mean by Social Change   108

The Direction of Change   113

The Form of Change   115

The Rate of Change   116

Chapter 7   Understanding Changing Society **119**

The Irony of Change   120

Characteristics of Traditional and
Modern Society   124

Beyond Modern: The Post-Industrial
Society   131

Four Types of Political Organizations as
Problem Solving Devices   135

PART IV   CONFLICT AND THE POLITICAL SYSTEM **143**

Chapter 8   Creating and Organizing Power **145**

Toward a Creative Politics   145

Before We Continue   148

The Nature of an Expanding and
Contracting Power Base   149

Making People Aware of Problems   152

The Organization of Power   159

Chapter 9   Using Power **165**

Who Should Rule the Society?   166

Who Does Rule the Society?   171

Two Interpretations of the American
Political Scene   176

Responsible versus Responsive Politics:
A Summing Up and Evaluation   179

Getting it All Together   182

PART V   CONSENSUS AND THE POLITICAL CULTURE   185

Chapter 10   **Making and Changing Political Attitudes**   187

Learning Attitudes About Politics:
Political Socialization   188

Changing Attitudes   194

Two Alternative Political Lifestyles:
Citizen and Subject   201

A Brief Summary and Afterthoughts   206

Chapter 11   **Changing Political Culture**   209

The Use and Abuse of Political Consensus   209

Changing Political Culture: When
Does a Society Change its Mind?   212

Charismatic, Coercive, and Creative
Leadership Styles   216

The Revolution is Over — And Now
What?   219

PART VI   TOWARD A CREATIVE POLITICS   225

Chapter 12   **Politics, Problems and Proposals**   227

The Good Society   228

Creative Politics: Toward the Solution
of the Problems of Post-Industrial
Society   234

Some Proposals for Adaptive Change in
Post-Industrial Society   240

PREFACE

**SOME THINGS I WANT TO SAY
BEFORE YOU READ THIS BOOK:**

I began thinking about and writing this introductory political science text with a dimly perceived but persistently felt realization that my students were no longer reading textbooks. What follows is my attempt to adapt to the none too gentle criticisms of introductory readings by many of my own students.

I have come to see research and teaching as two entirely different kinds of tasks even though as many others were, I was brought up on the myth that a "good researcher is also a good teacher." I now see research as the task of creating information from subjective human experiences. The teacher has the very different task of reconverting such information back into subjectively valid human experience which students can incorporate into their own lives. This conversion of objective information into subjectively understood experience is at the core of the student demand for "relevance." I believe that the teacher can only help students in the process of subjectively experiencing objective theories and data to the extent that he is able to evaluate that information through his own world view. Quite simply, I do not see the teacher as one who passes on information to students, but as one who judges that information and attempts to communicate the meaning such information has given his own way of seeing and evaluating the world about him.

Such logic leads me to impose myself heavily in the substance and writing style of this text. The text is meant to provide students with a way of looking at the often grim realities of politics and a society in which they must survive by understanding, making choices, and acting. It serves as an evaluative framework with which student and teacher can bring together the diversity of our discipline's research and thought, and apply it to living in this mass technological society.

PART I

BACKGROUND FOR STUDYING POLITICS

CHAPTER 1

PROBLEMS, PEOPLE, AND POLITICS

INTRODUCTION: THE PROBLEM AND
SOME SOLUTIONS

These notes serve as an invitation and warning—an invitation to examine and to become aware of the most important human endeavor of our time, and a warning about this book. I am attempting to influence your thinking about and acting in politics. This book, as all others, is affected by the way the author looks at the world. The reader must be aware that what follows is my interpretation of politics and its analysis.

It seems necessary to introduce this book by spelling out the general problem with which politics must cope. Further, I want to make explicit my purposes and values, which affect how I understand these problems and how I interpret research being done on them. What is the problem?

Garrett Hardin, in an article for *Science* magazine, discusses what he terms the "tragedy of the commons."[1] Hardin dramatizes the problem by calling attention to a hypothetical village situation in which each member of the community raises ten cows on a common pasture. It is readily conceivable that as the individual cattleman contemplates the addition of more cattle to his herd he calculates that profits from the additional cattle will be his own, while costs of supporting them will be shared by all the villagers. Assuming the existence here of a "profit motive" and individual rationality, it becomes reasonable for the individual to continue adding cattle. The tragedy of this rational decision is that every individual reasons to the same conclusion. And as each individual adds cattle to those already grazing on the commons, the pasture is rapidly destroyed.

The dilemma so simply clarified in this hypothetical situation involves on the one hand individual goals, and on the other the needs of the community. The questions raised in this example are similar to those which have always confronted politicians and political theorists. These same problems are of vital concern to our own society. Complex analogies to the tragedy of the commons can be found in almost any aspect of social behavior.

We might choose to examine the problem of world population in similar terms. In this case individuals are making "rational" decisions to have children in their own pursuit of religious, economic, and social values. The impact upon the total community is one of overpopulation. Serious scholars of this problem have warned that the population explosion is the most crucial issue of our century. Simply, there are going to be too many people to feed, clothe, and house.

In a more personal example the same dilemma exists in the family situation. Young people, pursuing values such as independence, social mobility, different religious norms, or pre-marital sexual relations, often find that the achievement of these goals is at the expense of the needs and values of the family as a whole. There are thousands of situations which could be used to demonstrate conflict between individual and collective goals. For present purposes we are concerned with identifying and examining solutions.

What we are talking about here deals with how people and countries survive conflicts between individual demands and the interests of the larger community. There are at least four solutions. Perhaps better ones will occur to you. These four are: (1) the technological solution, (2) the natural solution, (3) the behavior control solution, and (4) the "value change" solution.

---

1. Garrett Hardin, "The Tragedy of the Commons," *Science*, 13 December 1968, pp. 1243-48.

The Technological Solution

One of the most elemental aspects of the American experience with problem solving has been a faithlike confidence in science, technology, and knowhow. Whether the solution concerns cotton gins or cybernetics, we have come to believe that there are few tasks, if any, that cannot be accomplished by applying the knowledge and skills of science. Whether we want to reach the moon, wage war, or raise healthy children we seek and often find the solutions through expanding technology.

In the metaphor of the commons we conceptualize a technological solution as one of simply expanding the resources of the common lands so it is possible to sustain the increasing number of cattle. We can imagine better fertilizers to improve the quantity and quality of grass on the pasture, different breeds of cattle more nearly adapted to the limited resources of the commons, the development of food supplements for the people and cattle, and on and on in a spiral of technological magic.

This kind of solution is particularly satisfying from Western civilization's view of man as using his environment to further his own interests. One of the reasons we in America have been naive and unresponsive to our problems is that we have been dramatically successful in making available almost infinite resources. This ability to discover new resources has made it possible for each individual to pursue his own goals without having to deny the interests of the society. Quite simply, if resources are for our purposes infinite, or at least if the capacity to produce such resources is infinite, there is no problem. Each individual pursues that which he values, and because the valued goods are almost inexhaustible, he gets what he wants without denying others in the society the same benefits.

We are only dimly aware of social and economic situations in our country in which people are unable to produce such nearly infinite supply of valued goods or symbols. Such problems do exist. Poverty, race, population, pollution of air and water, and the arms race all may have technological solutions, but little solving has been done so far. Aside from those problems with which we have neither the will nor the way to solve using technology, there are also the problems created when we do solve by technology. For instance, we have met the demands of many people with mass production techniques that require little human effort. As a result many workers have been displaced, and it becomes a new and extremely difficult problem to retrain them for productive lives in other occupations. We met the problem of transportation with production of automobiles which now threaten our survival. They are the largest polluters of the air.

Technology is a solution to many "problems of the commons," but it appears that technological solutions only beget new problems. From such a conclusion, there is a basis for at least looking to other solutions.

The Natural Solution

This second solution to the commons' problem appears both novel and grotesque only because it is foreign to our usual way of looking at the world. The notion of being natural indicates that the solution does not involve human intervention. It in no way indicates a moral judgment.

Let us consider what might be the outcome of the dilemma of the commons if there are no attempts by men to solve the problem. It is inevitable that as the number of cattle on the land increases to a point beyond the capacity of the pasture to sustain life, the cattle will die of starvation. It is also imaginable that most of the cattle and many herders will not survive the famine years. At a time when enough have died to eliminate the overpopulation there will be pasture to support the more fortunate herders and their cattle. One might further guess that survivors will once again increase the size of their herd, have more children and eventually overpopulate the commons with similar grim consequences.

It is not difficult to extend the logic of such a "natural cycle." The continuing development of terrifying weapons by individual countries pursuing their national interest of "self-defense" in turn leads to an exhaustion of human and natural resources for dealing with other problems. In such a way the society is left prey to famine, poverty, disease, pollution, and other problems aside from defense. There are some cheery commentators suggesting quite seriously that if we have a nuclear war there will be enough survivors to rebuild. Even the problem of nuclear war has a natural solution!

This type of natural solution appears ugly and unacceptable to most of us because it relegates man to a position of no more importance than other organisms in the environment. We are a product of Western culture, which contains a deeply rooted belief in the dignity of man and his "right" to survive by using reason and work to intervene in the natural environment. Given this high priority upon the value of human life, it follows that the kinds of solutions to the problem we are most likely to accept must involve some form of human intervention. Technology is one form of intervention, as are the following two alternatives.

Controlling Behavior as a Solution

Maybe it comes from a distorted sense of American culture, but the notion of using social control for solving problems is almost as repugnant to most Americans as is the natural solution discussed above. Deeply ingrained in American thought is the idea that individuals striving unencumbered by political control can overcome most hardships. Perhaps this fantasy of individual initiative is a passing phenomenon in our political culture, but it remains deeply enough instilled to preclude in many people's minds the intrusion of government into the process of contending with social disruptions. Evidently many people in this country still believe that government's anticipation and planning for impending crisis by writing laws and adopting a public policy is almost un-American. How could political control be used to solve the tragedy of the commons?

Again we can imagine that if the villagers, recognizing their mutual problems, had banded together they might have decided to pass a local law controlling the number of cattle a particular herder could have. The law could have been passed, someone given the responsibility to enforce the law, someone else given power to adjudicate grievances arising under the law, and the villagers could have continued to survive. Clearly, the individuals in the village would have had to give up some portion of the valued goods they sought in order for the village as a whole to survive.

Our contemporary political scene offers many examples of the use of political controls for the solution of our problems. We are taxed in order to have money to meet common needs such as defense, welfare, services, education, and health. We have used political controls to work on problems too difficult for individuals to handle, but only when all else seems to fail. When we can no longer cope with a problem with means acceptable to most Americans, when the crisis becomes overwhelming, then we are willing to accept some kind of political intervention through laws and public policy to bind people to modes of behavior necessary for the community's good. With some thought we can see that political control as a solution becomes most necessary in areas where technology has been unable to expand resources. Given finite or limited resources, some form of political solution is required to prevent social disintegration in the crisis.

We are willing to use political control only when the crisis has become so severe it can no longer be ignored. The failing of such solutions in our society is that we still have little sympathy for using control over behavior to *prevent* bad situations from becoming worse. There are few people in this country today willing to support a political program involving a policy limiting the number of children to a single family. And yet such a form of political control might prevent a population crisis in the future. We will accept political control in *response* to crisis, but we have real fears of using control to anticipate and prevent developing problems from reaching crisis proportions.

We have discussed a solution to the problem of the commons which involves expanding the resources available to individuals, another which abandons the events to their "natural" consequences, and a third possibility which requires controlling individual behavior for collective interests. Still a fourth solution can be considered.

The Solution of Changing Man's Values

In the dilemma resulting from the conflict between individual pursuits and public interest, the solution of changing man's values seems to be a double-edged sword. On one edge changing man's values appears to be the least coercive and most humane solution, while on the other edge it appears the most repugnant of the several possibilities discussed. Before evaluating this alternative, let us consider how it could work.

Returning to our village scene for a final time, if the villagers understand their problem is rooted in the "profit motive," they can set about changing that value. They might decide as a community to teach their children and reteach the adults to accept the value of the common good of all villagers as having a higher priority than does self-interest. If they are successful in bringing about this basic change in values a cattleman in the village will be more concerned about maintaining and enhancing the common resources than in improving his individual lot. As a result individuals will discipline themselves in such a way as not to destroy the common resources of the village. With this genuine concern for the good of all villagers, there is no sense of self-denial. In this case the villagers will be controlling their own behavior according to their consciences and attitudes, rather than by laws.

Counterparts of this solution exist at the present time. There are many agencies, public and private, seeking to *reeducate* the population about the problems of birth control, poverty, pollution, race, and arms control. Their major theme is that people must understand that problems of great magnitude require individual sacrifice for solution. You may recall this same theme from President John Kennedy's now classic statement in his 1960 inaugural address, "Ask not what your country can do for you, but what you can do for your country." His appeal was aimed at encouraging individual sacrifice for the common good. This particular solution is perhaps the most acceptable of all the alternatives given for conflict between individual and collective needs. On the other hand, it has a truly terrifying potential.

We might describe such potential with the term *social manipulation,* simply substituting the connotations of propaganda for those of education. Thus, we can easily envision a society much like that in George Orwell's *1984,* in which people are directed totally by agencies of the government through highly sophisticated, mind-controlling mass media and propaganda techniques. It is this side of value change which makes it potentially terrifying as a solution. For if we accept the method of changing people's values as a way of solving our problems we run the risk, however small, of inviting political tyranny over the minds of citizens.

In this sketch of major elements in the problems facing our society today, we have examined the strengths and limitations of four alternative solutions. Hopefully, many of you have begun to discern of my values and attitudes about politics in the foregoing analysis. When teaching introductory courses in political science I begin the term with a brief self-analysis which encourages students to evaluate for themselves the material and analysis presented with full awareness of my own prejudices and values. I believe this kind of exercise is even more critical in a book read by new students of politics. Perhaps the single most important skill you can acquire while reading a book or taking a course is the ability to understand how people's values affect their attempts to explain events going on around them. Whether you are reading newspaper editorials or magazine commentary, listening to television news broadcasts or to politicians' speeches, or reading books such as this one, you must continually strive *to evaluate the source of the information as being separate from the content of the information.* You need not accept any of what follows because you agree with my values, nor need you reject the arguments because you dislike my values. Rather, you need to be able to separate what I have said from who I am and to use that understanding to accept or reject the ideas and analysis. In so doing, you will reason to your own conclusions.

The following sketch of myself may appear a bit novel or pretentious to many people, but I think it a necessary prerequisite for reading and evaluating this text. I offer it with the purpose of facilitating your appraisal of what I have thought.

ABOUT MY VALUES: THE GOOD LIFE, GOOD SOCIETY AND CREATIVE POLITICS

After all the build-up, what follows may seem disappointing. It is not meant as a life history but more as a listing of personal beliefs and thoughts about politics, political science, teaching, and the world I live in. I believe politics is the single most important avenue for insuring mankind's survival.

Politics is a way for individuals and for society to cope with the challenges of a continually changing physical and intellectual environment. Saying that politics is a way for people to cope with change and to adapt for their own survival is not helpful unless I specify both the ways in which such coping and adaptation occur as well as their purposes.

Individuals, in order to increase certainty about themselves and their world, cope with and adapt to continuing change in their environment by making and influencing choices. Every man has a need for some certainty or predictability about himself and what goes on around him; obviously some people can tolerate more uncertainty than others, but we all need some level of assurance about what is happening. For instance, upon leaving high school and entering a new and uncertain world, young people make choices about college, marriage, occupation, and other possibilities so that they may increase certainty in their lives.

We become more human as we engage in the process of understanding ourselves and our society with the purpose of making choices about how we will act to confirm and expand this understanding. It is also clear to me that we can fulfill our needs for certainty without making choices. We can increase our certainty by the uncritical acceptance of religious, political, social, or scientific explanations about ourselves and the world. We can also increase certainty by accepting dictates (from parents, teachers, and political leaders) that tell us what we are all about as people and society. All these ways of increasing certainty may or may not be useful in helping us effectively cope with our changing environment, and they may or may not permit us to make choices about how we act in relation to change. For myself (and I believe for others as well), the good life is one in which I come to understand myself and my society and am able to realize that understanding through making choices about how I will act to confirm or expand my self-concept and world view.

If the good life for individuals involves understanding of self and society and making and acting upon choices based in that understanding, then the "good society" must necessarily be one that makes available opportunities for such learning, choice-making, and action. These are my basic values about the good life for individuals and the good society. It should be clear that others may hold different values. Some people may assume that the values of the good life and society include physical welfare. Other people may assume that the good life and society are relatively free of conflict, violence, and instability. And still other people may prefer a life and society in which people are restrained from acting out their basic selfishness and evil impulses. There are many different conceptions of the good life and society. I have tried to make mine explicit. It will help you evaluate much that I have written in the rest of this book.

Now I need to clarify in some detail the relationships I see among such notions as the good life for individuals, the good society, and the processes of politics.

I have suggested that the good life begins with understanding ourselves and our society. In a real sense this book is an attempt to provide some understanding about society and politics and other aspects of the world. But here I need to specify more clearly my beliefs about what we need to understand about ourselves—things internal rather than external. Those things about ourselves which we need to understand include physical and psychological needs. What do I think these needs are? The physical needs are biological requirements for survival. They include such things as air, water, sleep, and food. The satisfaction of these biological needs is generally accepted as a requirement for our survival. Not so generally understood, particularly in our society, are the psychological needs we have. The satisfaction of these needs, just as with the biological ones, is necessary for our survival. In the same sense that physical survival depends upon meeting biological needs, human development and living are dependent upon meeting psychological needs. So what are these psychological needs?

We need to be relatively certain about who we are and to be able to accept that fact. We also need to be able to act and to think in ways that will confirm and expand what we know and accept about ourselves. The good life that I have defined is not some distant end-state of affairs that we may someday achieve, but is rather a process in which we can actively engage right now. So, for me, the good life does not involve what we do in order to achieve some Utopia, but what we are and can become in the process of making choices to satisfy our needs.

There are really two kinds of choices being discussed here. Personal choices are those we make which affect our own lives. Public choices are those made by the society and its political processes which also affect our personal lives. The basic theme with which I have chosen to begin this book is that there is often a conflict between individual choices and public choices. With some reflection we become agonizingly aware that in our present society public choices have as much if not more impact upon our personal lives than the individual choices we make.

As our government, which is the primary institution for making public choice, decides to value such priorities as defending our national security against the "threat of communism" by fighting in foreign lands, or as our government decides to spend greater and greater amounts of our human and natural resources to construct weapons for war, or as our government decides to spend less of its resources upon human survival and welfare, it makes public choices and decisions which bind us to future courses of events which will have a dramatic impact upon our own and our children's lives. In the light of this fact the good life for individuals cannot be obtained merely by our being aware of and accepting ourselves and by making choices and acting out their consequences in the attempt to confirm and expand our self-awareness. The good life also requires that we have some ability and opportunities to control the public choices which to an ever greater extent affect our personal lives. The good society is one that not only makes available opportunities for individual learning, choice-making, and action, but, and perhaps more importantly, makes available opportunities for affecting the decision-making processes for public choice-making. It is in this context that I have come to think of politics as the means we use to control ourselves and others. If this is politics, what I have chosen to call a "creative politics" is one in which people have more opportunity and ability to make choices which not only control their lives but the society's future as well.

With these criteria of the good life, the good society, and creative politics in mind, we are now equipped to evaluate our society and its politics in terms of whether it furthers or retards the development of such criteria as I have described. In other words we can evaluate our society as getting better or worse by the extent to which it enables us to make personal choices which give meaning to our lives, and also as it enables us to affect the public choices which control and determine much of our future.

In the same sense that it is impossible to fulfill ourselves without being aware of who we are, it is also impossible to have a creative politics without being aware of how politics operates. The balance of this book is an attempt to explain the processes in our society which must be understood and controlled in order to design and bring about a creative politics, the good society, and to engage people in the good life.

If in this secular age one can have a faith, mine is politics. Decisions that have been and will be made about the quality and the very fact of life itself will be made politically. Whether we decide as a society to launch ourselves into the hell of nuclear fury, to reach for the stars through space exploration, or to set about the task of improving the conditions of mankind, political decisions will shape much of history yet to be written.

I have also some beliefs about the discipline of political science which affect what I write in this book. I believe that our actions and attitudes as political scientists can also be evaluated by the extent to which those values and activities contribute to making choices and to having more control over the future. I will expand upon this notion in Chapter 3.

As to my beliefs about teaching, I do not really believe that a teacher can teach anyone much of anything. I believe that whether I am in a classroom or writing a book I can only encourage certain motives, attitudes, and behaviors which permit meaningful learning. The basic motive for learning is that of problem-solving. And the most necessary ingredient for problem-solving is a critical and sympathetic skepticism. This skepticism requires trust and a tolerance of uncertainty, qualities often lacking in both students and teachers.

Just a few more words about my general world view will suffice to the extent that it affects what I write. I tend to be pessimistic about the trends shaping the future of our society. As a government we are little more than a historical experiment. The experiment has thus far proved in many ways to be man's most successful attempt to solve problems in a just and equitable manner. But past problems are overshadowed by those problems yet to be confronted. There exists in my mind the possibility that if we fail in this political experiment we will come to the conclusion that has plagued man through the ages. As so many have before us, will we escape individual responsibilities and freedoms for the security of tyranny and dictatorship?

As responsible human beings, we must anticipate, plan, and carry out programs of public action to solve our problems as well as those of the world community. Or, we may well be left with the bitter evidence of an era which proved to be no more than a fragile, interesting, and unsuccessful period of human experimentation in justice and freedom.

Saying all of this, I am still optimistic about human nature. My optimism derives more from a faith in what man can be than from any evidence of what he is likely to do. I like to think that as man faces the challenges of complex societal change he will use these problems as a means of establishing his existence as being human, different from other organisms, a cause as well as a consequence of the changes which mold life itself. Hopefully, the narrative will be useful in the evaluation of the following material. And this leads to a discussion of the conceptualization and organization of the book.

With the present chapter serving as a prelude, Chapter Two introduces some of the background of the discipline of political science. Chapter Three attempts to evaluate both what political science studies and how it carries out such studies. But before we turn to these matters we need some further clarification of political processes.

SOCIAL CONTROL IN HUMAN ORGANIZATION

We can continue by stating that *"politics" means the ways we control ourselves and others and are controlled by others as we adapt our thinking and behavior to decide how to solve problems arising from changes occurring in our shared environment.* Now we can re-examine the four solutions to the tragedy of the commons to see which of them qualify as political, given the requirements of our definition.

Neither the technological nor the natural solution is political. The technological solution is an attempt to increase the capacity of society to produce valued goods and does not involve the ways people use to control one another. The natural solution does not involve any human intervention for control or any other purpose. However, the third and fourth solutions are attempts to control human thinking and behavior to solve problems resulting from change. By our definition then, these two solutions are political in that they involve control over human behavior. The behavior control alternative as we described it controls man's behavior through laws and public policy which bind that behavior. The fourth solution, that of changing man's values, is an attempt to control behavior through changing the way individuals think they should behave. We need to examine this question of control of human behavior in greater detail.

It might help to think of political control as being divided into two types—external controls and internal controls. One type of political control derives from sources external to individuals in the society. For instance, when people's behavior is controlled by the existence of laws, police, parents' dictates and group pressures, their behavior is being controlled externally. It may be useful to think of these external controls as having the common characteristic of operating as a sanction, positive or negative. Positive sanctions operate to control people by rewarding desired behavior traits, while negative sanctions operate to punish undesired behavior traits.

Much of students' behavior is controlled by rewarding them with good grades, status positions among their fellow students, and a degree which allows them access to the most sacred of social awards—a good salary. In order to gain all of these wonders a student has only to be well behaved, studious, dedicated (or perhaps conniving). On the other hand when a student behaves in some undesired manner (i.e., undesired by professors or deans) he can be punished with bad grades, no degree, suspension, and perhaps by being denied access to a professional occupation.

Various positive and negative sanctions are available to the society to regulate behavior of members, but clearly there are not enough "policemen" to watch everyone all the time, so we need to look at other forms of social control which are operative in stable societies. This other form I have termed *internal control*. It is a kind of control which is internalized into the habits, social mores, and individual consciences of a society; that is, internalized into individual thought processes. Internal controls operate within the individual and make external control unnecessary. The most obvious examples of such internalized controls are such things as religious norms (e.g., Thou shalt not kill, or steal), social traditions (doing something because your father and his before him did it that way), and values learned in the family. We could enumerate many examples of internalized controls, which makes the point that individuals, through innumerable ways, learn or internalize attitudes about what is appropriate behavior, and this knowledge in turn serves to control their actions in society.

If we understand social control as deriving from both external and internal sources, it becomes possible to construct a typology of social organizations around varying levels (distributions) of these two types of control. What we are going to do is not nearly as difficult as the previous sentence makes it sound. The following diagram will help clarify this point.

Figure 1 is an illustration of three different hypothetical societies, each with a different distribution of external and internal control operative.

FIGURE 1

**THE RELATIONSHIP BETWEEN RATIONALITY
AND SOCIAL CONTROL**

PRE-RATIONAL SOCIETY	RATIONAL SOCIETY	IRRATIONAL SOCIETY
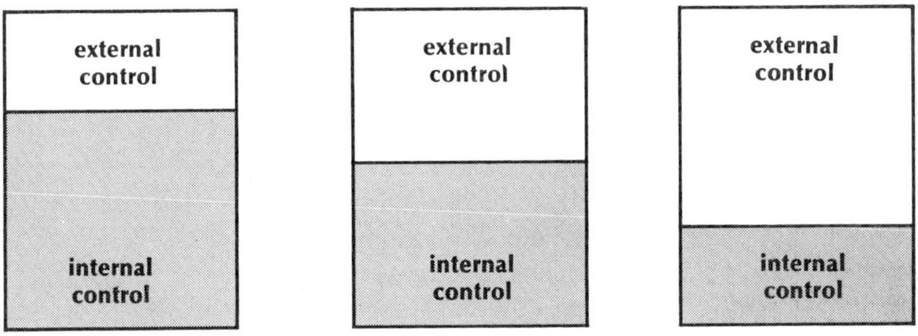 external control	external control	external control
internal control	internal control	internal control

Perhaps more detail about each type of social organization will clarify the typology above, but also I need to explain why I have chosen to equate varying degrees of rationality with these three distributions of external and internal control. As illustrated in the diagrams in Figure 1, pre-rational social organization is characterized by a preponderance of internalized control and a minimum of external control. Irrational society reverses this with a preponderance of external control and a minimum of internal control. What I have called rational social organization is constituted of a balance between the two types of control.

Hypothetically, in a pre-rational society we would expect to find most of the social behavior resulting from ingrained traditions and mores about how individual members of the society should behave. Peasants work the fields and obey the members of the aristocracy, who work the peasants and give orders. This hierarchy occurs because it is the way it has always been. Usually such traditional behaviors are supported by elaborate mythologies about the "divine right" of the aristocracy to lead and the not-so-divine right of the peasants to follow. In any case little external sanction is necessary because most of the people in such a society have internalized these modes of behavior as being the proper way for them to behave.

Another type of society is one which secures very little control from obedience and loyalty, but which for the most part derives control from threats and coercion. In such a society the rulers rely primarily upon their police and armies to coerce behavior consistent with the leader's goals for the society. These societies are usually further characterized by extensive efforts to destroy or to break down traditions and social mores and to replace them with the new regime's definition of social behavior and citizenship.

Finally, then, we turn to the example of a society which is composed of approximately equal parts of internal and external control. In such societies there are clearly many behavior traits which do stem from loyalty and individual willingness to accept the legitimacy or appropriateness of the rulers and regime, but at the same time conflicts erupt that require external control for their resolution. We could go on to supply further detail and illustration of these three types of societies, but for the present it is sufficient for you to have these distinctions in mind so that we now can turn to the problem of relating these hypothetical types of human organization to rationality.

Let us look at the notion of rationality. We do not need a sophisticated discussion of rationality, but we do need to ascribe some meaning to the term. We can think of rationality as choosing the most appropriate alternative of several possibilities for achieving a chosen goal. Both the goal and the means of achieving the goal must result from a choice among available alternatives. In other words your choice of going to college was rational to the extent that it was considered as one of several alternatives available to you and you decided that it was indeed the most appropriate way to gain some chosen life goals you have. Few human decisions ever approach fulfilling such a procedure, but some decisions approach this requirement more closely than others. Perhaps your decision to go to college was more rational than your decision to take this particular course, for instance. The same principle is true for the collective decisions which bind societies to specific policies pursuing a collectively chosen goal. Some decisions are more rational than others. With this notion of rationality in mind we can relate the pursuit of rational policy-making to the distribution of external and internal control in the society.

Central to the argument here is that rational political decisions by definition must involve the availability of alternative choices about goals and means to reaching these goals. If we examine pre-rational society it becomes evident that in such social organization choices are not available because behavior is determined by existing patterns or traditions of living in the society. On the other hand, what I have termed irrational social organization is also characterized by a lack of available alternatives in that a particular elite makes the decisions, which may be planned and calculated but are primarily a function of the elite's understanding of the alternatives. Hypothetically, such a society has difficulty getting information and alternatives from dissenting or opposing groups. Putting down dissent or conflict may preserve the elite's power, but it also reduces alternatives available from opposing sides that might otherwise enter into the equation of rational decision-making.

We are then left with the examination of the case in which there is a balance between external and internal controls. In this case there is enough internal control to allow stability, but not so much as to preclude dissent and conflict, which would require the imposition of external control. The conflict among opposing viewpoints increases the number of alternatives in the decision-making process. If the conflict is not put down with coercion it becomes more likely that the conflicting views will increase the rationality of the decision-making processes.

There is one further point that needs making. I have chosen to use the terms *pre-rational, rational,* and *irrational* to suggest the outlines of what may be a very brief history of social development. It makes sense to think of the transition through these three types as being one from early forms of social organization (pre-rational), which have yet to develop the levels of conflict required to ensure more rational decision-making, to the second type (rational). As the internal controls of the pre-rational society break down under the forces of development and modernization, conflict increases to the point where a balance between internal and external controls exists—that is, a rational social organization exists. It is also entirely conceivable that if these increasing conflicts created by the breakdown in internal controls are not adequately resolved, then external controls will become necessary to hold the society together. This leads to a preponderance of external control as in the irrational society—society which I term as being irrational in the sense that the elites within the society have consciously chosen to return to a form of human organization similar in many ways to the form of the pre-rational society. The difference is that the irrational form is bound by coercion rather than tradition.

It is not my intent to argue for some inevitable historical sequence of events, but to ignore the possibility is foolish. It is my belief that such a transition is not inevitable, nor even necessarily probable, but that our ignorance may promote its occurrence. If such a historical transition from pre-rational through rational to irrational social organization does exist, we must understand it to control it. *We do not have the choice of being free or being controlled.* We are already controlled by complex factors, many of which are beyond our awareness. *Our choice is to be aware or to be ignorant. Awareness of those conditions which control us gives us the ability to control these conditions and our own existence.*

This problem of awareness is disproportionately large. It is an appropriate challenge to a new student of politics.

Having established the proportions of the problem, we can now turn to the study of politics to understand its processes and how they may contribute to facilitating or retarding a creative politics and a better society. We begin with a brief sketch of the development of the discipline of political science as it has given its attention to the analysis of these problems.

Summary

In summary, just as in the illustration of the commons, the problem facing present society is the conflict between the pursuit of individual interests and the collective good. We have discussed four solutions, two of which are political—changing behavior and changing values. They are political because they involve the ways in which men are controlled and the ways they control others as they try to solve common problems. The way in which a society is ruled has to do with the distribution of external and internal controls. If it is ruled with a preponderance of internal controls, it is a pre-rational society. If internal and external controls are utilized more or less equally, it is a rational society. If it is controlled externally the result is an irrational society.

Politics is a way to affect our own and our society's future. A creative politics and good society help individuals make choices and have more control over their own lives.

CHAPTER 2

SCIENCE AND THE STUDY OF POLITICS

SOME BACKGROUND ON THE
DISCIPLINE OF POLITICAL SCIENCE

What is the discipline of political science? What is science? Where are we going in the study of politics? We need some answers to these questions before we proceed.

The last chapter was a statement of my personal beliefs about people, society, politics and the solution of problems. We examined some alternative solutions to the problem of individual and public choice, and then related both the problem and the alternative solutions to the process and purpose of politics. I see politics as being the major vehicle for solving the most critical problems we have today. This chapter is intended to provide some better understanding of the discipline of political science. Here we will be concerned with how political scientists have studied the problems they thought significant. We will look at the influence of science on the ways political scientists have studied problems generally. The third chapter will attempt to evaluate scientific political analysis by placing it in the context of other approaches to research, and we will return to the problems and concepts involved in political analysis in the fourth chapter.

If we begin this part of the discussion by identifying the purposes of studying politics, it may provide some understanding of the discipline of political science. Many political scientists would agree upon such purposes as evaluation, planned reform, description, and explanation of political events and activities. There has been disagreement as to which of these objectives is most important. Each goal has advocates among political scientists today. The varying importance of these purposes as well as their existence reflects both the change and continuity in the history of the discipline of political science.

As were the earliest Greek scholars, students of politics are in pursuit of the ingredients of the "good life" for individual citizens in a community. We seek to understand which type of political organization best ensures individual pursuit of valued goals while maintaining the common good. This emphasis on evaluating alternative goals and political organizations used to gain these goals can be identified as a normative inquiry. The purpose of such inquiry is to evaluate, prescribe, and plan the best form of political life for the society. Normative political analysis deals with such questions as: What means should rulers use in ruling? What goals should the rulers and the ruled have for their society? When should individuals revolt to preserve their rights? When should government coerce to maintain the public interest? For centuries prior to our own scholars sought answers to such questions in fragile, if eloquent, methods of speculative reasoning based in individual insight and understanding.

Just prior to this century, as the study of politics emerged in this country as a formal discipline of political science, the analysis changed to emphasize the description of political organization rather than the evaluation of means and ends. Evidently, political scientists assumed that the fundamental questions concerning the best form of political organization had been answered by the existence of the United States as a workable government. Given this assumption it was logical to shift from evaluating alternative governments to describing the institutions and organizations of our own government. The question was no longer, What is the best form of government for men? Rather it was, How can political scientists more accurately describe the organization and operation of our particular government? They were intent upon describing legal institutions and political organizations such as constitutions, laws, executive offices, and legislatures as well as the less formal organizations associated with American government—such organizations as political parties, pressure groups, and economic elites. If description was not the only activity of political science in the early decades of this century, it was certainly the most important. The discipline was still in the business of evaluating and planning, but only as to the improvement and reform of our political institutions and organizations as democratic mechanisms. Political scientists worried about corruption and inefficiency in city government, the replacement of political bosses with civil servants, and the most efficient organization of public administration. In general political scientists searched for ways to make our government a better way of achieving the "good life" for citizens.

Perhaps the accumulated disillusionments of depression and World War II provided the conditions for the next shift in the focus of political inquiry. A rapidly changing world with cold, warm, and hot wars, young, developing countries, and old, undeveloping countries shattered many assumptions and forced old questions back into the minds of many political scholars. Not only the previous answers but also the methods of arriving at these answers became suspect. Some political scientists came to distrust the methods and goals of previous political analysis. These political scientists were convinced that different assumptions and methods were needed to understand the exploding complexity of the postwar world. One major response to such thoughts has been to rely more heavily upon science to solve these difficult problems.

This shift in emphasis was focused primarily upon scientific explanation, whereas previous stages of political inquiry had emphasized evaluation, planning, or description. This is not to suggest that scientific analysis does not involve description, evaluation and planning—it most certainly does. But this newer approach seeks to use description to explain the whys and hows of politics, in order to evaluate and plan a better society.

In this brief sketch of the development of the discipline, the intention is not to suggest any necessary direction in the changing emphasis from goals of evaluation and planning to goals of description and finally to goals of scientific explanation. Rather, different approaches have been necessary for the different social and intellectual conditions existing throughout history. Being a complex and varied discipline, political science incorporates all of these goals for political analysis. Some political scientists, acting as philosophers, attempt to understand, prescribe, and justify what individuals and society should be doing. Others prefer to describe accurately the historical and institutional context from which our present political structures and policies have developed. In order to achieve planned reforms and influence public policy, a growing number of political scientists are taking a more active part in political action and policy analysis. And still others are persuaded to focus their efforts on the construction of a science of political behavior. None of these practices is exclusive of the others; therefore, as in most professions, political scientists act in a variety of roles. The advisability of the use of scientific procedures to study politics has been the center of debate among political scientists since the earliest days of the existence of a formal discipline in American universities; it may be useful to examine the approach in some detail.[1]

WHAT IS SCIENCE?

How does one know what he believes to be true is actually true? In thinking about this question you may conclude that you have different ways of knowing what is true or credible. In day-to-day situations we make decisions that are based on varying kinds of beliefs about what is true. Some beliefs which affect our choices about an appropriate course of action we consider true for us, if not for others, because we have faith in their certainty. Religious beliefs are usually of this sort. These are truths held as self-evident.

Other beliefs are derived from authoritative sources. In other words we hold these beliefs because something or somebody credible to us says they are true. Such sources include parents, teachers, close friends, textbooks, holy writings, editorials, or a widely held common belief. For instance, I may believe democracy to be the best form of government primarily because many people I know share this belief. Or I may believe what the President says about a particular policy issue because I expect information from this authority to be credible.

Our ability to reason provides still another way of knowing. One philosopher discussing these matters has called such beliefs derived from reason as constituting "a priori" understanding.[2] He claims that beliefs " ... of this sort have not usually rested upon any observed facts, at least not in any great degree. They have been chiefly adopted because their fundamental propositions seemed 'agreeable to reason.' This is an apt expression. It does not mean that which agrees with experience but, that which we find ourselves inclined to believe."[3] It may appear entirely reasonable to me that people who neither read nor write should not be able to vote. Of course, were I illiterate the proposition might seem less reasonable. In any case many of our beliefs derive from this "obviousness" to our concept of reason.

---

1. Albert Somit and Joseph Tanenhaus, *The Development of Political Science* (Boston: Allyn and Bacon, 1967), pp. 27-30.

2. Charles Peirce, "The Fixation of Belief," in *Basic Problems of Philosophy*, ed. D. J. Bronstein et. al (Englewood Cliffs, N. J.: Prentice-Hall, 1955), pp. 40-50. This discussion is a rather loose interpretation of Peirce's typology.

3. pp. 46-47.

Each of these three ways of knowing shares the common property of not requiring evidence to make it acceptable. We accept beliefs from faith, reason, or authoritative sources without asking that they be supported by the evidence of observed experiences. But many beliefs do rest upon evidence, and thus provide a fourth way of knowing.

We know that some things are true because we experience them. When we see, hear, or somehow perceive events, we are most likely to accept beliefs derived from these experiences as true. Beliefs derived from observed experiences are called *empirical beliefs.* We are most confident of empirical beliefs. Once we are "shown," we are fairly certain we know. And because we are so certain of beliefs based on observation we run headlong into a major problem. If I distinguish between two types of empirical beliefs it may be easier to understand the problem. Both common sense and scientific beliefs are based upon observation, but there are critical differences in the manner in which the man on the street derives and accepts empirical beliefs and the manner in which the scientist derives and accepts empirical beliefs. The problem is, since both kinds of empirical beliefs come from observation of events and objects it is sometimes difficult for people to understand why the researcher's information and explanation is more credible than the conclusions of anyone who has observed similar occurrences. In other words, is not the scientist just talking in a more complicated way about observations which are already obvious to everyone? Paul Lazarsfeld, in a similar discussion, answers the question in a persuasive manner.[4] He lists the following statements and explanations, which are typical of research findings in social science:

1. Better educated men showed more psycho-neurotic symptoms than men with less education. (The mental instability of the intellectual as compared to the more impassive psychology of the man-in-the-street has often been commented on.)
2. Men from rural backgrounds were usually in better spirits during their Army life than soldiers from city backgrounds. (After all, they are more accustomed to hardships.)
3. Southern soldiers were better able to stand the climate in the hot South Sea Islands than Northern soldiers. (Of course, Southerners are more accustomed to hot weather.)
4. White privates were more eager to become non-coms than Negroes. (The lack of ambition among Negroes is almost proverbial.)
5. Southern Negroes preferred Southern to Northern white officers. (Isn't it well known that Southern whites have a more fatherly attitude toward their "darkies"?)
6. As long as the fighting continued, men were more eager to be returned

4. Paul Lazarsfeld, "The American Soldier: An Expository Review," *The Public Opinion Quarterly* Vol. 13, no. 3 (Fall, 1949), pp. 377-404.

to the States than they were after the German surrender. (You cannot blame
people for not wanting to be killed.)[5]

After allowing the reader some time to read through these statements, Lazarsfeld goes on to establish the position taken by scientific
researchers in the following way:

> We have in these examples a sample list of the simplest type of interrelation-
> ships which provide the "bricks" from which our empirical social science is
> being built. But why, since they are so obvious, is so much money and energy
> given to establish such findings? Would it not be wiser to take them for granted
> and proceed directly to a more sophisticated type of analysis? This might be
> so except for one interesting point about the list. *Every one of these statements
> is the direct opposite of what actually was found.* Poorly educated soldiers
> were more neurotic than those with high education; Southerners showed no
> greater ability than Northeners to adjust to a tropical climate: Negroes were
> more eager for promotion than whites; and so on.
>
> If we had mentioned the actual results of the investigation first, the reader
> would have labelled these "obvious" also. Obviously something is wrong with
> the entire argument of "obviousness." It should really be turned on its head.
> Since every kind of human reaction is conceivable, it is of great importance
> to know which reactions actually occur most frequently and under what condi-
> tions; only then will a more advanced social science develop.[6]

The point to the above discussion is that it provides some rationale
for gaining a clearer understanding of the activities involved in scientific
research and what such activities contribute to understanding politics.

The Process of Science

As creatures of a technological culture we have given an almost
religious significance to science. Science permeates our evaluation of nearly everything. If it is "scientific" then it is good, true and even a little holy.
If an advertiser wants to sell his product he uses either sex or science to
justify his claims about the product. Each side in a political debate claims
that research verifies its position, whether the issue be Vietnam, the urban
crisis, or fluoridation of drinking water. Serious thought reveals a notion
of science as a body of reliable facts or information which scientists are
busily storing away in computers and libraries. This can be called a substantive definition of science. In this view science is a body of accumulated
information.

Another conception of science emphasizes the activities of the scien-

5. Lazarsfeld, p. 380.
6. Lazarsfeld, p. 380.

tist as he examines and attempts to understand problems. This latter view, which can be referred to as a "process" conception of science, is the more attractive of the two. To clarify what this means, you might think of science as a sequence or process of interrelated thoughts and actions which are carried out in order to solve problems. It is what the scientists are doing and thinking that is important in this conception rather than the products of their activity. By watching the scientist at work we could observe three different types of operations that he carries out. There is no particular order in which we might expect this thinking and activity to take place, but the following stages are usually apparent in any scientific research: (1) identifying a problem; (2) theorizing about the problem; and (3) observing to test the theory.

Identifying a Problem

Learning begins with a problem. Problems make us ask questions. As long as we have "the answer" we learn little, but when we are unsure, as is often the case when facing new or difficult problems, we begin to learn. Science, being a form of learning, often enough begins with the researcher identifying and defining a problem by asking a question about the relationship between two or more events or conditions.

There are questions and then there are questions. Some questions can be answered by scientific research and others cannot. You might consider the following two questions: What is the relationship between socio-economic conditions of people and the likelihood that they will become involved in violent activity? Should people living under inhumane social and economic conditions have the right to use violence to improve their situation? Those are two very different kinds of questions. The first question or problem is concerned with the relationship between several variable conditions that can be observed and measured. The researcher can actually observe such variables as level of income, extent of formal education, and religious preference of people who are involved in types of violence such as strikes, riots, crimes, and revolution.

The second question, however, asks for justification of the use of violence. Is it right for people to use violence? This second type of question can be thought of as a normative inquiry since it deals with justifying an event by examining personal values or social norms. The answers to normative questions must evolve from an examination of our values and the values of others concerning such matters as justice, freedom, law and order, use of force, and rights of individuals. Such questions cannot be answered in a scientific manner. Science can answer questions about what the relationship between observable events is, but it cannot answer the question of what these relationships should be. You cannot see right or wrong, good or bad, or what should or should not be. These are matters of value judgment, not observation. Questions that can be answered by observation are empirical questions. Science begins with empirical questions about variable relationships. So—what are variables?

The scientist may want to conceptualize the events or objects in the relationship he is questioning as being either *dependent or independent variables.* The independent variables are thought to be associated with the dependent variables in such a way as to alter or have an effect on the way in which the dependent variables vary. You might consider the question above about the relationship between socio-economic conditions and participation in violent activity. A particular socio-economic variable such as income (which might vary from less than $3,000 to over $20,000 per year) might stand as the independent variable. The expectation is that the variation in income, from lower to higher, will affect the variation in probability that people will be involved in a particular form of violent behavior—possibly fist fights—a variable which can range from a person's never being involved to his being in a brawl every Saturday night.

Science deals with empirical questions about relationships among variables that can be observed and measured. This is the beginning of research. Once a problem has been defined in this manner it is possible to begin theorizing.

Theorizing About the Problem

First, you should be aware of what a theory is in order better to understand the process of theorizing. A theory is simply *an unconfirmed explanation of the relationship among variable events.* There are two key words in this definition— "unconfirmed" and "explanation"—we need to look at both to get a better grasp of this notion of a theory.

By saying that a theory is unconfirmed, I mean to emphasize a theory is not a scientific law or general finding. Theories exist to be tested by observing real events and then either to be confirmed or to be rejected. Confirmed, they become valid generalizations or laws. For instance, we seldom speak of a theory of gravity, but more often of the law of gravity, since this notion of physical science has repeatedly been confirmed by countless observations at different times and in different places. Most of the explanations we work with in the social sciences lack any great degree of confirmation, so presently we deal primarily in theory and only seldom do we have laws of political behavior.

The idea that a theory is unconfirmed is simple enough, but what of the notion of explanation? What is explanation? There are a couple of things that an explanation does. First it tells how observed experiences are ordered and second it tells how the experiences occur in that particular way. *In saying an explanation permits the ordering of experiences, I mean that it specifies the relationship among variables by explaining the problem in such a manner that, having information about the independent variables, we can make predictions about the dependent variables.*

I might try to explain partially the fact that some people participate in political activities more than other people by specifying independent variables such as age, education, occupation and political party support— factors which I expect to have an impact on the dependent variable, which is the extent of political participation. A successful explanation must specify how people of varying ages, jobs, levels of education and political party support are likely to vary in the intensity of their political activity. The key term in this part of the discussion is *prediction.* When the researcher can predict what will happen to a dependent variable by measuring and by knowing the value of an independent variable, he can say that he has gone part of the way to explaining the relationship. For example, political scientists know that people who are most intensely partisan in their political affiliation (independent variable) are most likely to vote (dependant variable). Thus political scientists partly explain the finding that some people are more likely than others to vote by predicting and by confirming through observation that those who feel most strongly about their political views will be the ones most likely to vote.

Many people have argued that prediction is the only criterion of a valid explanation,[7] but the explanation must not only order experiences (e.g., permit prediction of certain variables from other known variables), it must also provide a reason or tell why the particular ordering of experiences has occurred. To fulfill this part of the definition with the example above, it is necessary to provide reasons why age, education, occupation, and the intensity of party support might be expected to alter the likelihood of political activity. It may be suggested that as people get older they are free of many demands upon their time such as the demands of young children, and the pressure of finding jobs, so that they have more time to be involved in political activity. I could also reason that people from certain professions have more immediate interests in political affairs (e.g., lawyers, businessmen, and public officials) and are, therefore, more likely to be

---

7. A typical textbook definition of theory normally emphasizes the notion of prediction. For example, "Theories are general statements that apply to specific events. They unify facts into an integrated body of knowledge and help predict new events by deducing their occurrences from theoretical assumptions." Quote taken from Howard H. Kendler, *Basic Psychology* (New York: Appleton-Century-Crofts, 1963), p. 16.

involved, a fact which would explain why there might be a relationship between the variable of occupation and the degree of participation in politics. To complete this illustration I would have to think through similar reasons for and effects of each of the specified variables. But for our purposes it may be enough to say that explanation should provide both prediction and reason. The prediction itself is observable, but the reasoning can only be supported by the inference that if the prediction is correct then the reasoning is also. To the extent the explanation permits predictions which are confirmed, we move from theory (unconfirmed explanation) to scientific generalizations and laws (confirmed explanation).

As a footnote to this discussion it should also be pointed out that theories can range from general levels of explanation to very specific levels. A general theory such as Freud's theory of personality development attempts to explain many diverse relationships. A more specific theory deals with a limited number of relationships rather than with a great many.

In a real sense theorizing or the process of building a theory is the attempt to confirm the explanation of certain events. It is in this sense that science is theorizing. Confirming a theory involves observation and testing, which leads us to a third stage of the scientific process.

Observing to Test a Theory

To this point two stages in the scientific process have been identified, the first as defining a problem about relationships among variables, and the second as theorizing about how and why these relationships operate. As the scientist proceeds to the stage of confirming (or rejecting) his theory, he attempts to establish the degree of confidence he can have in accuracy of his theory. Does the theory accurately reflect the how and why of what is taking place in the real world? I mentioned earlier that people in general are most confident of what they observe, but the scientist is most confident of that which he observes systematically and under controlled conditions. He attempts to test by observing what has actually occurred rather than by relying upon more casual observations. The tools for moving from theory to valid generalizations are models and hypotheses tested by systematic and controlled observation. The terms *hypothesis, model, systematic* and *controlled observation* are central to the balance of this discussion. I want to use a simple illustration to orient the discussion of these terms.

Often enough students are interested in the problem of conditions affecting their performance on examinations—the how and why of flunking an exam. There are several independent variables which might affect performance on the exam, such variables as (1) amount of sleep; (2)

amount of time spent studying for the exam; (3) number of related courses taken; (4) writing ability; (5) intelligence; and (6) type of exam being taken.

I might then continue to theorize that all of these above listed variables affect the student's level of anxiety (the dependent variable) while he is taking the exam. Variables one through six above are independent variables affecting the dependent variable, the level of anxiety. I would then, in turn, argue that the level of anxiety could also act as an independent variable affecting the dependent variable, test performance. This example could be summarized in a "model" of the relationships I expect among the several variables identified to this point. The model appears in Figure 2.

FIGURE 2

A MODEL OF VARIABLES AFFECTING EXAM PERFORMANCE

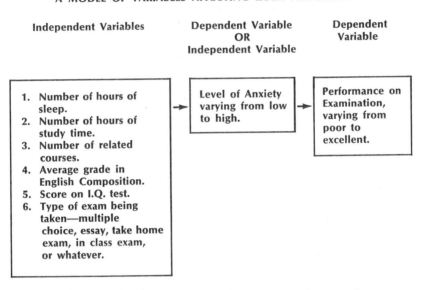

Independent Variables	Dependent Variable OR Independent Variable	Dependent Variable
1. Number of hours of sleep. 2. Number of hours of study time. 3. Number of related courses. 4. Average grade in English Composition. 5. Score on I.Q. test. 6. Type of exam being taken—multiple choice, essay, take home exam, in class exam, or whatever.	Level of Anxiety varying from low to high.	Performance on Examination, varying from poor to excellent.

The model orders the relationships among the variables. The reasoning is that students who have not slept, studied, taken exams in related courses, learned to write, and have low I.Q.'s, are more likely to be anxious about taking the exam, and therefore, are less likely to do well on it. With this in mind I can state several "hypotheses" which are suggested in the theory so far:

1.   People with less sleep than usual have higher levels of anxiety than usual.
2.   Students who study less than other students for an exam have higher levels of anxiety.

3. Students with fewer courses in a related area than other students have more anxiety about taking exams in a given course.
4. Students with poor writing skills have higher anxiety about taking exams than students with strong writing skills.
5. Students with lower I.Q.'s have higher anxiety about taking exams than students with higher I.Q.'s.
6. Students who are worried about a particular type of exam will have higher anxiety about taking that type of exam than students who are not worried.
7. Students with high levels of anxiety will do worse on a particular exam than students with lower levels of anxiety.

In each of these hypotheses I have specified a directional relationship between two variables. In the last one, I have said that as an anxiety (in this case it operates as an independent variable) goes up, the performance on the exam will go down.

The next step, and one of the most critical, is *operationalization* of the hypotheses. That is, I must provide a set of operations which the researcher can carry out to observe whether the relationships I have specified among variables exist. For example, to operationalize hypothesis number 7, I might suggest the researcher use some particular way of measuring anxiety, such as a set of attitudinal items which have been designed to reflect variation in anxiety level (e.g., Taylor Manifest Anxiety Scale), and that the measure of the dependent variable might be the student's score on the Graduate Record Examination in the student's major area of study. The operational hypothesis would be that the higher the score on the anxiety scale, the lower the score on the Graduate Record Examination.

To this point I have defined a problem, theorized about the how and why of the relationships identified in the problem, and developed an operational hypothesis to permit the observation and measurement necessary to test this hypothesis against what is actually taking place in the exam situation. But the observations of real events used to test the hypothesis must be made in a *systematic* way and under *controlled* conditions. To explain what I mean by this it may be useful to start with a fairly clear idea of what the ideal design is for testing any hypothesis.

Controlled Observation

For the scientist, the logic of a controlled experiment involves the demonstration of the effect of the independent variable upon the dependent variable while controlling for the possible effects of many other variables which might alter the situation. In other words in the above example I have to show that anxiety alone causes the impact upon test performance. The illustration in Figure 3 should help clarify the discussion.

FIGURE 3

A REPRESENTATION OF AN EXPERIMENTAL RESEARCH DESIGN

	Test Performance at time one	Test Performance at time two
Experimental Group	**A** average of exam scores for the experimental group on first attempt	**B** average of exam scores for the experimental group on second attempt
Control Group	**C** average of exam scores for the control group on first attempt	**D** average of exam scores for the control group on second attempt

If I were to follow this experimental design I would have to select at random two groups of students as experimental and control groups.[8] Random selection of the subjects for the two groups permits the assumption that the two groups are not significantly different on any particular characteristic in any systematic way that could bias their scores on the examination.[9] After the groups were selected, they would be given the Graduate Record Examination, and the average score on these exams for the two groups should not differ in any important way at one time (i.e., the average scores in cell A should approximately equal the average scores

8. Random selection simply means that everyone in a given population of subjects has an equal chance to be a part of the sample drawn from that population.

9. The assumption is based on the notion that if any subject with his many different personal traits is equally likely to be in the groups then there is no reason to expect that one group has any more or less of a particular trait than the other group.

in cell C). Anxiety could then be induced into the members of the experimental group by telling them they had all failed to pass the exam and would have to take it over again. The control group members would simply be asked to take the exam again. If the hypothesis is correct, the average score from each group at time two should show that the experimental group, which was exposed to anxiety did substantially less well than the control group, which was not exposed to the stimulus of anxiety (i.e., the average score in cell B should be significantly lower than the average score in cell D).

This then would be the ideal way to test the hypothesis, but it is not always possible to carry out this relatively demanding set of operations. We might want to vary from this ideal method in order to test the hypothesis with less expenditure of effort. The further we depart from this method the more risk we take that our conclusions are erroneous.

Perhaps the easiest way to test the hypothesis is to give a group of students both a Graduate Record Exam and a test such as the Taylor Manifest Anxiety Scale, and then to divide the total group into those who score high or low on the anxiety scale and to compare the scores on the Graduate Record Exam for these two groups. The expectation is that the group with high anxiety scores would have lower test scores than would the other group. Figure 4 represents this type of research design. In such a design we would expect most of the subjects to locate in either cell A or D; that is, we would expect those people who score low on the anxiety scale to score high on the Graduate Record Exam.

FIGURE 4

**THE RELATIONSHIP BETWEEN ANXIETY AND EXAM
SCORES FOR A SINGLE GROUP OF SUBJECTS**

Taylor Manifest Anxiety Score

	either Low	or	High

		either High	cell A	cell B
Graduate Record Exam Score	or			
		Low	cell C	cell D

Or we would expect those who scored high on the anxiety scale also to score low on the exam. If these relationships do occur, then we have support for the hypothesis that the higher the anxiety of the students, the lower their ability to do well on examinations. On the other hand, if the subjects tend to be evenly distributed in all four cells, then our hypothesis would not be supported by the research. A third possibility is that most of the subjects would be in cells B and C. This not only would deny the hypothesis, but it would suggest that the opposite of what we thought was true (i.e., higher levels of anxiety improve performance on exams).

This is obviously a much simpler design, although it departs rather severely from the ideal experiment, and therefore the researcher may not have as much confidence in his findings as he might have had in the experimental design.

Systematic Observation

I have tried to clarify what is meant by making observations under controlled conditions. In addition, we should discuss the point of systematic observation. When I say that the observation of the scientist should not only be controlled but also systematic, I might more clearly say that the observations should be truly representative of the groups or population about which he is attempting to generalize. For example, if the analyst wants to generalize about the effects of anxiety on American students, he will have to pick random samples of students from schools throughout the United States. Obviously this is a difficult way to test the hypothesis, so he will probably be content to work with more convenient samples of students drawn from more limited populations, such as students at one or more universities instead of students from throughout the country. In this case the researcher can only say that the relationship holds for students at a certain university, even though he may be fairly confident that it will hold for most university students, at least those in this country.

The reason for attempting to use a large sample selected at random is to reduce the possibility of observing only that which is likely to confirm the hypothesis. For example, if I only use a small sample of students whom I know well, they might form a very biased sample of students who are not representative of the total student body. Any result of this research will be biased by the fact that all of the students are people I know. This fact might result in their level of anxiety varying in a systematically different manner in the research situation than it might for students I do not know. Again, the researcher is attempting to test hypotheses in such a way that the findings can be generalized to include a broader number of events and that the findings will also be more likely the result of the hypothesized variables rather than of an extraneous variable.

This discussion should give you a better idea of the rigor of scientific research, and some appreciation for the manner in which research findings in science are developed. It should be fairly clear by this time that science does differ from common sense and the casual observation of events.

Now that we have a better understanding of science, we can turn to the further examination of the use of science in the study of politics. Political scientists who emphasize the use of science are usually labeled as using "the behavioral approach."

BEHAVIORAL POLITICAL ANALYSIS

There is no simple definition of the "behavioral approach." We can begin by pointing out that it is an attempt to use scientific procedures in the explanation of man's political behavior. Characterizing behavioral political science as a "persuasion" to use science does not help a great deal.[10] It may be more helpful to list some of the things behavioral political scientists are doing:

1) The persuasion to use science identifies the political behavioralists as a part of a broader effort to develop the behavioral social sciences. Political scientists with a behavioral orientation have joined with psychologists, anthropologists, economists, sociologists, and others to explain why and how people think and act in social situations. Because they assume there are similarities in the behavior traits of people, and in a variety of situations, including political ones, they find it valuable to draw upon related areas of research in other social sciences in order to exchange theory and findings about human behavior. A first characteristic of the behavioral approach is its reliance upon research in other social sciences in analyzing political events.

2) A second characteristic is that political behavioralists are seeking to understand individual and group behavior as it is affected by history, laws, institutions, and ideas. But the primary interest is in the thinking and behavior of people and not in the laws, history, philosophy, or institutions which affect them.

3) A third identifying trademark of the approach is its emphasis upon methods rather than upon the substance of political inquiry. We need to clarify this difference. Typically, political science has been subdivided into a number of fields of study (e.g., the substance of politics) which vary greatly. Generally, they include such areas as public administration, Ameri-

---

10. Heinz, Eulau, *The Behavioral Persuasion in Politics* (New York: Random House, 1963). p.

can government (national, state and local), international relations, public opinion, political parties and pressure groups, comparative government and/or politics, and political theory. This list suggests the diversity of fields which may be included in political science. The behavioral approach is not a separate substantive field within political science, but rather represents a concern with methods of research used to study these diverse fields.

4) This emphasis upon research methods and science has led to several additional characteristics of behavioral political science. As science emphasizes asking questions and theorizing about answers which can be tested by observing events, so does the behavioral approach. Therefore, a fourth characteristic is the importance of defining problems in a manner permitting the researcher to observe the answer. Scientists generally are attempting to understand *what is* (i.e., that which can be observed) rather than *what should be* (i.e., that which must be judged); the behavioralists are particularly interested in "empirical" questions that can be answered by observation of realities, and not in "normative" questions, the answers to which depend upon individual values or ideals. Behavioralists are explicitly trying to keep their values from influencing their research and thinking.

5) A fifth aspect of the behavioral perspective is the emphasis upon theorizing. This is possibly the single most important distinguishing characteristic. Behavioralists view theory as a tool in the process of understanding, and not the substance of man's understanding or a set of truths enduring for all time. Theories serve as a best guess about what is going on in the political world. They are subject to continuing observation, testing, and correction so that they may more adequately explain events. As more evidence is found to support a particular theory, it permits more confidence in that explanation. An explanation about human behavior may hold for different historical periods or different cultures, but it is still subject to modification if changing conditions so warrant.

Theory, as most tools, can be used in different ways. Some people use theory as a way of making sense of a variety of observed events. In other words, they make a great many observations and then attempt to explain these facts by *inducing* from the data some interpretation of what has taken place. For instance, we could try to explain why people vote for one political candidate rather than for another by asking a lot of voters what things affect the way they vote and then by analyzing their responses. Other theorists prefer to use theory in a *deductive* manner. They may start with a theory which helps them to make sense out of complex problems. This theory can then be tested by developing logical consequences of the theory about the real world, and by checking these expectations against what is actually occurring. So, we might theorize that voters are rational and vote for that candidate who does things most likely to further their desires. We could then ask people about their views on issues and ask them who they voted for in order to see if their candidate did support legislation consistent with their position on the issues. Researchers can use both inductive and deductive procedures in solving research problems, but the important similarity among behavioral theorists is the agreement that there is a necessity for theorizing in the process of understanding political events and situations.

6) Since behavioralists view theory as a tool for research that must be tested by observing real events, they are necessarily involved in the construction of better techniques for making observations and analyzing the results of these observations. A sixth characteristic of the behavioral approach is the concern with methods of research design, data gathering and analysis. These are some of the characteristics of the behavioral approach to political analysis. But now we need to consider some of the limitations of this approach.

LIMITATIONS OF THE BEHAVIORAL
APPROACH

My purpose in pointing out these criticisms is not to defend or attack the behavioral approach, but to make you aware of its limitations and problems.

The behavioralists have been criticized for trying to develop general theories to explain political behavior in a particular culture. The argument goes along these lines. Social scientists have consistently observed that human behavior is relative to the place and time in which it occurs, so it is logically inconsistent to seek for a theory which generally explains human behavior regardless of where or when it occurs.

The behavioralist might respond that there is little doubt that specific behavior traits of people are influenced by place and time; however, the level of generality of a theory has more to do with what one looks at rather than with what one sees at a particular place and time. If we look at the question of how people use their votes to control leaders, then the theory and observations are necessarily confined to countries where people vote. But if we choose to look at the question of how people exert control over their leaders, it is possible to develop theory and make observations which are applicable to situations in which people vote as well as situations in which leaders rule until a stronger chief can be found among the tribal members. The more general the theory, the less useful it may be in explaining specific behavior traits, but the more useful it may be in understanding the differences and similarities in human behavior at varying points in time and space. Behavioralists are interested in different levels of theory from the very specific to very general. The criticism points out the need of the behavioralist to define carefully the level of generality while being cautious of generalizing too far from limited theory or of inferring too specifically from broad theory.

A second criticism is that behavioralists are attempting to make predictions about human behavior in order to test their theoretical explanations, but that every time they predict a type of behavior it is possible that people will become aware of the prediction and act either to confirm or to deny what has been predicted. In other words, the prediction itself will influence human behavior independently of the explanation used by the scientist in his analysis. A most common example of this possibility occurs in the prediction of election outcomes by commercial pollsters. Many people have felt that the polls cause people actually to change their votes either by wanting to vote for the winner or by wanting to vote for the underdog.

I do not believe it. First, people are unlikely to be reading the literature of political science journals (it is hard enough to get students to read them) where most predictions are usually made public. But even if they are aware of predictions, as they are in the case of public opinion polls about politics, it is a little hard to believe they will actually change their behavior either to spite or to delight some college professor or pollster. But even assuming they do know about the prediction and do actually change their behavior, it would appear that one type of behavior change (either to get on the band wagon or to help the underdog) is just as probable as the other, so that they will cancel each other out.

The criticism suggests an additional problem which must be kept in mind. Human beings are aware of being analyzed and this may have an effect upon their behavior. This fact must be kept in mind as one analyzes results of any experiment.

Behavioralists are further criticized for being naive in their attempt to be objective and value free in their analysis. In fact, they, as any other people, have values and no matter what they say these values will affect how they conduct their research as well as how they interpret the findings.

Behavioralists would answer that they have values, and their first attempt must be to make these values explicit so that the potential impact on analysis can be recognized by other researchers. In this way people with differing values can examine the published research to see if the results are more a function of the researcher's values than of his observations. The crucial task of constructing a science is to make findings public so that the research can be replicated by other scholars to see if the conclusions are valid and reliable or only thinly disguised preferences about what should be. Values are important to behavioralists in choosing the research problem and in applying research findings to policy matters.

But behavioralists think that the actual conduct of the research must be as free as possible of bias or the research findings become little more than statements of personal beliefs. It is clear that a further limitation in using scientific procedures is the problem of objectivity. The researcher must be aware that his own subjective biases may be affecting his interpretation of his findings.

A fourth criticism is that behavioralists are overly concerned about finding out what is rather than what should be, and appear to be overlooking the most important problems of our times in order to observe a trivial political event. The really significant problems have to do with how people should act and not with how they do act; therefore, the argument goes, they are wasting valuable time on trivia when they should be examining critical issues of human concern.

Behavioralists reply here that for centuries scholars have argued to little avail about what should be. As students of human behavior they are attempting to develop some understanding of what is actually occurring in order to make more informed and practical judgments about what should be occurring. They find no necessary incompatibility between trying to get more objective information about political events and at the same time being committed to acting toward the solution of the problem.

The last criticism I want to mention is in many ways the most difficult to answer. It states that behavioralists are attempting to develop a science of human behavior which can be used to manage and control society and that this pursuit is morally wrong. In other words, if they somehow manage to predict human behavior from research (which critics argue cannot be done because individuals are unique and unpredictable) it will be possible to use such knowledge to manipulate people.

Behavioralists argue that people are not free. They are controlled by a multitude of varying conditions which social science has only recently begun to understand.

People are controlled by sociological, economic, psychological, geographic, and political forces which exert influence on their every behavior trait from early childhood to death. It is not a matter of being free versus being controlled by a mad social scientist. It is a matter of being controlled by causes of which people may be ignorant or by causes of which they may be aware. To be ignorant is to assure that certain factors will continue to control them. To be aware gives people the ability to intervene to control their own lives. There are risks involved in understanding anything, including human behavior, but the positive value is that behavioralists may construct the elements of a sane and livable society. These are only a few of the limitations of using science to understand political behavior, and we will continue with a more general evaluation in the next chapter.

CHAPTER 3

EVALUATING THE STUDY OF POLITICS

AN INTRODUCTION TO A CRITICAL APPRAISAL

Does the scientific analysis of "democracy" give you any more control over your life? If you think back to the discussion in Chapter 1 you may recall that I said that I thought of the "good life" as one in which individuals make choices to have control over the events which influence their lives, and of the "good society" as one that facilitates this kind of human endeavor. Whereas Chapter 2 was a description of the development of political science as placing most emphasis upon the continuing trend toward scientific political analysis, this chapter is intended to be a critical appraisal of both the subject matter and of methods of studying politics. Such an evaluation involves a brief overview of the subject matter being studied by political scientists and the methods they have used to

This overview is necessary in order to consider whether present political inquiry contributes toward people having more control over the events which affect their lives.

The following discussion will suggest that the subject matter of political analysis has been permeated by the belief that democracy as practiced in this country is the "best" form of government to ensure the good life for people. Further on, we will find that there is a growing belief among political scientists that science is the "best" method for understanding the theory and practice of democracy. Then we will discuss what I believe to be a newly developing but extremely serious skepticism about both of these widely shared beliefs. It will be your task in this reading to evaluate for yourself the strength and merit of these beliefs, weighed in with the balance of the skepticism about them. First we can turn to an evaluation of the subject matter that has been central to political analysis in this discipline.

WHAT POLITICAL SCIENTISTS STUDY AND TEACH

In this section I want to describe briefly some of the major fields of subject matter in the discipline of political science, then to suggest what I think is the central focus to all of the various fields of teaching and analysis.

You should be aware that there are no standard definitions of the fields of research within the discipline of political science. Different faculties at different universities have chosen to teach and to conduct research in some fields rather than in others and to emphasize one field over another. But there are some fields of subject matter that have been and continue to be central to any curriculum of political science. We need to look at these fields in more detail.

It is possible to begin by broadly classifying the subject matter of political science as falling into two major categories—the politics external to a society and the politics internal to a society. Most current study falls under one of these classifications. The major exception is the field of political theory, which we can discuss separately.

Under the heading of "politics internal to a society" we find such courses and research fields as constitutional law, the analysis of federal, state and local courts, judicial behavior, Congress and the state legislatures, executive branches (usually the presidency) and leadership, public administration in bureaucracies and in large organizations, political parties, pressure groups, community politics, public opinion and voting behavior, political socialization, and the study of public policy. In the major fields of research and teaching falling into the category of "politics external to a society," we find such areas as comparative government and/or politics, area studies (e.g., Southeast Asia or Latin America), and international relations. This listing in no way exhausts the subject matter of political science, but the list does illustrate the diversity and breadth of political analysis and teaching. We need to get some grasp of what these different courses and fields of research are about.

The courses taught and the research being done in both of these categories result from traditions as well as from newer theoretical and methodological interests (i.e., the behavioral approach). Tradition dictates that we offer courses and conduct research concerning the major institutions of government. In the category of "politics internal to a society" we typically find that courses dealing with the major institutions of American government are divided according to the level of government at which they exist—national, state and local levels. Given this tradition, the new student of political science is often introduced to the subject matter of politics by courses emphasizing American government and state and local governments. Both of these types of courses attempt to describe briefly the major institutions of government such as Congress, the courts and the presidency, the structure and operation of various state legislatures and municipal governments, and material on political parties, pressure groups, public opinion, and public policy.

With this introduction to the subject matter the student then may take advanced courses dealing with specific institutions of government. He may take Constitutional law in which the content of the course has to do with Supreme Court decisions from the early foundations of the court to the present. He may take a course dealing with Congress, with the emphasis placed upon understanding the organization and operation of the U.S. Senate and House of Representatives as these bodies seek to construct laws. He may find courses available on the presidency in which the subject of the powers, both formal and informal, of the president are studied in detail, with attention given to the way presidents have organized their decision-making and particular decisions they have made. Often enough there are courses dealing with public administration in national and state bureaucracies. Here the attention is placed upon the way in which public bureaucracies are structured and upon how they operate to implement public policy. Closely related to courses on public administration are courses dealing primarily with public policy, that is, the study of the various issues and policies which have dominated the work of major political institutions (e.g., defense policy, welfare, education, and environmental problems).

Concerning state and local levels of governmental institutions some political science departments offer courses in state legislatures, courses which are normally comparative in nature. They attempt to compare the ways in which different state legislatures are organized and the manner in which they operate. There may be courses on state and local courts. There is usually at least one course on municipal politics, examining forms of city government. Urban problems are analyzed and related to the general question of the cooperation or lack thereof between cities and other levels of government.

Many of the courses dealing primarily with the institutions of government remain in the college curriculum because of the tradition in political science that our major concern is with the operation and structure of governments, particularly American governments. But there are also a host of courses usually offered which are not studying the constitutionally created institutions of government, but are investigating the institutions in our society which have grown from extralegal origins. Such institutions have come to assume major importance. Here we find courses on political parties, courses emphasizing how such parties recruit and elect officials to serve in the major institutions of government. Sometimes such courses include material concerning the types and activities of pressure groups. Such groups are normally viewed as being a part of the informal processes of politics that attempt to influence public law. They influence by "helping" political parties in recruiting and electing officials, but they also attempt to influence the process of developing public policy.

These are some of the more typical courses offered, as well as some of the research areas existing in many departments of political science.

There are other courses that fall under the heading of "politics internal to a society" which have been added to satisfy the interests of behaviorally oriented members of a faculty. Normally included are courses dealing with judicial, legislative, or executive behavior. The effort is to view these fields with the emphasis being placed upon the behavior of officials in each institution rather than upon the structure and operation of the institution itself. So, for instance, the courses deal with the behavior and attitudes of judges, or with different types of legislators in order to see to what extent these factors are important in the analysis of politics. There are also courses on public opinion and voting behavior that emphasize the study of the ways that individuals and groups in the society come to hold the opinions that they do and the ways that these opinions affect their political behavior. Behavioralists also have offered courses in community politics in which they typically use the local community as a small world to see how elites and people in a community behave. Still another course of more recent origin is concerned with the study of political socialization —the study of the ways people learn to become a part of the political system and the attitudes they acquire about government and politics.

Courses and research dealing with "politics external to a society" usually involve at least three areas—international relations, comparative politics and political systems of particular countries. The subject of international relations normally includes such courses as international organizations (e.g., the United Nations, the League of Nations or other major agencies of importance to the relationships among sovereign nations), foreign policy, which emphasizes the development and acting out of policies of one government or group of governments, and diplomacy, a course in which emphasis is placed upon the history of bargaining among nations, upon treaties they enter into, and upon the individuals who have been critical in carrying out such settlements and agreements.

We also usually find courses dealing with comparative government or politics. These courses and research areas traditionally have compared the major governments of the world. These courses at one time were heavily influenced by the behavioral orientations to broaden their subject matter to include the politics as well as the governmental institutions of such societies. In this kind of analysis, growing numbers of studies and courses deal with political processes of other societies, such as the operation of pressure groups in other countries, the operation of their political parties, the attitudes of people and elites in other societies toward politics, and the values and behaviors of people in different kinds of societies. A more recent emphasis in the comparative field is reflected in the attention given to the so-called developing nations of the world, with political scientists studying the efforts of other countries to become industrialized. This emphasis upon developing countries and areas of the world has largely been non-comparative, using case studies of particular countries as the basis for analysis. It might be expected that as more area studies are completed we will find more attempts to compare the different emerging nations with one another.

The one field of teaching and thought that I have not discussed yet, since it does not neatly fit my classification of politics as being either internal or external to a society, is the field of political theory. Tradition in our discipline has brought with it an emphasis upon theory, and theoretical courses are a part of most political science curricula. Normally such courses are a history of great political thinkers about politics (e.g., pre-Socratic thinkers, Plato, Aristotle, all the way through contemporary political philosophers). Given the behavioral emphasis, "theory" courses have focused upon the student's understanding the theories of classic thinkers in terms of how they might contribute to better understanding of present-day politics. Rather than being a field of its own, political theory becomes a source of ideas that may be tested by researchers.

This brief description of the research and teaching areas in political science in no way exhausts the possible courses and research in the discipline, but it does illustrate the diversity and breadth of what is being done by political scientists, particularly in this country.

In concluding this section I will suggest that all of the different courses and research fields we have talked about have an underlying focus. The focus results from the assumption that democracy as practiced in our country is the best form of government.

Given this assumption, most of the material being taught and researched in political science has dealt with the ways of maintaining and improving our democracy. Typically, courses and research dealing with the internal politics of our society have been attempts to understand better how our democracy operates, and what kind of institutions, human behaviors and values make it operate as it does. In studying the politics external to a society, we have typically emphasized in international relations how our democracy can survive in a world containing non-democratic countries that either compete with or attempt to dominate us. In comparative studies we have tended to emphasize the ways that our democracy is different from other governments, with a view to possible reforms to make our democracy better, but more typically to demonstrate the unique capacity of our democracy to do further human good. Finally, our analysis of the emerging nations has been dominated by the attempt to understand how they can become more like our own democracy.

Without asking you to agree or disagree with this interpretation of the major focus in the study of politics, I now want to turn to the ways that political science has studied these subjects. Again, we will need to start by giving some brief sketch of the different modes of analysis available to researchers in our discipline.

HOW POLITICAL SCIENTISTS STUDY PROBLEMS

As in the last section, in which we attempted to simplify the discussion of the variety of subject matter in political science by saying that we would classify what is being studied into two major categories—the politics internal and external to a society—here we will attempt to describe the many different methods of political analysis by suggesting that they can be classified into three categories. First we will discuss experimental research methods, then comparative methodology, and finally case studies and historical analysis.

It is my assessment of research in political science that under the influence of the scientifically oriented behavioral approach the trend is toward using experimental and comparative methods rather than the more traditional case studies and historical analysis. Even though I believe this trend toward being more "scientific" (i.e., using experimental and comparative methods) is going to continue, this is not to suggest that the significant problems can be approached only by scientific analysis.

Research must begin with the identification of a problem, a review of the existing information about that problem, and an assessment of the purposes and consequences of the research. With this beginning the analyst is better able to choose the type of research method most appropriate to dealing with the problem he is attempting to understand. It seems clear that certain problems can be studied in a more scientific manner than can others, but this is not to say that only scientific research is valid. We use the method most appropriate for the problem being analyzed. It is the study of a problem that is most important. The type of research method is secondary, in my mind, to the attempt to solve the problem under investigation. Now we can turn to the first mode of research.

Experimental Research Designs

In order to illustrate this discussion of scientific or experimental research design, I will use a particular problem as an example of the way in which this research method works. We might begin by identifying the problem of the impact of leaders upon followers. Given this problem, we might be interested in the ways that the "style" of leadership affects the extent of agreement about issues. Specifically, we might want to investigate how variation in the independent variable "style of leadership" affects the dependent variable "extent of agreement about issues."

We can conceptualize "style of leadership" as varying between the autocratic and equalitarian extremes. We can conceptualize the followers' opinion by the extent of their approval of a number of issue positions which the leader represents to them. Operationalizing our variables, we might say that we will identify autocratic leadership as a style that involves the leader simply repeating his opinion about particular issues in an attempt to dictate to the followers what they shall believe. Equalitarian leadership involves a style in which the leader and followers discuss in some detail their opinions on issues. The dependent variable could be operationalized as being a list of statements about issues (for instance, issues of pollution control, defense spending, or welfare spending) with which the respondent will be asked whether he agrees. With this conceptualization and operationalization in mind, we might hypothesize that the more equalitarian the leadership style, the more likely that the followers will agree among themselves about the issue. If we demonstrate this relationship, we also show that autocratic leadership is less likely to promote consensus. With these theoretical considerations formulated we now turn to the problem of gathering data to support or to reject this hypothesis.

There are two variations in experimental research one may use to gather the necessary data in the most scientifically valid manner. First, we will discuss the laboratory experimental design and then the field experimental design.

If we were to construct a laboratory research design, we might start by selecting three random samples of citizens from registered voter lists in the particular community used for the research. One group (experimental group A) would be exposed to the independent variable of autocratic leadership, the second group (experimental group B) would be exposed to equalitarian leadership, and the third group (control group) would not be exposed to any leadership style. The members of all three sample groups would be paid for their attendance at a series of discussions about major political issues. Each group would meet once a month for a period of six months. At the first meeting we might give a "pretest" to each subject about his approval or disapproval of a series of issue positions. If our random samples were indeed random, we should find no significant differences among the groups as to the extent of their approval or disapproval of the issues. Group A would continue through the series of discussions with a leader who would be instructed not to discuss the issues under question, but merely to reaffirm his own opinion on these issues. Group B's leader would be instructed to create and to encourage discussion and communication about these issues among the members of the group. Finally, group C would simply be required to meet six times to discuss the issues, without any leadership for the group.

At the end of the six months period, all three groups would again be tested with the same opinion approval test given at the beginning. The expectation is that if our hypothesis is correct, we would find significantly more agreement among the subjects in group B (the equalitarian leadership group) than among the subjects in group C (the control group), and the members of the control group would show more agreement among themselves than would the subjects in the autocratic group. We might also expect the opinions of the subjects of the control group to show no substantial change from the first session.

If all of these expectations were confirmed we might then conclude several things. We might conclude that both Group A and B showed changes and that the control group did not. Therefore, our conclusion would be that leadership does have an impact upon followers' opinions. We might also conclude that equalitarian leadership styles are more likely to increase the level of agreement among subjects, while autocratic leadership styles have the effect of decreasing or of not affecting the subjects.

This then is a controlled experimental design which would test the hypothesis about the impact of leadership upon follower opinion. The problem is that these kinds of laboratory designs tend to be unrealistic. The people in the research laboratory know they are not involved in real life situations, and they may act differently than they do normally. The strength of this research design is that it is rigorous and closely approaches the standards for deriving scientific findings. Because of the problem of artificiality, many researchers have thought it necessary to get out of the laboratory and into real-life, field-research situations.

A field–research design to test this hypothesis could be constructed in the following way: We might focus upon communities as the base of the research. Since we cannot expect people in different communities to form truly random groups, we have to control for variables other than leadership which might be operating to affect the extent of agreement among the people. We could do this by matching communities on a number of variables that we might expect to have impact upon the people's opinions. That is, we could attempt to choose communities in which there are approximately equal distributions of such variables as socioeconomic status, religious affiliations, cultural context, jobs, and population. By choosing communities where there are approximately equal proportions of these major variables, we could be relatively confident that people in each community would be affected in about the same way by these variables. We then could choose the communities not only on the basis of their being matched on these several variables but also on the basis of significant variation in the leadership styles of the city leaders. A field experimental design is one in which communities are matched by the above variables. If one of the two selected communities were initiating a public relations program to discuss policy questions with voters, we could then test the level of consensus about issues among a random sample of citizens of both communities at "time one" and then wait until the community having the public relations discussions has had its program under way for a period of time. We could then test to see if there were significant differences in the levels of opinion consensus in the public relations community and the other community after a period of time (i.e., "time two"). If we found significant differences in the level of consensus we could conclude that the community where leaders had more equalitarian leadership style (discussing issues with citizens) did in fact have a higher level of consensus among its citizens than the community without the public relations program.

Such a design is rigorous in that it involves controls for confounding variables (by matching) and also involves the demonstration that the independent variable does affect the dependent variables over time. But there are still problems. We are not sure of the controls. There may be other variables of which we are unaware affecting the level of consensus, and for which we have not made provision in the experiment. There is also the difficulty of finding communities which meet the criteria of matching, as well as of having the variation in leadership styles. This design is difficult to carry out properly.

The laboratory research is more rigorous, but often unrealistic. The field research is realistic but is also more difficult to carry out. For these reasons it may become necessary to utilize other research methods which in one way or another approach experimental design but lack its precision and control.

Comparative Methods

There are a number of ways of making comparative analyses. Each way should be considered for its different strengths and weaknesses. We might compare the same group of people over a period of time. This way is commonly referred to as a panel study. The group of subjects for research form the panel, and each time that we study the panel, the occasion is called a wave. One may study a panel of voters in a community by administering a questionnaire every year. Each yearly administration of the questionnaire is considered a wave in the panel.

The advantage here is that we can assess the impacts of natural changes in leadership styles in the community over a period of years (e.g., each time the city administration changes) upon the same people (i.e., the panel). This fact allows us to be confident that we have controlled for many confounding variables simply because we are using the same people under varying conditions. We gain relatively good control over individual variation, but we have no control group to indicate if the changes we note over time are a function of the changing leadership rather than of other variables. We are therefore less confident of our results. This type of research is still difficult to carry out, and extremely slow in producing results since the analyst has to wait until several years pass in a community study before drawing any conclusions about the effect of leadership styles on the opinions of the panel of subjects.

Because of the expense and time involved in panel studies, another type of comparative study is even more frequently used. This type of study involves the comparison of different groups at different points in time. At "time one" we might test to find the level of consensus among a random sample of people in the community, and at a later time we might return to the community (as before, after a change in administration) to take another random sample of people to interview. In this case we are able to say that changes in the style of leadership have an impact upon the citizens in the community, assuming that we do find significant changes, and that the differences have occurred after the impact of the experimental variable. But we do not have the rigor of the control used in the panel design. In other words, the people in the second random sample may be different from those in the first group, not because of the impact of changed leadership, but because they are simply different individuals. However, this research is much easier to carry out, since it does not involve keeping track of all of the subjects in the panel over a period of time. Again, this type of study is time consuming in that the researcher must wait for an administration change to get results.

A third type of comparative study simply involves the comparison of two different groups operating under different kinds of leadership styles. This type of design can be carried out with relative ease since it simply involves finding two groups of people with different leaders (one autocratic and the other equalitarian) and comparing the level of agreement about policy preferences of the two groups. But there are severe problems introduced in this type of study. First, we are not sure that leadership style has caused any observed differences since we do not have before-and-after data. In other words, we might have observed the same differences even if leadership styles were the same in both communities. We do not know what each community was like before it was exposed to the different leadership styles. Such designs are easier to use, and common to political science.

Still another type of comparative study involves the comparison of people's present opinions with their past opinions, as they recall them. This type of study might be used after a change in administration in a community, and it might be conducted by the researcher simply asking a sample of people if they now have different opinions than they did in the past. The problem with "recall data" is that it is usually selectively recalled and people remember things differently than they actually were. This type of study nonetheless does involve some attempt to get at changes over time.

Still another type of comparative study is conducted by the researcher simply taking a sample of people and comparing their opinions with what might be expected by "chance" in a random population. In this case we have only one group, which we divide into those who show high agreement over particular issues and those who show low agreement. Then we see if those people who tend to agree have been actively involved in discussing public issues with leaders. If the differences in the amount of communication with leaders between those who agree and those who disagree could not have occurred by chance alone, then we can attribute the difference to discussion of issues with leaders. Finally, we can turn to case study and historical analysis.

Case Study and Historical Analysis

Case studies and historical analyses are often the least acceptable of types of research in terms of producing scientifically valid conclusions, but they are quite often the most acceptable because they can be made amenable to a wide variety of political problems which cannot be researched in any other way.

The case study is perhaps the most common type of political analysis in our discipline. Case studies utilize many different kinds of data collection techniques. The researcher selects a particular political situation which appears to conform in many important ways to the type of problem under research. He might pick a university which has a particular type of leadership style apparent in its administration (autocratic or equalitarian) and then collect various kinds of data on the impact of that style of leadership upon the attitudes of students and faculty. Common kinds of case studies involve presidential decisions, analysis of committee operations in Congress, and the study of particular kinds of cases before the Supreme Court. The major virtue of these studies is that they can be conducted in political situations not easily amenable to more systematic kinds of data collection techniques (e.g., it is difficult to get the President of the United States to fill out a questionnaire for a study). The major disadvantage is that these studies are usually carried out in such a way by the researcher that it is very difficult to compare the results of one study with the results of other studies. This disadvantage can be partially corrected if several such studies are launched by researchers utilizing a common approach, but this coordination seldom occurs.

Finally, we need to consider the historical approach to political analysis. The adoption of research techniques utilized by previous historians to study political situations is still a very common kind of analysis. In other words, a particular political situation is studied over the period of time in which it took place, the researcher using available data (i.e., private letters, documents, biographical material, and newspapers) to attempt to piece together the sequence of events which have occurred. One might study the life of a particular leader with a strong autocratic personality to determine if his style made for widespread support of his positions on issues. There are several limitations of this type of analysis. The most obvious is that the technique is confined to the particular events or person under investigation. It has the same disadvantage as the case study does in that it is difficult to compare findings with other studies, and it rests upon data which are not easily replicated in other studies. Its major advantage is that it does direct the researcher's attention to the time sequence of events, which is required to make some informed guesses about the relationship among events. And it does recognize the important point that much of what occurs in any situation is a function of the unique conditions in that situation. This type of analysis tends toward emphasis upon the unique aspects of a particular problem, while the comparative approach tends to emphasize the common elements in different kinds of political situations.

In the preceding portion of this chapter I concluded the description of the subject matter of political analysis by suggesting the underlying assumption of our attention to politics has been that democracy as practiced in our society is the best form of government to ensure the "good life" for individuals. In a similar manner I think there has been an underlying assumption which limits our choice of research methods to study these political processes and institutions. In my opinion this assumption is that science particularly and objectivity generally are the best ways in which to approach the understanding of politics. Regardless of whether we are talking about scientific (i.e., experimental) research, comparative methods, or historical and case study analysis, the emphasis in all three approaches has been and continues to be upon removing the researcher and his values from the research situation. The researcher must remain objective and free of values or biases in his observation and interpretation.

The argument for objectivity and value neutrality is essentially that to be accurate as an observer and analyst, the researcher must be attempting to see and explain what is going on, not as he might prefer it to be happening, but as it actually occurs. As was suggested in the last chapter in which we discussed the behavioral episode in the discipline of political science, there is a continuing debate as to whether it is possible for the researcher to be objective and value free. However, without returning to that kind of argument, I think an even more serious question is raised as to the consequences of such objectivity and value neutrality in research, even if such attitudes are possible. With this description of both the subject matter and the methods of political science completed, we can now turn to the much more difficult problem of evaluating these matters.

EVALUATING THE SCOPE AND
METHODS OF POLITICAL ANALYSIS:
SOME SOURCES OF SKEPTICISM

In order to evaluate anything, we must first have a basis for judgment. My criterion for evaluating what is being done by political scientists is whether it contributes to the creation of the "good life." The "good life" is one in which individuals can make choices and have control over their own lives and their society's future.

With this criterion in mind, we can turn to the question of evaluation. I have argued that democracy as practiced in this society has been the focus of analysis in political science, and that objectivity and value neutrality have been seen as necessary qualities for carrying out that analysis. The question is—Does democracy as we know it in this country and objectivity as practiced by political scientists contribute to your having more control over your life? We will begin with an examination of the notion that democracy in our society does in fact facilitate individuals having control over their lives. Some of the research suggests that our system does not measure up.

The following statements seem to be at the very core of what we believe is good about our democracy: (1) As citizens, we are represented by the public officials we vote for; (2) We are governed by laws, not by men; (3) Our interests are represented by the political party we choose to support; (4) Democracy operates in our local communities; and (5) It is the government, run by the officials we elect, which makes the policies affecting our lives.

Much of the skepticism about democracy in this country has arisen from research on the political institutions and processes in our society, the same institutions and processes which we have believed support and verify the above statements. I will not attempt to describe in detail here the research or the theories which have created the skepticism. Instead, I want to give you a brief look at the conclusions of the research.

Most people in this country believe that we are assured of democratic representation by the fact that we cast our votes for the person who most nearly represents our interest. One of the most thoroughly investigated areas of research is that of voting behavior. And its conclusions are most pessimistic. Research has shown that a large segment of the American voters are simply not aware or informed enough to make a rational decision about candidates or issues. If they cannot make such choices, then how do they elect office holders who truly represent them? The answer seems to be—they do not. Because he is ill-informed or deliberately confused, it is impossible for the majority voter to elect officials who will carry their interests into public policy. A major assumption of democracy is that the will of the people is implemented through their representatives in government. According to the research, this theory of democracy is not confirmed in the practice of voting in this country.

But, no matter, we are governed by laws, not men. A great deal of research has been done on the behavior of judges in the court system. Here we find the attitudes, values, and biases of judges are as important in determining their decisions as are the law and judicial precedents.

Democracy requires the courts to interpret the law of the land, independent of personal values, and to make decisions based upon law, not upon individual values. Democracy should be controlled by laws, not by the whims or caprice of particular men. According to the research, political, social, and other values held by judges have a great deal to do with the way that they interpret the law. Certainly these findings suggest that the theory of the operation in our society of "constitutionalism" (e.g., laws governing man's behavior) is open to serious debate. Here is another assumption about our democratic processes not confirmed by the research.

Another area that we have believed contributes to our representative democracy is that of political parties. Supposedly, the voter chooses to support the political party which best represents his interests. And his choice of party makes up for any lack of information about particular candidates. However, upon investigation, we find that only the elites within a political party organization have any real understanding of the different sides of an issue. The vast majority of voters are unable to distinguish between the parties, let alone choose the one which best represents them. And yet most people do support one party or another. How do they decide which party? Apparently they do not decide. Rather, studies show, voters "inherit" their party affiliation from their parents. In light of this, it is difficult to perceive political parties in our country as contributing to the operation of a representative democracy. Although the parties recruit candidates, they do not seem to facilitate people controlling their own lives or government.

In order to understand the workings of democracy better, political analysts have studied small communities and cities. These studies have resulted in a growing debate over whether American communities do operate in a democratic manner. One view, supported by research, is that there is no democracy in our communities. Rather, decisions are made by a small elite of business interests who manipulate the public. These "power elite" theorists argue that the formal political institutions such as elections, political parties, or elected officials are little more than frills provided to appease the public. Another group of analysts, pluralists, conclude there is more than one elite (i.e., multiple elites) in a community. These multiple elites, formed around different interests and activated by issues, determine public policy in the process of competing, bargaining, and compromising with each other. Therefore pluralists do feel that the mass of people are indirectly represented. But decisions arising from the competition of elites is hardly what we think of as a truly representative democracy.

Still another group of theorists greatly influenced by their study of large corporations and economic elites have concluded that the politics of a society is largely irrelevant. The major institution is the large corporation.

This focus upon corporations and economic power has led to still another source of skepticism about our democracy. While some theorists have attempted to understand the real importance of corporations and economic elites in determining the public policy, other theorists have arrived at perhaps the most startling and provoking of all the analyses of our society.

According to these theorists, corporations are determined by even more fundamental processes or imperatives than we have suspected. Although the terms may be different (new industrial state and the corporate state) the analysis is similar as is the conclusion, that the question of democracy is irrelevant to our society. They argue that there is no separation between public and private sectors of our society. Instead the two sectors are merged into one giant or corporate structure in which all institutions serve the same basic goals of greater production and consumption. To this end, we have been caught up in a frantic technological spiral requiring more careful planning and the manipulation of people so as to assure the consumption of products without major loss to the producers. In a sense, then, no one is in control of the system—neither the corporations, business elites, nor a set of elites, and certainly not citizens. The system is running us. We have become the products of our own technology and economics, which demand an ever increasing conformity in order for us to continue. The major forces in our society are the values which support the expanding production of goods and the consumption of those goods without the critical assessment of their worth. And we are all so completely captured by these values that the great technological machine continues, uncontrolled and unexamined, because we are bribed by a system that provides well for the majority of its people.

If research on the practice of democracy in our society has raised questions about the basic belief that it is the best form of government to ensure the good life for people, there also exists skepticism about the methods of research that we have relied upon so heavily. Our belief in objectivity is being greatly scrutinized. Although difficult to identify and discuss, these criticisms are even more profound. After reading Jacques Ellul's *The Technological Society*, or Herbert Marcuse's *One Dimensional Man*, I am left with unending sources of uneasiness about scientific methods specifically and objectivity in research generally.

The basis of this skepticism is that we have become servants of our own techniques. As we gain better ways of understanding our society through measurements, quantification of what we see, and the development of sophisticated techniques of research, we lose the ability to evaluate what we are studying. We are so involved in objectively observing society and so fascinated by our means to do so, that we no longer see these methods in relation to the goals of our understanding, such as evaluating what is good and bad in our society. Understanding and research have become a process of developing more methods and techniques, a process which has become an end in itself. In a real sense our pursuit of objectivity has in fact led us further from the kind of quest we should become involved in—the evaluation of ends and goals of our political system. We seem to be caught up in pell-mell attempts to justify our research by its precision and objectivity, rather than by its contribution to a valuable goal that we assert to be important.

This striving for objectivity and scientific precision has in large part removed us from our own understanding of ourselves and of our society. It has tended to diminish our awareness of the significance of individuals and their needs, feelings, and values. We have come to defer to the scientists, technicians and all other "experts" who have available to them the vast apparatus and scientific techniques. They are left to make judgments which we in turn accept as being more expert, therefore better than our own. We have lost our ability to criticize the experts. Experts are right. Experts have the information. Experts have the power. Individuals merely act out what the expert decides is best for them, and in so doing are relieved of the responsibility of deciding what is good and bad. The consequences of giving up our judgments are clear. We no longer value our own values. We no longer believe we know what is good for us or for our society. We have become servants of the experts, not because they have better goals or values, but because they have developed techniques of gathering the information which might be used to make such judgments. The more experts and expertise we have, the less control we have over the goals to be pursued. In summary, it seems we are developing a society in which we no longer have the capacity to evaluate where we are going and whether our direction is good. Deference to the role of methods and objectivity has resulted in our dismissal of evaluating human goals.

I have suggested that the most basic human goal ought to be the creation of greater control over one's life and the society that in part determines that life. By such a criterion the very pursuit of objectivity and science works against the individual controlling his environment. The individual becomes a pawn in a society that is dedicated to improving means rather than to evaluating ends. The individual is no longer a valuable and significant person, but merely an object to be related to the imperatives operative in a technological society.

These are some of the sources of skepticism about two of the most fundamental assumptions underlying the scope and methods of political science. We have found reason to question whether democracy as practiced in this country is the best government to achieve the "good life" for people and we also have found reason to be skeptical about science and objectivity as research goals. These are not easy matters to evaluate. You will have to think through for yourself what your opinion is. You might keep in mind the question which began this chapter: Does *scientific analysis of democracy* give you any more control over your own life?

What Research in Political Analysis Should Be—Action Research

What I have been describing in this chapter is a more or less traditional view of political analysis. In this section I would like to suggest what I believe is wrong with this mode of analysis, and an alternative which I prefer for both moral and professional reasons. I raise the question of morality in this context because of my personal conviction that the problems in our society are of such critical nature as to require the creative and informed efforts of all of us to solve as well as study problems if we are to survive. I think it is time for intellectuals, researchers and students alike seriously to evaluate why they are doing the research they are doing.

Before considering a morally preferable approach to research, I need to characterize the traditional view of analysis. Traditional analysis has at its very core the notion of objectivity in making the observation about the relationships among variables. Part of the credo of traditional political analysis has been centered in the necessity for remaining aloof and objective in the analysis. This has usually been interpreted to mean that even though the researcher may have values and a deep concern about the problems he investigates, he must assume the posture of non-involvement in that problem. In other words, he must observe the problem or perhaps other people attempting to solve the problem, but he at all costs must remain objective and non-involved. It is argued that non-involvement in the problem makes it more likely that the researcher can make the judgments and observation necessary to analyze critically what is going on in the political world he is researching. If this is the essence of research I must confess I find the notion totally unacceptable in these times when every citizen has the deep and continuing responsibility to contribute solutions to the many difficult and complex problems facing us.

The approach I am persuaded to use might be called "action research." As the words suggest, the researcher not only identifies and theorizes about the problem which he finds significant, but takes action upon the problem in order to bring about solutions or preferred outcomes. Objectivity becomes essential when measuring the impacts or consequences of the researcher's intervention into the problem area. Whenever there is involvement in solving a problem, it is difficult to analyze objectively what was done and how successfully. I find this risk small indeed compared to what I consider the immorality of not accepting the responsibility for and attempting to solve the problems existing in our society. I would not disagree that students should remain objective and critical, but

I would emphasize that our objectivity must be employed in solving our problem. I believe that we are entrusted with the task of applying all our knowledge and understanding to solving the problems which overwhelm us. In my judgment it is the application of understanding that justifies our research efforts, as opposed to simply developing a warehouse of knowledge, hoping someone will use it for good purpose.

Let me give an example of the distinction between action research and the more traditional mode of analysis. Racism is a problem in this country. Given the more traditional perspective upon research, the researcher might attempt to focus upon some particular consequences of racist attitudes in this society. For example, he might try to appraise the effect upon electoral outcomes of people holding particular attitudes about black people. Or he might want to find out the extent of support for various kinds of poverty, welfare, and education programs designed to help blacks overcome their problems. There is no end to the amount of research that might be done and made available to policy makers. On the other hand, in action research, one could actively engage in the creation of a program aimed at changing racist attitudes within a community. Such solutions might include training programs for white parents on ways to raise their children to reject racist attitudes. Or, approaching the problem from another direction, programs could be created to bring disadvantaged students into a university. This assistance might involve developing support programs and curricula which meet their needs while at the same time attempting to provide an education that will permit them meaningful participation in the society. In both situations the researcher would attempt to identify, measure, and relate the different aspects of these programs. He would be concerned to find out what approaches are most effective in bringing about the impacts he desires. Further, he would research the consequences of bringing about these changes in the university and in the broader community.

From my view the political analyst involved in this manner is acting in a morally consistent way with the need to solve problems while at the same time accumulating knowledge.

I am convinced that the researcher, with his knowledge and understanding of problems, should not simply stand back and watch "mad men" achieve mad consequences. Quite simply, I find it morally unacceptable to remain in an ivory tower when the kinds of problems we face do not afford us the time to wait for someone else to save us. As students and citizens in this country we have the deep and profound responsibility of abdicating our neutrality to become directly and actively involved in the solution of problems, while at the same time maintaining our commitment to objectivity, precision, and scientific rigor to the extent possible.

PART II

A WAY OF LOOKING AT POLITICS

CHAPTER 4

POLITICS IN CONFLICT, CONSENSUS, AND CHANGE

I believe that we are losing control of our own lives and of our society's future in large part because we can no longer distinguish between what is possible and what is preferable—what we can do and what we should do. Yet the distinction is clear indeed. Just because we can do things such as attending college, fighting wars all over the world, or sending space ships to other planets, does not mean necessarily that we should go to college, fight wars all over the world, or send space ships to the planets. I might further suggest that just because we should do things does not mean that we can, but this point seems too obvious to belabor. If control is exerted in our lives as well as in our society through making choices, and if we can no longer distinguish between what we can and what we should be doing, then it is impossible to exert that control to gain either the "good life" or the "good society." I need to explain this in a bit more detail.

Perhaps, as some people have suggested in this age of technology, we have come to place so much emphasis upon learning how to do something and creating the capability to do it that we have forgotten why it is we have developed the capability, what we want to use it to accomplish, and whether these purposes are good ones. It seems that we have come to accept a social ethos that says, "If we can, then by all means let's get it done." And it is in just this way that our spiraling technological capability usurps and devalues our human need to have choice and control of our lives. It is as if our technology and science have provided us with means, and that somehow in doing this have also provided a justification for using those means without evaluating them. Nothing could be further from the truth.

We may have the capability for producing enough material conveniences to destroy our environment, or to produce the biological, chemical, and nuclear weapons to destroy the world, or to produce enough people to consume all our resources to feed and care for them, but none of these capabilities seems to justify doing any of these things. On the other hand, there are many things that we as a society are not as yet capable of doing, such as feeding the hungry people in this world or providing meaningful work for people in our society, but this does not mean to me that we should not be trying to do them.

We must no longer tolerate the belief that what we can do defines what we should do. We must be able to choose the ways in which we are going to utilize our capability to bring about valued purposes, and at the same time we must use valued goals to choose what capability we want to develop. If we cannot make such choices, then surely we are no more than cogs in a giant machine over which we have little control, and in which there is little purpose beyond self-perpetuation. We must not allow human purposes to be distorted or destroyed by our pursuit of technological capability.

Saying this, it also becomes clear that we must know what our capabilities are in order to be able to make judgments about the ways to use them. In this sense we must also know how politics operates in order to be able to evaluate and choose the ways we are going to use these political processes to create a better life for people. This chapter is my explanation of the ways in which politics operates. With this understanding we then are better able to make choices about the ways we want to use these processes. Knowing how it operates permits us to choose whether to change it, leave it alone, or get away from it all together. With this context we can now survey some of the major concepts used in political analysis and relate those concepts to the ways in which politics operates.

I think it is fair to say that political science is attempting to explain both human behavior and thinking as they relate to politics. In a sense the entirety of this book is an elaboration of this statement. In the present chapter we will review some of the concepts used by political scientists to understand human behavior and thinking. We will find that these concepts have the common focus of trying to explain control over human behavior. We will see that the concept of power is used to analyze the ways that external controls operate to affect human behavior, and that the concept of attitude is used to understand how internal controls determine human behavior. This then brings us to the definition of politics that I have suggested. Politics is a study of the ways people control and are controlled as they adapt to a changing environment. But first we can review the concepts relevant to understanding human behavior, and then go on to concepts concerned with human thinking.

CONCEPTS RELEVANT TO POLITICAL BEHAVIOR

Contemporary political analysis has placed primary emphasis upon human behavior as the focus of research. Perhaps the greatest proportion of our theorizing has been directed to the problem of distinguishing political behavior from other kinds of human activity. I am not sure this effort has been well directed, but nonetheless it is necessary in this assessment to clarify how political scientists distinguish their subject matter from what economists, sociologists, psychologists, and other social scientists are studying. The definitions of political behavior are as numerous and as diverse as their advocates, but these definitions have a common concern with the concept of power. I think there is little disagreement with the statement that power is the primary unit of analysis in the study of politics, but let us consider what some leading political scientists have to say about this matter. Vernon Van Dyke says, "Politics, then, becomes a process taking place within and among groups—a process in which power (influence and control over others) is gained, maintained, and used."[1] Before his death, V. O. Key Jr., one of the most esteemed political scientists in this country, defined politics as power. He argued, "Politics as power consists fundamentally of relationships of superordination and subordination, of dominance and submission, of the governors and the governed. The study of politics is the study of these relationships."[2] Another prominent political scientist of some time ago, George E. G. Catlin, spoke of ". . . politics as a study of the act of control, or as the act of human

1. Vernon Van Dyke, *International Politics* (New York: Appleton-Century-Crofts, Inc., 1957), p. 6.

2. V. O. Key Jr., *Politics, Parties, and Pressure Groups,* 4th ed. (New York: Thomas Y. Crowell Co., 1958), p. 5.

or social control."[3] Harold D. Lasswell, perhaps the major figure in the development of the behavioral approach to political analysis, states simply, "The study of politics is the study of influence and the influential."[4] Another central figure in political science, Robert A. Dahl, defines politics in the following way: "A political system is any persistent pattern of human relationships that involves, to a significant extent, power, rule, or authority."[5] He further argues " . . . that influence is a *relation among* actors in which one actor induces other actors to act in some way they would not otherwise act."[6] He uses the notion of power to specify a particular type of influence. For Dahl, power is the special kind of influence that involves extreme positive or negative sanctions.[7]

In these several conceptualizations of politics we find a repeated theme of power having to do with individual and group behaviors that cause other people and/or groups to change the way they normally behave. For example, people pay taxes, are drafted, buy certain advertised products rather than others, and take final examinations as a result of their involvement in power relationships with others.

Having identified political behavior as consisting of actions which change others' behavior, the next step is to locate the most likely places where one can observe power relationships among individuals and groups. Here we again find some consensus among political scientists as to which activities are most likely to involve political power. Another contemporary political theorist, David Easton, has specified this location of power relationships in his definition of political science. He suggests, "The study of politics is concerned with understanding how authoritative decisions are made and executed for a society."[8] Without trying to overindulge in jargon, I may say that each word in this definition introduces important considerations which you will need to bear in mind. For present purposes, we can be satisfied with understanding that for many theorists, political behavior and therefore power relationships are to be found and observed in processes of human activity which *distribute* (or in Easton's term *allocate*) advantages or disadvantages among people in society and in *general acceptance* by people of these distributions. Such distributions of

3. George E. G. Catlin, *A Study of the Principles of Politics* (New York: Macmillan Co., 1930), pp. 68–69.

4. Harold D. Lasswell, *Politics* (New York: Whittlessey House, 1936), p. 1.

5. Robert A. Dahl, *Modern Political Analysis* (Englewood Cliffs, N.J.: Prentice-Hall, 1965), p. 6.

6. *Ibid.,* p. 40.

7. *Ibid.,* p. 50.

8. David Easton, "The Analysis of Political Systems," *Comparative Politics: Notes and Readings,* eds. Roy C. Macridis and Bernard E. Brown, 3rd ed. (Homewood, Ill.: The Dorsey Press, 1968), p. 87.

values require decisions as to who gets what (e.g., status, prestige, income, safety, and deference). The sequence of activities which have as their primary function the distribution of values are frequently referred to as decision-making processes. And it is in such decision-making processes that political scientists are most likely to observe individuals and groups acting out power relationships in an attempt to get others to defer to their particular desires.

To return to the previous example, it is relatively easy to think of paying taxes and going into the military as behavior traits resulting from decision-making processes involving powerful individuals and groups. The laws and policies resulting from governmental decision-making are only a part of the political picture. The manufacturer of an advertised product as well as a college professor makes decisions to change people's behavior. The manufacturer spends large amounts of money to get people to buy his product, and the professor imposes grade sanctions to get students to study in his course.

So far we have identified political behavior as that behavior oriented to the exercise of power in society, and we have specified that such exercise of power is most likely to be found in decision-making processes. We are left with one more major concept to introduce in this assessment of the analysis of political behavior, the concept of system.

A political system is a collection of power relationships at some particular moment in time in the process of making decisions. There are several alternative definitions of political system which we should consider.

David Easton was one of the first to introduce this notion of a political system. He states in his book, *The Political System,* ". . . that the phenomena of politics tend to cohere and to be mutually related. Such phenomena form, in other words, a system which is part of the total system and yet which, for purposes of analysis and research, is temporarily set apart."[9] Gabriel A. Almond and James S. Coleman elaborate upon this theme and point out " . . . that the political system is that system of interactions to be found in all independent societies which perform the functions of integration and adaptation (both internally and vis-a-vis other societies) by means of the employment or threat of employment of more or less legitimate physical compulsion."[10] In less formidable language Frank Sorauf states, "What we have been calling the political system may also be viewed as a series of consecutive activities which culminate in the

9. David Easton, *The Political System: An Inquiry into the State of Political Science* (New York: Alfred A. Knopf, 1959), pp. 96–97.

10. Gabriel A. Almond and James S. Coleman, *The Politics of Developing Areas* (Princeton, N.J.: Princeton University Press, 1960), p. 7.

making of authoritative, binding decisions ('public policy').''[11] Sorauf continues to relate the notions of system, decision–making, and power by arguing that "One can, in fact, imagine a rough hierarchy of these arbitrative, goal-setting systems, the ones at the top having broader coverage and more potent enforcement power than those below them. The system of social control at the top of the hierarchy we call the political system.''[12]

For the purpose of becoming acquainted with major concepts it is necessary only that you understand that a political system is a collection of behavior traits oriented toward the exercise of power (causing others to behave in ways they would not otherwise behave) in which the power relationships are dependent upon each other. In concrete terms you can imagine this concept applying to legislative systems (e.g., Congress, state legislatures, city councils, and parliaments), judicial systems (e.g., the United States Supreme Court, state supreme courts, and other federal, state, and local courts) and executive systems (e.g., the office of president of the United States, corporate managers, city mayors, and prime ministers).

Congress provides an excellent example of a political system. These lawmakers are constantly considering bills and making decisions (i.e., passing bills into law) that try to change the way people behave. There are many groups and individuals attempting to exert control over congressmen in this process, and what one group or individual does in the process affects what others do. These behavior traits are oriented toward controlling others and are interdependent. In this sense we can use the concept of a political system to describe behavior traits in the legislative process.

The foregoing has been a brief review of some major concepts relevant to the analysis of political *behavior;* the following is an attempt to define some major concepts about human thinking as it relates to politics.

CONCEPTS RELEVANT TO POLITICAL THINKING

Political scientists have been somewhat hesitant to deal theoretically with the phenomena of human thought. The rationale for this hesitancy lies within the rules of scientific procedure. Science directs its attention to that which can be measured by the direct observation of researchers. Human thinking is not observable. The best that can be done is to infer about thought processes from behavior traits that can be observed. Variables

11. Frank J. Sorauf, *Perspectives on Political Science* (Columbus, Ohio: Charles E. Merrill Books, Inc., 1965), p. 5.

12. *Ibid.,* p. 3.

which cannot be directly observed but must be inferred from the observation of other variables are called hypothetical variables. Hypothetical variables are not new to science, but they have always been a source of uneasiness. When the scientist makes inferences without direct observation, the processes of reason and presumably bias and error become disproportionately important. Social scientists have been advised by many to avoid concepts that involve variables that cannot be observed, and to remain true to a science which rests most comfortably upon that which is directly perceived.

Perhaps it is a sign of intellectual maturity that social scientists are now moving beyond the limitations imposed by a too severe definition of our procedures. They are more willing than in the past to admit the complexity of the human calculus and to focus upon behavior as a product of a highly sophisticated thinking organism. The central concept borrowed to begin the analysis of man's thinking as it relates to politics is the attitude. As power was the primary unit of analysis in the investigation of political behavior, the attitude is the unit of analysis in understanding human thought.

Political scientists have borrowed the concept of attitude from social psychology and it has been defined in different ways, but there is general acceptance of the basic notion that an attitude is *a predisposition to behave* in a similar manner in varying situations which the person confronts.[13] By the phrase "a predisposition to behave," political scientists mean that the person is more likely to behave in one manner than in some other. For instance, I have an attitude about wearing ties to lecture classes—I do not like to wear them. Therefore, I am less likely to wear a tie in a classroom situation than is someone with a more positive attitude about ties. Of course, there are multitudes of attitudes about all kinds of social and physical objects making up the environment. *The collection of attitudes that an individual has can be thought of as his attitudinal system.* Here we are using the term *system* to describe the interdependency of an individual's attitudes in much the same way we used the concept of system to describe the interdependencies among power relationships in the decision-making processes.

As before, political analysts are not concerned about every attitude in the individual's attitudinal system, and it makes some sense to say that they are most interested in those attitudes which predispose individuals to behave in particular ways in political processes. As they are concerned in the analysis of human behavior with power relationships among people,

13. For a more detailed review of several conceptual notions about attitudes see Milton Rokeach, "The Nature of Attitudes," *International Encyclopedia of Social Sciences* 1 (New York: Macmillan Co., 1968), pp. 449–570.

they are also interested in the analysis of human thinking, beginning with attitudes which predispose people to act as they do in these power relationships.

When people interact with each other in political systems, many of them share attitudes as to what particular behavior traits they are most likely to act out. We can conceptualize a collection of individual attitudes held by members of a group or society (i.e., attitudes about how they will behave in the political system) as being a political culture. Political systems can be conceptualized as the way people behave toward one another in power relationships, and a political culture permits the analyst to conceptualize about the predispositions causing them to behave that way. It is possible to think of the political culture of a student body in a university as including attitudes many students have about the ways they should behave toward the administration, toward teachers, toward police on campus, and toward student government.

This notion of political culture is relatively new to political analysis but a recent work of pervasive influence in our discipline has included the following definition:

> The term political culture thus refers to the specifically political orientations—attitudes toward the political system and its various parts, and attitudes toward the role of self in the system. We speak of a political culture just as we speak of an economic culture or a religious culture. . . . When we speak of the political culture of a society, we refer to the political system as internalized in the cognitions, feelings, and evaluations of its population.[14]

This completes a brief sketch of some major concepts being used by political scientists to construct theories about human behavior and thinking as they relate to politics. If the above assessment is indeed a reflection of the conceptual foci of political analysis, then there is a central theme which can be inferred from this survey. Both the analysis of political behavior and attitudes have the common characteristic of being concerned with control over individual and group behavior. Perhaps you have already noted the similarity between the concept of power and attitude discussed above and the notions of external and internal control introduced in the latter part of the first chapter. Power is external control over behavior while attitudes are internal controls over behavior. Now it is possible to construct some theoretical elements to organize the study of politics.

Power is defined as being the major unit of analysis in theorizing about processes of external control, and attitudes are central to understanding processes of internalizing control among people in society.

---

14. Gabriel A. Almond and Sidney Verba, *The Civic Culture* (Princeton, N.J.: Princeton University Press, 1963), pp. 13–14.

With this link established between the problem of the distribution of internal and external control in society introduced in Chapter One and the major concepts being used by political analysts we can now proceed with the task of theorizing about relationships and reasons helpful in understanding politics.

SPECIFYING THE INGREDIENTS OF POLITICS

Several times in the preceding chapters I have said that I think of *politics as the ways or processes*[15] *by which people control themselves and others and are controlled by others as they make or influence choices about how they will solve problems arising from conditions in their environment.* Perhaps the real utility of a definition such as this is that it points out what elements we should be looking for in politics. So what are some of the ingredients which this definition specifies as being political?

The definition tells us to look for ways people control and are controlled in their choice-making. In other words, we need to examine the notion of power (external control over people). Here I think there are two distinct political activities we need to understand. The first kind of political activity includes actions that create power for people as they come into conflict with and attempt to control what others are doing. The second kind of political activity involving power is the use of power to resolve conflicts over what the group or society is going to do about its common problems. As people attempt to solve their shared problems arising from changing circumstances, they act to create power and to use that power to manage or control others so that the resulting solution (e.g., the public policy which will be binding upon all the people) is most consistent with their particular interests, values, and purposes.

But it should already be clear that people are not only controlled by power relationships external to them, but that they are also controlled by attitudes and by the ways they think about things. So the definition tells us to look for ways that people are controlled by their attitudes. As with the notion of power, we specified two kinds of activities external to people —the creation and use of power—and we now can specify the processes that are involved in the ways people are controlled by their attitudes. First, we need to understand the ways that people learn or internalize the attitudes they have about politics. When we talk about individuals learning

15. We use the concept of process to refer to interrelated events taking place over a period of time. That is, there can be a process of making steel, a process of thinking, a process of making decisions, or whatever, as long as the events referred to are somehow tied together and taking place over a period of time.

about politics, we refer to political socialization, and in the same sense we can conceptualize about how many people in a society learn similar attitudes as the making of a political culture. So we need to understand how individuals and collections of people learn common attitudes which control the ways they act in politics. But we cannot assume that such attitudes never change once they are formed, so we need to examine the ways that individual attitudes and political cultures are changed and in turn how that fact affects people's behavior traits.

Finally, the definition tells us that politics also involves change in our environment, which generates needs for adaptations in the ways we behave (i.e., public policy changes). In other words, change is fundamental to politics. Man is both the product of and the producer of change. He is the product of environmental changes which result in his producing public policies (or adaptations in collective behavior) that create further changes in the environment.

Now that we have identified some of the various ingredients which were defined as being political, we need to bring the pieces together in a more concise way in order to theorize about the relationship among these elements. I have identified the creation and use of power as political activities in that they control the behavior of people. We learned earlier that such external control over people's behavior (i.e., power relationships) can be conceptualized as being a political system. You will recall that a political system is a collection of power relationships at some particular time in a decision–making process. So our concern with using and creating power (i.e., external controls) in the process of making public policy adaptations to environmental changes leads us to look at the political system.

The two most important variable characteristics of a political system are the extent to which conflict is perceived by people in the system and the effectiveness of people manipulating that conflict to reach solutions. So we are asking two different questions about conflict as a variable characteristic of the political system. What is the level of conflict perceived by people in the political system, and how effectively is that conflict manipulated to bring about policy adaptations or solutions? The political system has two variable characteristics which affect the ways that external controls operate in our society. The level of perceived conflict affects the degree of power that can be created in a society, and the manipulation of these conflicts involves the use of power to make public policy adaptations binding people to some particular solution.

In the same sense that we used the concept of political system to think about external controls in society, we can use the concept of political culture to think about the internalized controls. As the level of perceived conflict and the effectiveness of conflict manipulation are the major variables of concern in the political system, the extent of political consensus and the effectiveness of consensus formation and change are the major variable attributes of a political culture. We can think of consensus as being the extent of shared agreement among the attitudes held by a collectivity of people. So the variable of consensus needs to be examined by asking two different questions. What is the extent of political consensus, and how effective is the society in forming and changing that level of consensus?

The balance of this chapter will elaborate upon these notions of conflict in the political system, consensus in the political culture, and environmental changes affecting the political system and culture through public policy adaptations that bind people to changed ways of thinking and behaving. In this way conflict, consensus, and change become central to our analysis of theorizing about politics.

There is nothing new in this attempt to analyze politics by focusing upon the concepts of conflict, consensus, and change. Indeed, the primary reason that I have selected these concepts as the tools for organizing an introduction to political analysis is that they are themes often suggested by students of politics as central to their work.

Generally, though, political scientists have been more intent upon talking about conflict while giving less attention to consensus. I am attempting here to bring both of these notions together with the concept of change as a way of theorizing about diverse themes of political analysis. A few examples from current literature will support this choice of concepts for inclusion in a theory.

E. E. Schattschneider in a classic analysis of politics argues, "At the nub of politics are, first, the way in which the public participates in the spread of conflict and, second, the processes by which the unstable relation of the public to the conflict is controlled."[16] For Schattschneider, the creation of conflict and the management of that conflict among the people involved is central to political analysis. As further illustration I refer to two textbooks for political science, both of which argue that political science is primarily investigating conflict and its resolution.

Robert Dahl in his text *Pluralist Democracy in the United States* says that man's existence as a social being is controlled by three "contradictory tendencies." He feels that man needs fellowship and so forms communities, but that man is unable to live in a community without conflict; therefore, communities must adjust these conflicts. Dahl then defines political activity:

> The third stage in this dialectic is the turning point from man as a social animal to man as a political animal. For if conflicts are to be settled, somewhere in

16. E. E. Schattschneider, *The Semi-Sovereign People* (New York: Holt, Rinehart and Winston, 1960), p. 3.

the community there must be individuals or groups with enough authority or power to secure—if need be to compel—a settlement; to make sure that the parties to a conflict abide by the judgment of the rule, the will of God, existing rules, their own agreement or law. At any rate, human communities do not seem ever to have existed without some such powers without, that is, political institutions.[17]

Dahl agrees that the settlement of conflict and the power to enforce or manage such settlements are the essential ingredients of political problems. Dan Nimmo and Thomas D. Ungs argue in their introductory text that politics can be thought of as the way social conflict is regulated in the community. They say, "In this sense, we define politics as a series of human activities related to adjusting social disputes, a series manifested in patterned form."[18]

I am not suggesting that political scientists, particularly those cited above, have been unaware of the importance of consensus as well as of conflict in the understanding of politics. Indeed, both Dahl and Nimmo and Ungs point out the importance of political consensus to political analysis. Nimmo and Ungs suggest that conflict and consensus are related in the following manner: "This working consensus helps define the issues that must be resolved and the effective limits of political conflict at any given time."[19] Certainly political scientists are aware of the importance of consensus to political analysis, but their tendency has been to define politics as conflict and its control. The direction I am taking emphasizes the necessity of thinking about politics as composed of conflict, consensus, and change, not just of conflict by itself.

Seymour M. Lipset, a political sociologist, suggests a similar conception by defining politics as an interplay of conflict and consensus in his discussion of "democracy" as a political form.

> Surprising as it may sound, a stable democracy requires the manifestation of conflict or cleavage so that there will be struggle over ruling positions, challenges to parties in power, and shifts of parties in office; but without a consensus—a political system allowing the peaceful "play" of power, the adherence by the "outs" to decisions made by the "ins", and the recognition by the "ins" of the rights of the "outs"—there can be no democracy. The study of the conditions encouraging democracy must therefore focus on the sources of both cleavage and consensus. [20]

17. Robert A. Dahl, *Pluralist Democracy in the United States* (Chicago: Rand McNally and Co., 1967), p. 7.

18. Dan Nimmo and Thomas D. Ungs, *American Political Patterns* (Boston: Little, Brown and Co., 1967), p. 11.

19. *Ibid.,* p. 27.

20. Seymour M. Lipset, *Political Man* (Garden City, N.Y.: Anchor Books, 1963), p.1.

Consistent with this vein of thought Robert C. North has more recently stated rather bluntly ". . . that all human relations may be viewed as interlaced by two closely related processes—the conflictual and the integrative."[21] He elaborates this statement with the following argument:

> Whenever two or more individuals or groups come into contact with each other, they may choose to make their relationship primarily conflictual or primarily integrative (i.e. cooperative, supportive, agreed upon). If the initial relationship is primarily conflictual, there will nevertheless emerge at least a few minimal strands of understanding and reciprocity—rules of combat, or perhaps only an agreement to disagree. If, on the other hand, the initial relationship is primarily integrative, it is certain that conflict will develop—if for no other reason than the demands of the association itself as they compete with the preferences of individuals and component groups.[22]

It is of considerable importance that one of the leading contemporary "conflict theorists," Lewis Coser, has concluded that both consensus and conflict are essential to understanding social dynamics.

> Peace and feuding, conflict and order, are correlative. Both the cementing and the breaking of the cake of custom constitute part of the dialectic of social life. One is hence ill-advised to distinguish sharply a sociology of order from a sociology of conflict, or a harmony model of society from a conflict model. Such attempts can only result in artificial distinctions. The analysis of social conflicts brings to awareness aspects of social reality that may be obscured if analytical attention focuses too exclusively on phenomena of social order; but an exclusive attention to conflict phenomena may obscure the central importance of social order and needs to be corrected by a correlative concern with the ordered aspects of social life. We deal here not with distinct realities but only with differing aspects of the same reality, so that exclusive emphasis on one or the other is likely to lead the analyst astray.[23]

It is my intent in this conceptualization of politics to take the good advice of Professor Coser while at the same time extending the logic to include also the interrelatedness of change with conflict and consensus. To do this I need to make two assumptions explicit before proceeding with this model of politics.

The first assumption is that environmental changes are inherent in society. Change can be so slow as to be barely perceptible, as it often is in traditional societies. It can also be so rapid as to defy the ability of people in the society to cope with its effects. The rapidity of change in industrial

21. Robert C. North, "Conflict: Political Aspects," *International Encyclopedia of Social Sciences* (New York: Macmillan Co., 1966), p. 226.

22. *Ibid.*

23. Lewis A. Coser, "Conflict: Social Aspects," *International Encyclopedia of Social Sciences* (New York: Macmillan, 1966), pp. 235–236.

society has become so commonplace that it hardly needs further comment. Change exists in all societies, but the rate of change varies from very slow to extremely rapid.

There is a distinction between environmental changes and adaptive public policy changes. Environmental changes can be thought of as differences occurring between two points in time in the physical, social, and cultural characteristics of a society. Such differences can be a result of natural events (e.g., population growth, earthquakes, floods) or they can be the product of human intervention into the environment (e.g., technology, industrialization, urbanization). Adaptive policy changes, on the other hand, are a result of man's intention to control the human condition in order to adjust social priorities and to distribute resources to meet these priorities. That is, adaptive policy changes are changes made in political processes for the purpose of coping with the problems arising from environmental change. The most obvious example is public policy changes made by ruling groups to bind people to different modes of behavior than previously existed in order to cope with changing environmental conditions in the society. This notion of adaptive policy changes is consistent with the second major assumption I am making, which deals with human nature itself.

I am assuming that the essential quality of man's nature is his adaptive capability as he attempts to increase predictability for himself and for his society in an uncertain world. Man does not simply calculate means and ends. Nor does he mechanistically respond to environmental stimuli, nor does he simply balance realities and instincts. Man's behavior and thought are with purpose. Smith, Bruner, and White clearly articulate this assumption concerning human nature.

> The human being, according to this approach, is not governed by a rational calculus, nor is he a blank slate on which experience traces its inexorable mark. Nor yet is man an ingenious machine translating physical stimuli into bodily responses. Like all animals, he is an organism, a system of life processes that somehow maintains its identity in active interplay with its environment. An organism is never passive, but survives and grows through constant striving, responding selectively to relevant aspects of its environment, and reaching out to incorporate, modify, fend off, or attain. Final passivity is death; in life there is always striving to maintain the delicate adaptation of needs of the organism to its environment.[24]

These are the assumptions, one about society and one about man. Change is inherent in society. The rate of environmental change varies

---

24. M. Brewster Smith, Jerome S. Bruner, and Robert W. White, *Opinions and Personality* (New York: John Wiley and Sons, Inc., 1956), p. 30.

along a continuum ranging from a rapid to a slow rate of change. Adaptive changes also vary along a continuum of effectiveness (i.e., more or less effective adaptations). Purposeful striving to cope with the environment and therefore to increase certainty is inherent in man's nature. Man is a problem-solving animal. And the fundamental challenge to his nature is change.

With these assumptions explicit we can proceed to sketch, first with broad strokes and then in finer detail, this concept of politics as involving processes of conflict, consensus, and change.

A SKETCH OF THE THEORY

My purpose in this section is to use the assumptions, definitions, and distinctions already established, as well as some others, to lay out the general outlines of this way of understanding politics.

Environmental changes, however rapid their rate, have the consequence of changing the experiences of people in the society. People learn from their attempts to cope with these changing experiences. This learning is internalized in the form of attitudes or predispositions about appropriate behavior. To the extent that the experiences of a person vary a great deal, and the rate of environmental change is rapid, it is necessary for that individual to learn new attitudes about the appropriate behavior for these different circumstances. For example, the environmental changes occurring as a society becomes more industrialized and less agrarian require the people in that society to learn how to get along in the world by working in factories and by living in cities rather than by farming and by living in rural areas.

Of the many attitudes that people learn from their changing experiences, two sets are most important to the politics of that society. The first set of attitudes is about individual preferences—preferences concerning which goods and symbols are to be valued over others. In other words, individuals learn *value priorities* in terms of their particular views of the good life. As a consequence of continual experiences with a "cold war" they may learn to value protection of the community as a first priority, pursuing economic values as a second priority, education of the young as a third priority, and the welfare of others in the society as a still lower priority. Given different circumstances or conditions, they might learn an entirely different set of priorities. In any case, people learn what is of greater and lesser value given their individual experiences in their way of life.

The second set of attitudes relevant to politics is formed as people learn who will benefit from the allocation of resources. I can best illustrate the distinction between these two sets of attitudes by the example of white and black militancy in the United States during the 1960s. White radicals appeared to be questioning the basic value priorities in the society and devaluing the most highly valued goods and symbols in affluent, middle-class America. The black militants appeared to be more concerned with becoming a part of the groups benefiting the most from the already existing value priorities. In other words, the black leadership seemed more concerned with moving into suburbia than with "dropping out" to form a new and different social order.

People learn, as a consequence of coping with their changing environment, *what is to be valued* and *how valued benefits are to be distributed among the people.* All people do not learn the same attitudes from the same experiences. Depending upon who they are and upon where they are in the social context, they will learn different attitudes from the same environmental changes. The ghetto resident learns to cope with urban renewal beautification projects in an entirely different way than does the member of the Chamber of Commerce. The more diverse the experiences in society and the more rapid the rate of change, the less likely it is that people will have similar attitudes either about priorities or about the distributions of benefits.

So far, I have been talking about individuals coping with their changing experiences in relationship to attitudes relevant to politics. If we shift from the individual to the social level by focusing upon the political culture rather than upon individual attitudes (you will recall that political culture has been defined as a collection of attitudes held by people in a society relevant to political action in the society), we can now investigate the extent to which there is agreement in the collection of attitudes existing among the individuals in a particular society. In other words, the extent of agreement or consensus is a variable characteristic of a political culture. The collection of attitudes in a society may be mostly in agreement or they may be virtually in total disagreement (i.e., either high or low consensus). What I am suggesting is that as the rate of change increases there is less possibility of consensus among people. As rates of environmental change increase, the level of value consensus decreases. As value consensus in the political culture decreases, the internal social controls are less effective. People no longer agree as to what is appropriate behavior, so they are no longer controlled by internalized norms. With fewer internal controls working in a less effective manner, it becomes necessary for the leaders to raise the level of external control in order to maintain order in the society. Decreasing consensus leads to increasing conflicts and disputes in people's behavior. Conflict increases to the extent that people have different and incompatible attitudes about what is appropriate. This context of increasing conflict has to be accommodated or resolved if the society is to survive.

Rising conflict has to be coped with by individuals. At this point I draw upon the assumption I made concerning human nature. Man requires predictability in the events occurring around him so that he may have a meaningful conception of himself. Given this assumption there will be a general demand from the people in a society for order and control of the level of conflict so that they can once again rely upon the ordering of the social context to permit their own life pursuits on relatively certain and predictable terrain. Conflict is fraught with uncertainty about the outcome, and uncertainties are the stuff of which alienation and apathy are composed. Such uncertainty and fear are the essential ingredients in the disintegration of human personality. In order to reduce these uncertainties and to increase the predictability of events it is necessary for the society to resolve conflicts.

Various groups and institutions in the society have the primary function of resolving conflict. To the extent they are successful in creating adaptive changes (i.e., new policy and law about what is appropriate behavior), conflict can be resolved. Of course, if these social agencies are not successful in making such adaptive changes, then the society continues to escalate the conflicts to the point of the eventual destruction of the entire social system.

In order to continue this discussion we can assume that conflicts are resolved by agencies making adaptive changes. In turn, then, these adaptive changes must be enforced through the continued use of external controls, since they have yet to be accepted or internalized by most of the people in the society. The society must expend resources in coercing or "bribing" people to accept the adaptive changes in values and benefits distributions. Such external controls are costly, thus reducing the amount of resources available to solve further problems. Therefore, it is necessary for the society to shift the weight of control from external controls to internal ones if it is to progress. In other words, there are *other groups and institutions in the society which have the primary function of forming and changing consensus.* As these agencies operate to "teach" members of the society what is now the appropriate behavior for them in light of the adaptive changes, people internalize these new modes of thought and behavior. The extent of agreement about what is appropriate increases. Other human agencies operate to reinforce this newly forming consensus and to maintain its basic tenets. Consensus begins to increase. *The society now completes a cycle of environmental changes lowering consensus, increasing conflict, and achieving a new consensus as adaptive conflict resolution is internalized.* The cycle has taken time to occur and during this time period new environmental changes have already taken place. Once again these changes erode the newly emergent consensus even before it is totally accepted by all members of the society.

What I have just sketched here essentially are spiraling cycles consisting of increasing environmental changes, decreasing consensus, increasing conflict, resolved conflict, and a new consensus, which is in turn decreasing.

This completes the theoretical view of politics as being composed of relationships among processes of change, consensus, and conflict. In the next section I want to offer a more detailed examination of the processes, variables, and relationships set out in this sketch.

CHAPTER 5

USING THE THEORY TO COPE WITH
A REAL PROBLEM

I think people want to become purposefully engaged in coping with changes in their environment, to make personal choices, and to influence public choices which determine how they will act out their lives. They need to live in a society which helps them to do this. Society helps them by providing opportunities for them to learn about themselves and about the ways in which their society operates. With this understanding they are better able to meet personal needs and to affect social goals in the confrontation with change.

I believe that politics is the way in which a society copes with change. I want the politics of our society to be creative—creative in the sense that it permits people to gain more control over their lives and society. I believe that these values are more likely to be realized if you have a better understanding of politics. This understanding permits you to affect choices that control your own and our society's future.

In the last chapter we reviewed concepts being used in political analysis and related them in a theory about politics. In this chapter I want to clarify that theory by using it to explain a particular political situation, and to make you aware of how such understanding can be used to cope with real life problem solving. I see this as the beginning of a process of being able to make choices and to take control of our lives.

Perhaps the best way to clarify this explanation of politics is to begin with the major variables discussed in the previous chapter.

VARIABLE 1: *Rate of Environmental Change:* This variable is designed to be a composite of such changes as increases in the rate of technological development, the rapidity of population movement from rural to urban areas, the rate at which the country becomes industrialized, and the rate of population growth. All of these changes can vary from lower to higher rates of change.

VARIABLE 2: *Level of Political Consensus:* Here we are concerned with the extent to which peoples' attitudes about politics agree. Of particular importance are attitudes having to do with value priorities (what people consider most important) and distribution of benefits (who will get that which is valued). This collection of shared attitudes—political culture—can be characterized as having either a higher or a lower consensus. That is, the level of political consensus about value priorities and benefit distribution can vary from practically total agreement to almost complete disagreement among people.

VARIABLE 3: *Level of Perceived Conflict:* This variable refers to the number of individuals and groups who perceive the disagreements involved in the lower levels of consensus. There are a wide variety of indices of the perception of disagreement, such as the number of people involved in protest and social movements, the number of incidents of public violence in the society, the number of political assassinations, the size of police and military forces required to maintain order, and the number of civil and criminal cases pending in the court systems. The level of perceived conflict varies from no perception of disagreement to wide perception of disagreement.

VARIABLE 4: *Effectiveness of Conflict Manipulation:* Given the rising levels of perceived conflict, this variable describes the extent to which groups, individuals, and/or institutions are successful in manipulating the conflict toward solutions which result in actual modification of social behavior. We will need to assess such phenomena as interest groups (e.g., corporations, military, religious, labor, management), para-military organizations, government institutions, and agencies. Effectiveness can vary from a modification of all behavior in the society to no change in peoples' behavior at all.

VARIABLE 5: *Number of Adaptive Public Policy Changes:* Here we are considering the number of new rules, public policies, laws, and/or executive dictates that can be enforced in the society. Such changes are adaptive to the extent that they can be enforced by the body creating the new rule. I am not saying such changes are just, equitable, or honorable, but if they can be enforced and if people abide by them, they are adaptive changes. This variable can range from no such changes in a particular period of time to a nearly infinite number of such rules.

VARIABLE 6: *Effectiveness of Consensus Formation and Change:* Finally, we need to consider the extent to which groups and institutions are successful in forming and changing agreement among people's attitudes about the legitimacy of the adaptive changes made. Such agencies as families, schools, churches, high status groups, work groups, and various public and private groups attempting to influence people's thinking may have the effect of increasing the legitimacy of new rules or of decreasing the acceptance of such rules in the minds of most people. If most people come to accept the new rules as legitimate, these agencies have been highly effective, and if not, the agencies are considered to be ineffective.

Having specified the six major variables in this theory we can now construct a model depicting or illustrating the interrelationships of the variables. A first model, shown in Figure 5, displays the basic relationship among three of the variables—the rate of environmental change, the level of political consensus, and the level of perceived conflict. Figure 5 illustrates the relationship between these three variables in the following way: as the rate of environmental changes increases, the level of political

FIGURE 5

**BASIC MODEL OF THE PROCESSES OF CONFLICT, CONSENSUS
AND CHANGE**

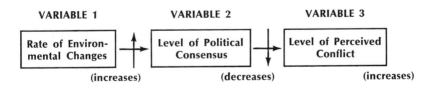

VARIABLE 1	VARIABLE 2	VARIABLE 3
Rate of Environ- mental Changes	Level of Political Consensus	Level of Perceived Conflict
(increases)	(decreases)	(increases)

consensus decreases, a fact which results in increasing conflict over priorities and distribution of benefits. We can now use an example to clarify what was just said.

THE UNIVERSITY AS AN EXAMPLE OF
THE MODEL AND THEORY

There are innumerable examples that might be used to illustrate this theoretical view of the processes of politics. I might use the example of a complex industrial society, a simple social organization such as an urban community or tribal society, or any one of a multitude of situations involving politics. I have chosen the university to illustrate these political processes. I have done so for two reasons. First, the university involves experiences and phenomena which are familiar to you, and second, one of the central arguments made in this text is that politics is inherent in any social organization.

The universities in this country during the mid-1960s were caught up in the spiraling events in the world about them. These events strained the existing consensus about what university policies should be. The major environmental events included the greater emphasis placed upon higher education by competitive Soviet technology and scientific achievement, the greater influx of new students as a result of the population boom, the fact that college education was becoming a normal expectation for a greater number of high school graduates, and the increasing intervention of Vietnam protest and civil rights movements into the quiet halls of the academic world.

These events are just a few examples of the escalating rate of change impinging upon the university communities during this period. Our theory suggests that as the rate of environmental change increases, the level of consensus about value priorities and benefit distributions decreases. Quite simply, there will be less agreement among the members in the university community as to what the university should be doing.

Examples of this breakdown of existing consensus are evident today in student demands that the universities respond to serious social problems by becoming involved in the solution of such problems. These demands are directed toward redefining the university as an instrument of social change rather than as a place of ivory halls and ivy. It is safe to say that there is considerable disagreement with new attitudes about higher education among many members of the university community as well as in the public at large. For many people (including a great many students) the university is still the place to educate the young and to produce necessary professional people for the society. The old consensus concerning higher education is under attack by new ideas about what the university should be doing. As the disagreements magnify among members of the university as well as between the university and the public at large, conflicts erupt. Groups and individuals attempting to impose their definition of the university's purpose by controlling the thinking and activity of those in the university typically polarize around two relatively extreme positions.

On the one hand are those wanting to transform the university into an instrument of social and cultural change, and on the other are those seeking to maintain the status quo of value priorities and advantages.

Two quotes seem best to illustrate the breakdown in consensus which was occurring on many campuses during the mid-1960s. The first is a quote from a speech by Mario Savio made during one of the "universities confrontation" in the fall of 1964 at the University of California at Berkeley:

> It is a bleak scene, but it is all a lot of us have to look forward to. Society provides no challenge. . . . American society in the standard conception it has of itself is simply no longer exciting. The most exciting things going on in America today are movements to change America. America is becoming ever-more the utopia of sterilized, automated contentment. The "futures" and "careers" for which American students now prepare are for the most part intellectual and moral wastelands. This chrome-plated consumer's paradise would have us grow up to be well behaved children. But an important minority of men and women coming to the front today have shown that they will die rather than be standardized, replaceable, and irrelevant.[1]

The second quote is taken from a speech by R. F. Dussalt made during the same revolt at about the same time as Savio's speech.

> The organization which I represent, University Students for Law and Order, was organized as an alternative course of action to the so-called Free Speech Movement. We believe that the FSM has exceeded the limits of protest acceptable to the majority of students at our university.
>
> There is no need nor is there any excuse for civil disobedience on this campus. Those students involved demand protection of their rights while at the same time they are violating our rights.
>
> As an organization USLO does not pretend to know solutions as to the varied and complex problems which presently confront us as students. But one fact is undeniably clear—that unless we are willing to express ourselves as a responsible body, we have no right to expect the continued financial support of the community at large.
>
> We therefore request that you express your moral support for our viewpoint

---

1. Seymour M. Lipset and Sheldon S. Wolin, eds., *The Berkeley Student Revolt* (Garden City, N.Y.: Anchor Books, 1965), p. 219.

by signing the petition which is now being circulated and by disassociating yourself from the FSM.[2]

The incompatibility of these respective student attitudes is clear, and the ensuing conflicts are a matter of recorded and somewhat tragic history. Confrontations, police brutality, student riots, bloodshed, and general chaos reigned. However, in most cases the conflicts were resolved and stability emerged. This emergent stability leads to an examination of the next stages in this theoretical spiral of politics.

The theory to this point indicates that as the rate of environmental change increases, attitudes change, and because people selectively perceive changing conditions, a wide diversity of attitudes results. That is, consensus declines among people as to what are the appropriate ways to behave. Specifically, the political consensus about value priorities and allocations decreases, and as this fact is perceived, conflicts escalate and groups seek to redefine priorities and the allocations of benefits by attempting to control what others are thinking and doing. The crucial question is—Can the rising level of conflicts be used to solve problems? In other words, can some group bring about a solution by taking advantage of the increasing awareness among larger numbers of people that there is a problem? People are motivated to bring about such solutions and to adapt to such solutions because of a psychological need for predictability. As consensus concerning appropriate behavior declines, people are motivated to form a new consensus defining in more predictable terms what is appropriate. Without such certainty individuals are deprived of one of the basic ingredients of the human condition—the need for certainty.

Before examining how conflict can be managed to create adaptive policy changes (solutions) and how these changes are to be legitimized in the minds of people, we need to clarify some of the distinctions being made in this argument.

First, we need to distinguish carefully between the *level of conflict* in the society and the *effective use of conflict* (i.e., manipulation) to bring about adaptive changes. The term "level of conflict" refers to the extent to which people perceive disagreement. The effective manipulation of conflict involves the creation of power and the effective use of power to control people's activity. Or as Schattschneider has said:

> Since politics has its origins in strife, political strategy deals with the exploitation, use and suppression of conflict.[3]

2. *Ibid.,* p. 226.

3. E. E. Schattschneider, *The Semi-Sovereign People* (New York: Holt, Rinehart, and Winston, 1960), p. 67.

He also contributes the following clarification to this discussion of effective manipulation of conflict:

All forms of political organization have a bias in favor of the exploitation of some kinds of conflict and the suppression of others because *organization is the mobilization of bias.*[4]

I have found his definition of organization, as the mobilization of bias, a useful tool in this theory. Power is created when people use their resources to bring about changes consistent with their "biases" or interests. Once power has been created by some organized group it becomes crucial that it be used effectively in order for their group's problem to be given highest priority and its solution accepted.

One more definition before we continue with the university situation as an illustration of these conceptual notions. The meaning of the concept of *stability* has caused some commotion among political scientists. I use stability to describe social situations in which individuals have relatively predictable life patterns. With this kind of definition it is clear that I conceive of social stability as being rooted in the characteristics of individuals. But these individual characteristics have impacts upon the society when enough people share either predictable or unpredictable life patterns. When most people in the society know what is going on and what is likely to happen in the future (i.e., there are high levels of certainty about present and future outcomes of their behavior) social organization tends to become more stable. When they are uncertain, instability and social disorganization result.[5]

I am not associating, as many political scientists do, the instability of a society with the presence of violence or with the rapidity of turnover of political rulers or institutions. Both violence and the rapid turnover of political institutions can be predictable occurrences to the members of the society. It is only when such events are unpredictable that instability results. We can now continue to illustrate the present conceptualization.

Figure 6 is a representation of the relationship among all the variables in this theory leading to stable social organization. The "cycle" presented in Figure 6 takes up where the basic model (Figure 5) left off—with rising levels of conflict in the society or in this case in the university situation.

In our university situation, the level of political consensus in the culture concerning what values the university should pursue and

4. *Ibid., p. 71.*

5. *See* James C. Davies, "Toward a Theory of Revolution," *The American Sociological Review,* 28 (1962), pp. 5-19, for a more extended discussion of this notion of instability and political revolution.

FIGURE 6

POLITICAL PROCESSES RESULTING IN STABLE SOCIAL ORGANIZATION

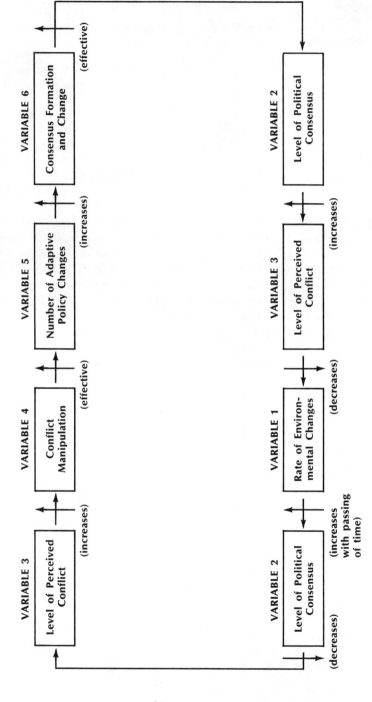

who should be gaining advantages from these priorities is beginning to disintegrate under the impact of environmental changes. As we would expect, conflicts erupt as groups perceive the disagreements over priorities, and the conflict is manipulated (i.e., power is created and used) as groups seek to define a new consensus consistent with their own interests and biases. Given the higher levels of conflict, the political cycle now merges into the stage where power must be created and used in order to bring about adaptive changes. In order for the rising level of conflict to be effectively used, organizations must form to mobilize shared biases and interests toward redefining priorities and controlling the kinds of adaptive changes that are to be made.

Typical groups involved in many of these university confrontations are the Students for a Democratic Society, black student unions, student government groups, administrative officers, faculty committees, tax payers' associations, alumnae, public officials of the state, and law enforcement agencies. Each of these groups is seeking to organize, that is, to mobilize into activity, the attitudes shared within their group to control the behavior and thinking of other groups within the community. Each of the groups involved utilizes varying amounts and kinds of resources in its attempt to control others. For example, student groups lacking such resources as money, authority, and status, often fall back upon another major resource, which is their ability to stop the operation of the university, in some cases by destroying university property. Other groups in the conflict, such as law enforcement agencies and public officials, have more traditional resources such as state and local laws which can be empowered with physical coercion, public opinion, which is in large part supportive of hard stands against student radicals, and mass media, which can be used to gain further public support. Faculty groups both for and against student demands have resources such as petitions, strikes, refusals to teach, and in some cases resignation from the university. The administrators of the university typically rely upon ill defined but traditionally accepted resources such as their authority within the campus situation—they are the groups expected by most people to make the decisions about how conflicts are to be resolved and about how budgets are to be allocated within the university community.[6]

All of these groups are attempting to mobilize personnel, energy, and resources to control the behavior and thinking of others involved in the confrontation. But they must use these resources to create power and use it effectively toward a solution. That is, decisions must be made as to which

6. Here, I am using *authority* to mean power relationships that are accepted by most people as being legitimate.

of the many problems will receive priority and as to what the solution will be. The traditional priorities include such issues as faculty tenure, raises, funding of research grants, curriculum, and the size of enrollment. All of these disputes have existed prior to the major confrontation brought about by student radicals' attempts to change the nature of higher education in this country. One of the primary purposes of the student revolt is the redefinition of university priorities. Student radicals seek to place the role of the university as an instrument of social change and a benefactor of the disadvantaged at the top of the list of issues to be resolved, having higher priority than granting degrees, hiring and firing faculty members, teaching, and research.

The success of their attempt to redefine the priorities is directly related to resources they can bring to bear in their manipulation of the rising level of conflict on the campus. In other words, student organizations are effective to the extent they can increase the level of conflict and manipulate that conflict to bring about the changes they want.

As an illustration, a typical confrontation might begin with a small number of students petitioning for redress of particular demands, with the strategy of forcing the university authority to counter with repressive and overzealous responses. Often what begin as reasonable demands for policy change become furious confrontations between police and students over entirely different issues such as the right of students to protest or the treatment of the students involved in protest. As new issues are introduced, more students are drawn into the mobilization of forces. The students become geometrically more powerful in the conflict situation. The effect of police attempts to control the student movements often gives the radicals the very power they lacked originally—the power of numbers with destructive potential. In such ways student movements become powerful groups in the decisions as to what values will be held and what advantages distributed via university policy.

In these advanced stages of conflict adaptive changes become necessary to resolve the emerging chaos with its inherent dangers for the existence of the university itself. In some cases, of course, the authorities have been able to control the activity of student groups, but in others, although police have held a monopoly of coercive power, a stalemate between opposing forces has resulted. Thus, a university can be so embroiled in chaos, brutality, and coercion as to make it impossible to continue to any purpose. At these points in the conflict, agencies are often created with the specific purpose of changing university policy to resolve the expanding conflict mobilized by the students. Usually committees are formed involving students, faculty, and administrators with the task of compromising the demands of groups in the confrontation. In some cases such committees are effective in bringing about changes in university policy. Such changes might include the creation of black studies programs, the acceptance of disadvantaged students into the university without minimum grade standards, financial assistance for such students, and basic changes in the curricula and faculty itself. Such adaptive changes are often resisted by other groups mobilized in the confrontation. Some student leaders have interpreted these changes as compromises of basic principles, while in other cases the faculty and administration have viewed the changes as destroying the very nature of the university. In any event, enforcement of the new policy often requires strong external sanctions to back up the university authority. And, in such situations, the university survives to the extent that external sanctions, such as firing malcontent faculty members or suspending students, are effective in bringing about conformity to the new policies. Over a period of time these changes have to be legitimized through a new consensus and through attitude change agencies within the university community.

Such agencies might include the university president, faculty spokesmen, highly regarded student leaders, student newspapers, and public officials, each expressing approval of the changes and pleading for acceptance of the changes in the name of progress. Stability results as the new definitions of consensus emerge, and the norms and behaviors of the members of the university community change as a result of the internalization of the appropriateness of these new policies. The changes can then be further supported by the student government, active peer group pressures and classroom teaching. In other words, the members of the university community have begun to accept as legitimate these new value priorities and distributions of benefits. Once these adaptive policy changes are accepted the university is able to relax the amount of external control necessary to enforce the changes, and the university stabilizes, awaiting new changes in the environmental circumstances that will lead to disintegration of the newly formed consensus and the ensuing rise in the levels of conflict.

What I have described in this particular sequence of events results in the stabilization of the university organization. It is not difficult to imagine an entirely different sequence of events with different consequences. By changing outcomes at any one of several critical points in the cycle we could expect different results.

For example, the rising levels of conflict on the campus might not be effectively manipulated by student leaders, a fact resulting in other groups maintaining the status quo or even in turning policy about priorities in entirely different directions. The consequence here would again be enforced stability but without the necessary adaptive changes in policy reflecting the demands of the groups in conflict. Such coerced stability would necessarily be momentary since it would be difficult to legitimize the lack of demanded change in university policy among the students seeking change. Such stability is the result of continual coercion rather than a redefinition of policy to bring about a new consensus. There would be certainty about outcomes of behavior in such situations, but the certainty would stem from fear and imposed sanctions rather than from agreement among the students. In other words, the problem has not been solved in such a situation since the solution has not been accepted by the people living in the community. One would expect continued attempts to mobilize conflict to bring about a change.

We might also imagine the consequence that students mobilize such power that the adaptive changes would have the effect of driving many of the other participants in the community away. Again consolidating such changes into a new consensus would be most difficult, if not impossible. We might further imagine that the levels of conflicts could not be manipulated because of lack of leadership. In such a situation the conflict would escalate sporadically, resulting in chaos, fear, and more uncertainty. In this kind of situation it is not difficult to understand that the members of the community might react by crying out for more external control to reduce uncertainty and increase "law and order." The cry would be for stronger external control to hold the fabric of the community together. Then the time is ripe for the man on the white horse, the strong, charismatic leader to dictate new policy to the community. Dictatorship inheres in chaos. The community gives power to coerce in order to escape chaos and uncertainty. With a certain relief they also escape freedom.

I want to remind you at this point that the foregoing analysis of the politics of the university confrontation has been intended primarily to illustrate and apply this theoretical framework which is used to organize the material in this textbook. It is obviously not an attempt at considering all the complex events in these situations, but rather is an attempt to provide examples of these basic dynamics of politics. I also want to point out that using this particular example places upon you the additional burden of translating these events and examples into other situations involving the processes of conflict, consensus, and change. I am arguing that any social organization confronted with changing environmental conditions operates to adapt to these changes through processes illustrated in the above example. Whether the organization be the federal government, state governments, local governments, international organizations, universities, parent-teacher associations, business corporations, or bridge clubs, the dynamics are basically the same.

To this point we have used the theory to classify and relate variable conditions in the processes of politics. But a theory should also be useful in diagnosing and prescribing solutions to problems arising in social organizations confronted by the challenge of change. The next section is an attempt to diagnose the same university situation and prescribe some suggested cures for these problems involved in change based on this theory of political dynamics.

I have many reservations about arguing policy objectives on the basis of an untested theory. But as is often the case in social sciences, few of our theories have been tested to the point of being reliable and valid explanations of events. I offer the following more as an example of what might be done to use theory in diagnosis and problem solving than as suggestions for policy implementation. I like to think that further research will verify the basic notions of this theory and the following policy reforms could be considered cures for the problems involved in social change.

USING THE THEORY FOR DIAGNOSIS OF AND PRESCRIPTIONS FOR THE PROBLEM

After some reflection it is apparent that certain processes identified in the theory are more subject to manipulation than are others. For instance, the rate of environmental changes in a particular situation may be largely beyond the control of human beings. But other variables in the theory are more susceptible to manipulation (e.g., the creation and use of power, the kinds of adaptive changes made, the ways in which legitimacy of the changes are created). Using the university as an example, we can begin by discussing each of the major variables in the theory in terms of the extent to which manipulation of those conditions might be advisable and useful in solving the problems of adapting to change.

First, you might consider the rate of environmental change. Most of the factors contributing to the rate of environmental change are largely beyond the control of the members of the university community. But some factors are not. For instance, a rising extent of outside intervention into the university confrontation is certain to accelerate these rates of environmental changes. As outside groups make more and greater demands, the university is more likely to be caught up in a rapidly rising rate of environmental change. At least in part this acceleration could be controlled. Assuming that we want to maintain the status quo of the university, the less intervention there is from outside, the more likely it is that the existing mechanisms of politics will be able to handle the problems of adaptation. The reverse is also true. If we wanted to change the nature of the university it would be necessary to increase the extent of outside intervention. One of the real paradoxes of the university confrontation is that at the time the university is being most sorely tested in its ability to accommodate change, state legislatures, public officials, and other such groups are most likely to be intervening in the situation. The result is an increase in the levels of conflict to such a point as to overload the rather fragile structures available to adjust the existing disputes in the university. Therefore, the general proposition is, the higher the level of conflict in a situation, the less likely that outside intervention will help solve the conflict. As we have seen, such intervention becomes an additional source for acceleration of the environmental change processes already operating. In other words, intervention merely increases the demands for change which are already overburdening the mechanisms that function to adjust to such changes.

The second and third variables in the framework—the level of consensus in the political culture and the level of perceived conflict in the political system—are again processes that are energized by the rate of environmental change and are largely beyond control. It is extremely difficult to control the ways people react to changing conditions and the attitudes they form in attempting to cope with such changes, and it is also difficult to prevent the formation of incompatible attitudes that make conflict more likely. However, the fourth set of processes in the theory, conflict manipulation (i.e., creating and using power), can be made subject to human control in order to create a more viable and adaptable social order.

It is clear that one of the major problems with universities attempting to cope with change during the 1960s and 1970s is that they have had few mechanisms for coping with the kinds of conflicts encountered. Universities have existed for centuries largely isolated from society. Once the universities became caught up in the rapidly changing conditions of a complex industrial society, agencies for the adaptation to conflict were required. Such agencies simply had not previously existed in the universities. In an analysis of a social organization and its ability to adapt to change, part of the diagnosis must be an estimate of the organization's capability for coping with rising levels of conflict. As political analysts, we should be most concerned with identifying mechanisms necessary for creating and using power in the confrontation and for making decisions as to which of the priorities will be responded to and as to how they will be responded to.

Several questions become critical at this point in the examination. Is there adequate leadership to bring about the creation and use of power to prevent the chaotic and random escalation of levels of conflict and violence? Are there agencies available to make decisions about which problems will be solved and which will not be? Are these agencies authoritative? Will their decisions be accepted by the parties in the conflict? If not, what kind of steps could be taken to create or enhance the authority of these change accommodating agencies? If there is not adequate leadership to manipulate the rising levels of conflict, it may make a great deal of sense somehow to engage and encourage such leaders among the conflicting parties. Rather than try to coerce, arrest, or eliminate the leadership of opposing groups it may be most important from the view of the total community welfare to preserve the leadership of opposing groups. This preservation will aid in the creation and effective use of power to resolve the conflict. The alternative is spontaneous and sporadic escalation of conflict no longer subject to control and likely to lead to the eventual destruction of the entire community.

Such questions as these might be appropriate at the early stages in the development of the conflict in the situation. It is also necessary to understand that a different diagnosis and prescription may be necessary at later stages in the political spiral.

It might be that the conflict had already escalated to such a point that without the implementation of strong external controls the organization would come apart. At the same time the political analyst is prescribing the imposition of strong external control such as the use of the military or police to enforce stability, he would also suggest that such steps are only temporary treatment. The cure for the problems lies in creating a viable mechanism for coping with conflicts, creating adaptive changes to the new conditions, and developing the idea of legitimacy among the members of the community for such changes.

Before leaving this part of the discussion I want to comment on the interplay of internal and external control necessary to maintain the community in the conflict situation from the viewpoint of this theory.

One of the points throughout this argument has been that as agencies within a social situation are incapable of translating conflict into legitimate policy changes that people will accept without being coerced, there is a greater need to impose external control for the continuation of the society. In situations in which conflict has been controlled by the rise to power of a dictatorial leader forcing obedience, the energy, talent, and resources necessary for this coercion deprive the community of its capability of making the adjustment that would truly begin to resolve the problems which gave rise to the conflict in the first place. Obviously the solution of these basic conflicts is the only way to bring about the stability of the system without a predominate proportion of external control. Yet the irony is that in the situations in which such solutions are most necessary, the community has the least capability for making the changes because its energies are being exhausted in simply maintaining rather than in changing the community.

Granted that we are interested in reducing the level of coercion in the community, it may make a great deal of sense in these situations for outside groups, agencies, or nations to increase the flow of resources into the coercive situation so that the additional resources can be used to make the necessary adjustments while existing resources are being used to control the society externally. It would be extremely naive to believe that the typical leader (whether he be president of a country or of a university) would always use these additional resources to develop and adapt his community rather than become a wealthier ruler, but on the other hand, without such resources there is no alternative available to the leader. It may be possible to earmark the additional funds being supplied in these situations for particular kinds of projects that in the judgment of the donors would be most likely to bring about the adaptive changes required. For example, rather than for state legislatures to cut back on funds to universities that have become largely coercive communities, it may be that they should increase funds, which would be given with the explicit purpose of improving undergraduate teaching, curricula, and of meeting other demands that typify many university confrontations. If this were done it is conceivable that the leader would find that as the basic conflicts are solved in legitimate ways he is no longer required to expend large amounts of resources to control the behavior of the members of the community. This would, in turn, lead to a relaxation of the external control in the community and make it more likely that viable mechanisms could be developed to stabilize the community without imposing external control.

If we move on to the next variable in the theory—adaptive changes —we see that it is clearly this aspect of the theory that is most susceptible to informed and intelligent human manipulation. The political analyst should be able to advise the kinds of policy changes which will be adaptive and most likely acceptable to the participants in the conflict. In other words, it is at this point in the political process that creativity, imagination, and thoughtful judgment are most critical, and ironically, it is also the point at which they are least likely to occur. Typically, conflict escalates rapidly to the point of accommodation. The adjustment is made in the context of crisis at an almost instinctual level rather than at the level of reasoned solutions. It may well be that an analyst would suggest the creation of a special agency with the specific function of developing contingency plans for the emergence of many possible, if not probable, conflicts in the community as well as for planning for normal development and expansion.

The last variable in the theory is again susceptible to human control. Here we need to consider the agencies which have the function of forming and changing the new consensus in the culture around the adaptive changes that have been made. The analyst would want to identify the most effective agencies in the community for forming and reinforcing the attitudes of students, faculty, and other members of the university community. It may be that student newspapers, university presidents, and faculty spokesmen are not effective in forming or changing new attitudes among the members of the community. The most effective agencies might be mass meetings of members of the community in which all sides could be heard and some kind of reasonable compromise solution could be reached that is acceptable to all people involved. Alternatively, it might be that informal groups on campus are most effective in the process of consensus formation and change, groups such as collectives, student organizations, and dorm councils. If this is the case, then such groups should be identified and given support in carrying out the necessary function of creating legitimacy for the adaptive changes.

These then are some of the questions and suggestions which can be raised by utilizing this particular theory in diagnosing university confrontation. The balance of this book will be organized around the major variables in this theory. Part III will deal with the concept of change, Part IV with conflict in the political system and Part V with consensus in the political culture. Part VI will analyze adaptive policy change.

PART III

UNDERSTANDING CHANGE

CHAPTER 6

UNDERSTANDING SOCIAL CHANGE

Social change is perhaps the most fascinating and illusory concept in political analysis. It is illusory because it has proved extremely difficult to understand or to utilize the concept in understanding human behavior. It is fascinating because it seems to many people to be the essence of the human condition. A multitude of ideas and questions arise in connection with social change. What causes social change? Does social change necessarily lead to a better society? Or does it lead inevitably to decay, stagnation and the fall of nation states? Can man survive in a changing world? Can man have an impact upon his own conditions given the seeming inevitability and rapidity of forces of change?

One of the most common statements among contemporary social commentators has been the claim that changes are occurring more rapidly and more profoundly than ever before. If such a comment is even partly true, the most serious question that I can imagine is—Can the society and the individuals in it plan to adapt to these tremendous changes? I believe that your survival and mine is more likely if we can gain some understanding of social change, both of the changes we must make in ourselves and our society and those changes that affect us regardless of what we do. The purpose of this chapter is to provide some tools for evaluating social change. We need to know what kinds of assumptions and what kinds of theories have been created by men who thought about and attempted to explain social change. With an understanding of how others have thought about social change, perhaps you will be able to make your own reasoned judgments about the ways that you and your society are going to confront the challenge of change.

There is a great deal of material we could discuss in this chapter. I have chosen to focus upon what I consider the most essential elements in thinking more intelligently about the nature of social change. First, I want to discuss sources of social change. What makes a society move? Next, we will consider assumptions about man in relation to social change. Is he good, evil, rational, or irrational? We will be looking into the ways such assumptions have affected the theorists' thought about the processes of change. In the last section of this chapter we will look to the kind of assumptions that have been made about the nature of change itself. And there we will investigate how these assumptions have also affected the way theorists have evaluated and explained changing human conditions.

THE SOURCES OF SOCIAL CHANGE

Before we leap into the discussion of assumptions and theories I should caution you that much of what we will discuss next lies in the realm of philosophy rather than of science. Some of these assumptions and theories have been partially tested by the observation of real events, but for the most part they remain largely the product of speculation and thought. I think most political scientists become a little uneasy when they begin to talk about concepts and theories dealing with such a complex matter as social change. This uneasiness results because such questions, for all practical purposes, are not subject to the rigor and protections of scientific methods. They are more philosophical than scientific. In any case these questions are of such significant proportions that we must consider them, regardless of our ability to present evidence either for or against most of what will be discussed in this chapter.

I can find no better example of this mystical and often mysterious quality of change than in the question about its sources. I might clarify by saying that when I speak of the sources of change I am raising the question of what causes change to occur. But we must be careful that we do not get into a "chicken and egg" type of question. We are not necessarily arguing that some particular event occurred first and resulted in social change. Instead, this section is reviewing some of the more common theories having to do with conditions associated with social change. Some of these theories will be relatively simplistic, specifying a single major variable that produces or influences change, while other theories will argue for a complex chain of variables, each in turn leading to or somehow creating change in a society. In any case we are examining one of the most significant of all questions to arise in political thought. What causes a society to change—to become something different and perhaps better than it was? What are some of the theories which explain the origins of change in society?

We may begin by distinguishing between two very general types of theories. The first type appears to explain social change by focusing upon conditions occurring within individuals that make them act differently, and as a result change the nature of society. The second type of theory tends to emphasize conditions external to the individual that make people respond differently and in this way lead to social change. We could think of the former type of theory as one in which individuals change society while in the latter theory the society is thought to change individuals.

Individuals Changing Society

One of the most simplistic if not simpleminded theories of social change could be referred to as the "great man theory" of social change. Many historians are particularly fond of pointing out that great dramatic changes in the conditions of man have occurred as a result of the ambitions, psychoses, and power drives of particular great men in history. Such theories often recount that General So-and-So led his armies throughout the known world, conquering all before him. Quite incidentally he brought about the most profound form of change in known civilization by introducing a new culture to the victims of his wars. Simplistic, yes, but simpleminded?—another kind of question.

There can be little disagreement that great men have had tremendous impact upon the way that societies have changed as well as upon the fact that they have changed. At the same time I am a little uneasy with such a simple notion of how change in history occurs. One might even suspect that such theories are more a product of what has been recorded by historians than of what has actually occurred. You will have to evaluate for yourself the worth of explaining social change as originating from the efforts of powerful, charismatic leaders working their will and way upon entire nations and civilizations.

A second theory of social change I want to consider has been developed by an economist seeking to explain how nations develop and change. Everett Hagen argues, persuasively I think, that individuals and groups who have lost their status and respect in a society become the generators of new cultures.[1] He argues that such individuals, and particularly their offspring, are continually seeking to regain their lost status in the society. And as the children of these individuals mature they find they are alienated and frustrated by the norms and social mores which forced them from their previous positions of high status in the society. Such people then are continually seeking to re-create their past status by innovating and attempting to get such innovations put into policy that will be consistent with their own perception of themselves as deprived but significant members of the society. They seek to change the society to regain their lost esteem.

Still a third view of individuals bringing about social change is that of David McClelland.[2] In his work, *The Achieving Society,* he suggests that what he calls the "achievement need" in individuals compels them to strive. He characterizes the need for achievement which he refers to as "*n* Achievement" in the following way:

> Our early laboratory studies showed that people "high" in *n* Achievement tend to work harder at certain tasks; to learn faster; to do their best work when it counts for the record, and not when special incentives, like money prizes are introduced; to choose experts over friends as working partners; etc.[3]

McClelland then continues to theorize that societies with concentrations of people having high need achievement are those most likely to be able to make the jump into the industrial cycle of economic development. These concentrations of high need achievers will supply the innovative personnel to bring substantial social and economic changes. He has historical data to support this part of the theory. In addition, his contention is that such achievement needs are instilled in cultural patterns in the society through child rearing that emphasizes independence and self-reliance on the part of the children in the family.

A fourth theory of change that fits in this general category of theories about change is the notion that particular ideologies are critical in bringing

1. Everett E. Hagen, *On the Theory of Social Change* (Homewood, Ill.: Dorsey Press, 1962).

2. David C. McClelland, *The Achieving Society* (Princeton, N.J.: Van Nostrand Co., 1961).

3. David C. McClelland, "The Achievement Motive in Economic Growth," *Political Development and Social Change,* eds. Jason L. Finkle and Richard W. Gable (New York: John Wiley & Sons, 1966), p. 140.

about social development. Here again the argument is relatively simple. Elites and leaders in the poorer nations have somehow learned ideas and political ideologies to bring about change in their society. Sometimes these ideas are basically those shared in Western societies, sometimes they are Marxist or neo-Marxist ideas about development, and sometimes they are based in movements stressing national pride and the necessity for self- and national development. But whatever the ideology, the theory argues that ideas, formed into national policy, implemented through leaders and elites, become the prime source of socio-political change in the country.

All these theories are relatively simple notions about social change and they all involve the common theme that change comes about as individuals, for whatever reasons, act to bring about social consequences. Now I want to turn to the second general type of theories about social change; those which tend to emphasize that changes occur as a result of forces acting upon individuals rather than as a result of individuals acting upon society.

Societies Changing People

To begin this discussion we need to focus upon what is perhaps the most common theory of social change existing in the world today. Karl Marx argued, and many contemporary neo-Marxists have argued, that a shift in the control over economic processes in the society is the basic force which moves society to change. As those who control the economics of the country (i.e., the owners) make decisions which will further their interests, greater profits, they necessarily exploit those who are not in control of those economic processes (i.e., the workers). In such a way the continuing exploitation of the workers by the owners leads to an increasing disparity in their relative positions on a scale of material well-being. As the disparity grows so does the discontent among the masses of workers. The ensuing struggle between the masses of "have-nots" and the elites of "haves" is the conflict which brings about change in the society. The "have-nots," becoming aware in this "class struggle" of their own deprived conditions, arise to throw off the control of the elites. As they succeed in the revolution they construct the new society by redistributing the basis of economic power among all the people. This redistribution of economic control also ensures the distribution of political power, which in turn prevents the accumulation of such powers in the hands of small elites. Without small elites in control there is no disparity between those who control and those who do not, and therefore no struggle or conflict. Thus, harmony prevails under conditions of "full Communism."

In this kind of theory the change which occurs does so not because of some individual action, but because people in the society are responding to their relative economic positions in such a way as to bring about change. Change is inevitable in such a theory. Just as inevitable as history itself. Given this view of the world it becomes clearer why Khrushchev said that the Soviets would bury the United States. He was expressing no threat or intent to attack the United States to bring about the burial. Consistent with Marxism, he was expressing the belief that the economic and political forces operating in all societies will eventually lead the United States, as all other countries, to the kind of class struggles described in Marxist theory and to the eventual development of communism in that country. Such arguments may stir Americans to fear the threats of Communists, but for Communists such statements are merely an interpretation of history more than an expression of intent to act in international relations.

Marxian analysis has found much acceptance and become very pervasive among social theorists and political leaders, particularly in the non-Western worlds of development. It has also been widely and severely criticized by many—particularly by non-Communist theorists.

Marxian theory is often referred to as the "poverty thesis" because Marx described revolution as the outcome of the "have-nots" (e.g., the poverty-stricken) revolting against the "haves" (e.g., the wealthy). The most common sense kind of criticism is that Marx did not foresee the possibility that the "haves" would share their profits with the "have-nots." The criticism argues that a management class has evolved in the capitalist societies that must maintain their corporations and not just their profits. In order to maintain their corporations, they must stabilize their labor relations by sharing profits, usually in the form of higher wages for workers. The poverty that Marx assumes for the workers never actually occurs because they become richer as the enterprise becomes richer. This fact is not so much an argument with the logic of the Marxian analysis as it is with the basic assumption Marx makes about the existence of an owner class whose sole motivation is to become more wealthy. The intervention of the management class is a substantial addition to the simple analysis of "haves" and "have-nots" offered by Marx. So the "haves," in the form of managements wanting to preserve their corporations, do sometimes share the profits with the "have-nots." Or so this argument suggests. You must make your evaluation.

A more persuasive criticism comes from theorists who have pointed out that social change or revolution does not typically occur in situations where there is a great deal of poverty. Quite to the contrary, these theorists would argue, revolution occurs after a period of relative economic prosperity among the masses of people. Such social theorists as Alexis de Tocqueville, or more recently Crane Brinton and James C. Davies, have pointed out this kind of contradiction to the Marxian analysis.

As Crane Brinton says:

Thus we see that certain economic grievances—usually not in the form of economic distress, but rather a feeling on the part of some of chief enterprising groups that their opportunities for getting on in this world are unduly limited by political arrangements—would seem to be one of the symptoms of revolution.[4]

James C. Davies has tried to combine both the Marxian notion of poverty versus wealth with the analysis of de Tocqueville that revolutions tend to occur not after periods of long-term poverty but after periods of relative prosperity.[5] He concludes that revolution occurs after a period of rising expectations when the people come to expect the government to deliver more and more need satisfactions. When, for whatever reasons, government is unable to satisfy these needs, there is a dramatic decline in the social welfare. For Davies, then, there is a period of relative deprivation or poverty that creates revolution, but this poverty is a psychologically felt phenomenon rather than an objective condition of the poorer classes in the society. Such deprivation is most likely to be widely perceived by people after a period when they have been receiving a great deal of material goods from their government, a period which is for some reason interrupted or is else not meeting their rising expectations.

Another theory of social change is that of William Ogburn. He argued for what is now a fairly common cultural lag theory—change is created by an ever developing tension between the material and non-material cultures in a society.[6] For example, as the technology (i.e., material culture) changes with ever greater rapidity, the social norms (i.e., the non-material culture) lag far behind in the pace of development. As a result the society is moved to change its norm structure to complement the technological developments. It is not quite clear in this theory whether it is the technological growth which creates the change or whether it is the different rates of growth. But in any case, Ogburn emphasizes, as many others do, the importance of technology in social development. In some ways such theories are little more than elaborations of the notion that man invents, technology expands, and society changes.

As Marxian analysis has been perhaps the most persuasive theory of social change in the non-Western world, various theories of economic development have been the most influential within the Western world, particularly influencing United States foreign policy toward developing nations. It is impossible to specify all of the different economic conditions

4. Crane Brinton, "From Anatomy of Revolution," *Perspectives on the Social Order,* ed. H. Laurence Ross (New York: McGraw-Hill Book Co., 1968), p. 525.

5. James C. Davies, "Towards a Theory of Revolution", *American Sociological Review,* 27 (1962), pp. 5-19.

6. William F. Ogburn, *Social Change* (New York: The Viking Press, 1938).

seen as prerequisites to social change and modernization. However, most of these theories assume a common set of notions. First, that economic development of the society leads inevitably to a modern industrial state. Second, that economic development is brought about by a series of economic changes within the society, changes usually involving the accumulation of capital in the traditional society that can then be used to bring about the industrial takeoff. In other words, the most serious restraint to modernizing the traditional society is that all of its resources are typically used simply to maintain the social conditions and none are left over to bring about development. So, a critical condition for change is that the elites in these societies must accumulate a large amount of capital savings that can be used to launch the new industrial enterprises.

Walter Rostow is among the leading economic theorists of this school. He specifies four conditions which must exist before the "takeoff" into industrialization can come about. First, there must be a transfer of resources from consumption or hoarding by the people in the country to investment in the productive capabilities of the society. This transfer frees capital to be used for industrial growth—the initial step toward economic development. Once the productive potential has been created, it is realized as consumers demand the products of that new industry. The second stage is the diversification of the industrial base beyond the initial source of goods—production of many different products. Third, to assure further development of the industry, profits from production and consumption are put back into the economy. Finally, there must be the creation of some kind of self-generating technology to sustain the new industrial capability. In other words, the existing production sources in the society must evolve the technology and expertise which can be used to create new and ever expanding productive capability. This knowledge will ensure that the country is producing its own resources, both material and technological, for further development.[7]

There is still another theory of social change which I find more provocative than most. Daniel Lerner's theory has become a classic analysis of social development.[8] He speaks of three types of mobility. Physical mobility, that is, the ability to move from one place in a country to another, frees man from his traditional position of being bound to the land. This freedom makes a second kind of mobility possible. Social mobility is spawned by physical mobility. Freed from particular roles or statuses (i.e.,

7. W. W. Rostow, "The Take-Off into Self-Sustained Growth," *Political Development and Social Change*, eds., Finkle and Gable, pp. 233-253.

8. Daniel Lerner, "Communication Systems and Social Systems—A Statistical exploration in History and Policy," *Ibid.*, pp. 195-205.

castes) in that society, man acquires social mobility. Now he can move in the social hierarchy much as physical mobility allowed him to move about in the country. These two prior conditions then allow a final form of mobility—psychic mobility. As physical mobility freed man from the land, and social mobility freed him from his position in society, psychic mobility frees man from constraints which his mind has imposed upon him. Now he may act to change himself.

There are many such theories that emphasize conditions of mobility as the very root conditions of a changing society. In all of these the idea of mobility involves the tearing away of the chains that have prevented man from achieving a different life style for himself and different form of society as a whole. Such variables as communications media have had revolutionary impact upon facilitating mobility in the traditional societies. Change involves changes in the condition of man's relationship to society and himself. As he is freed of traditional constraints he is capable of "becoming." In that process of becoming whatever his potential dictates, the individual changes the form and the nature of society as a result of society changing man's relations to it.

This concludes the discussion of the origins of social change. It is in no way meant to be an exhaustive discussion. It is suggestive of the wide variety of theories which exist. In my own mind the question of "why social change" is a fascinating and necessary intellectual problem. But more significantly, for whatever reasons, change *does* occur. For me, why change occurs is not nearly as important as the problem of what is to be done about it.

I have conceptualized politics as arising from environmental changes creating a diversity of life experiences, and in turn, people learning from these diverse experiences hold conflicting interests and values that cause conflicting behavior traits among the people in that society. Such conflicts must be resolved if the social order is to be maintained. Conflicts are often resolved by the imposition of external controls over people's behavior. These controls are man-made changes—or as I have termed them, adaptive changes—in public policy that bind people to different forms of behavior. These adaptive changes must be engrained into the culture of the society for the conversion of the control of human behavior from external or "political control" to internal or "psychological" control. That is, a new consensus must be created in the minds of people concerning the legitimacy of the policy adaptations which have required them to behave in a new manner. Then, since each individual is willing to comply with his own conviction that the changes he has made are appropriate ones, it is unnecessary to force compliance. With the emergence of a new consensus, the cycle of politics turns once again, as the continuing envi-

ronmental changes work to erode the newly formed consensus by producing a different set of experiences with which people must cope. Their
attempts to cope with the new experiences once again create conflicts
requiring external political controls that in turn require the formation of a
new consensus. And so politics spins on its way.

It is apparent in this view of politics that the notion of change, both
environmental and adaptive, is of critical importance to understanding
politics. Therefore, this chapter is devoted to understanding some of the
concepts and assumptions which are critical not only to this theory but to
our survival. The next two sections of this chapter deal with assumptions
about man and the process of change.

SOME THINGS WE MEAN BY SOCIAL CHANGE

Actually, when we think about social change we are calling to mind
several different notions and assumptions about the nature of change in the
human and social condition. It is important to make some distinctions
among these elements of change in our own minds before we proceed.
We can start to unravel part of this conceptual confusion by distinguishing
between change thought of as growth and change thought of as progress.
We will also discuss some assumptions about the nature of man that affect
the theories of social change. Is man actively making choices which control his future, or is he simply carried along by the tide of history as a pawn
of social and economic conditions in the society? Is man basically good?
Is man really not so good? Is he neither good nor bad, but perhaps of some
other essential quality? As we will be raising several questions about the
nature of man we will also be raising some questions about the nature of
change itself. Is change cyclical? Is it linear? Is it necessarily slow? Is
revolution the only real change?

Change: Growth or Progress?

The distinction between growth and progress is really almost simpleminded, but it is also a source of unending problems when one begins to
think about the different theories of change. When I suggest that change
can be thought of as growth, I am using the concept to *describe the
differences* occurring in some object, situation, or event between two
points in time. For example, a boy grows into manhood between 1970 and
1990. The gross national product of a society might grow from $50 billion
to $100 billion in 25 years. A population grows from a few billion people
to too many billion people in a short period of history. I could give
innumerable examples of the notion of growth that is often referred to as

change. But how is change thought of as growth different from change thought of as progress?

Progress, unlike growth, is change from one condition to a later, preferred condition. In this sense we are no longer describing what actually occurs over a period of time, but instead, specifying what we prefer to happen. Perhaps we need some illustration of the difference between growth and progress.

We can describe the differences occurring over time as a society changes (grows) from an agrarian, socio-economic configuration through some transitional stage to an industrialized society. But when we argue that such growth from agrarianism to industrialism will lead to a better life for the people in that society, we are specifying a future condition which we prefer (i.e., a better life for the people). But if we believe rural life to be the only "good life," this growth would not be considered progress. The point I am making is that it is necessary to distinguish in our minds the notion of growth from the notion of progress in order to analyze a theory of change and to see to what extent it is an explanation of change, or to what extent it is a projection of a personal value.

Is Man Active or Passive in Change?

There is a second fundamental distinction that we must make in our attempts to understand theories of change. This has to do with the way man relates to the changes taking place in his society. On the one hand there are those who believe that man is an effective agent in bringing about changes. He actively intervenes in historical processes and brings about conditions which are consistent with his own will or purpose.

On the other hand there are those theorists who would argue that change is inherent in the natural laws of society and history, and that man is little more than the effect of these causal forces operating in the social processes. These theorists are greatly influenced by the theories of evolutionary change common to natural science. In other words, change is caused by forces inherent in the nature of society, and man passively plays his role in a scenario of change written into processes over which he has no control.

Perhaps these two views of man's relation to change form just another way of asking the age-old question about whether man is an agent of free will or is determined by forces beyond his control. In any case there is little doubt that this kind of distinction has a profound influence on the way different theorists think about and explain change in society.

In order to give concrete illustrations to these notions of change we can turn to two relatively common theories of change. One such theory argues that man changes his society through technological inventions. In this theory man invents a major new form of technology and in turn creates new ways of coping with nature. With these new technological tools man brings about substantial changes in nature and in society itself. Man invents the wheel, and society changes as a function of the alterations in the technology of transportation. Man invents ways to use nuclear energy, and society changes as it accommodates to this tremendous change in the available power sources. Such explanations illustrate the assumption that man is an active agent in bringing about social change.

As an illustration of the opposite notion of change we can cite the doctrine of predestination. Here the assumption is that God is the ultimate controller of each individual's destiny. Man has only to play his role in the scene, and he is an effect rather than a cause of societal change. There are many theorists subscribing to this view of man as a pawn of forces beyond his control. Whether that force is God, or Freud's libidinal energy, or Marx's economic class struggle, these theories all leave man as an effect rather than as a cause of social change.

Is Man Good, Evil, or Something Else?

A third component of most theories of change is the assumption the theorists make about the essential nature of man. Is man good or evil? Does he have some other essential characteristic? This question of human nature has a great deal to do with the kind of inherent processes that will bring about change. Normally such assumptions are more important in thinking about progress rather than growth, but in any case they are important in thinking about change.

The theorist who assumes that man is by his nature good will tend to think of change (or more correctly progress) as consisting of those conditions that promote the liberation of man from social conditions that restrain his basic goodness. That is, man, although he is basically good, is enveloped in social conditions that prevent him from acting out his inherent goodness. Therefore, progress is promoted by relieving man of the conditions which constrain his progress toward being good. This kind of thinking is very much a part of present-day theories about the ways we should approach social problems. If we remove the social and economic conditions of poverty, poor people will assume positions of dignity and meaning in our society. In other words, poor people are not basically evil and therefore unable or unwilling to be good citizens. But their social conditions are such as to prevent them from being productive and useful members of the society.

A contrary view common to present-day thinking about the nature of man is that man is essentially evil, lazy, or conniving, and that regardless of social conditions he is out to do his worst to his fellow man. In this view it is necessary to impose greater and greater constraints upon man in order to prevent him from acting out his evil nature. So progress occurs to the extent that governments, traditions, and laws operate to control man and his natural urges to evil. The difference in these two views is apparent. On the one hand man progresses by freeing himself from social conditions which interfere with his basic nature, while on the other hand man progresses through the imposition of greater constraints which enable him to live in some form of harmony with his fellow man.

A third alternative view is that man rationally calculates his destiny in the process of social change. In this view man is assumed to have the capacity for objectively searching out information concerning alternative ways of achieving self-defined goals. He is actively seeking information which will permit his rational evaluation of the most effective means of pursuing his self-interests. Progress, then, occurs to the extent that there is a free flow of information in the society, a flow which is necessary to inform the individual's choice about appropriate means to his goal. There must be not only information to inform individual choice but there must also be the opportunity and freedom from constraints so that these individually defined choices can be acted upon. Thus, man is thought of as being neither good nor evil, but as a self-interested agent actively pursuing his interests to the collective good of the society. In other words, each member of the society is permitted to follow his own definition of the "good life," and the entire society benefits by his pursuits. In this argument progress is not so much the achievement of a preferred goal, but is a procedure that promotes whatever goals and interests the people in that society wish to obtain.

As there were contradictory assumptions about the goodness or evilness of man, there is also a competing assumption concerning the notion of man as being a rational agent. This fourth assumption about the basic nature of man pictures him as an irrational subject of hidden and largely unconscious instinctual drives that determine and dictate his behavior in society.

This view of man, most commonly associated with Freud's theories of psychoanalysis, has many contemporary versions among social scientists, but their similarity lies in the generally shared assumption that man does little at the conscious level to affect or control his own behavior. Progress, given these assumptions, is the unintended and accidental consequence of man's attempts to act out his very basic nature. There is variation in such notions as to nature of man. In some theories he is basically motivated by sexual urges that must be made acceptable in the context of social norms. In other theories he is motivated by aggressive or "killer" instincts to pursue actively the destruction of others and even himself. But in all these cases man is seen as striving to realize the nature which has been instilled in his own being even when that nature is socially or self-destructive. It is easy to comprehend why people who hold such theories may become pessimistic about the outcome of social development.

A fifth alternative conception of man's nature holds that he is a social animal. In this view man is thought of as a creature who learns under the impact of environmental circumstances to be whatever his immediate environment dictates. So man is neither good nor evil, neither rational nor irrational, but is quite simply whatever society defines him to be. Society will produce men who are good or evil, rational or irrational, depending entirely upon the characteristics being taught by the social institutions and traditions operative in the individual's life. Theorists adopting this posture argue that progress results from the creation of social circumstances and human conditions that teach the organism to become whatever is defined as good.

There are two further schools of thought about the nature of man that I would like to discuss before we turn to the question of the nature of change. Both of these views are compatible with the theory which I have been developing to this point in this text.

A sixth notion about the nature of man in some ways permits a bridging of some of the previous models. Abraham Maslow argues that man has no one central characteristic, but indeed is an organism involving a hierarchy of basic needs that he is compelled to satisfy. Maslow specifies five such needs, paraphrased here as (1) body needs, (2) safety needs, (3) need for love and belonging, (4) need for adequacy, security, self-esteem, self-enhancement, competencies, and (5) need for self-fulfillment, broader understanding.[9]

He goes on to argue that these needs form a hierarchy in the sense that man must fulfill the most basic need before he is aware of and able to fulfill the next level. As man is capable of satisfying the varying levels in the hierarchy he moves from a largely passive organism in the environment to an active, actualized human being engaged in promoting his own potential nature.

In this somewhat more complex view of man it is clear that progress requires social organization that will maximize individual chances to satisfy and fulfill the basic needs in the individual's hierarchy. To the extent that a society provides the satisfaction of these basic human needs, it is a society which progresses as each individual becomes actualized.

A last conception of man that I want to discuss is in part a notion of man which is consistent with Maslow's "self-actualizing" personality. M.

9. Abraham H. Maslow, *Motivation and Personality* (New York: Harper & Bros., 1954).

Brewster Smith, Jerome Bruner, and Robert White summarize this conception in the classic study of *Opinions and Personality:*

> The human being, according to this approach, is not governed by a rational calculus, nor is he a blank slate on which experience traces its inexorable mark. Nor yet is man an ingenious machine translating physical stimuli into bodily responses. Like all animals, he is an organism, a system of life processes that somehow maintains its identity in active interplay with its environment. An organism is never passive, but survives and grows through constant striving, responding selectively to relevant aspects of its environment, and reaching out to incorporate, modify, fend off, or attain. Final passivity is death; in life there is always striving to maintain the delicate adaptation of needs of the organism to its environment.[10]

It seems that what is described as a striving organism is very close to Maslow's notion of the self-actualizing human. So in part then, one could argue that the nature of man, whatever it is, depends in large part upon the nature of the society in which he exists. If the society has been helpful in promoting conditions which tend to fulfill man's basic needs, it is a society in which individuals may become the striving, adaptive, and creative organisms described by the above authors, and also individuals who are capable of achieving and defining a meaningful, moral life for themselves. This is one more definition of social progress.

Hopefully, it is now clear to you that when we speak of change we are referring not only to a process taking place over time, but to a process involving human behavior. It has been necessary to spend some time identifying the assumptions made about the nature of man and about how man relates to change—actively or passively. We have distinguished between the empirical concept of change, growth, or differences occurring between two points in time, and the normative concept of change—progress from some existing state to a future preferred state. With this understanding, we can proceed to identify and discuss some of the characteristics of the process of change itself. There are several kinds of questions raised here. Where does change go? How does it get there and how fast?

THE DIRECTION OF CHANGE

Nearly every political philosophy or theory dealing with the concept of change involves an assumption of the direction that change takes. The early Greek philosophers typically thought of change as cyclical. Observ-

10. M. Brewster Smith, Jerome S. Bruner, and Robert W. White, *Opinions and Personality* (New York: John Wiley and Sons, 1956), p. 30.

ing changes in nature, they assumed that changes in society were of the same kind. The seasons of the year, repeating over and over again, in a cyclical manner, and the life process itself, from birth to death to rebirth to death, made it appear to these philosophers that all change must be a process of the same events recurring repeatedly. A rather popular form of such an assumption is expressed in the trite thought that history repeats itself. This notion is still very much alive; for instance, many people believe that an economy is doomed to have repeating cycles of depression, stability, and inflation.

It is not difficult to understand why change was and is seen as a series of cycles. You might ask, what difference does it make? A great deal—for the consequences of assuming cyclical change are far-reaching indeed.

For someone holding this view it is very difficult, if not impossible, to see change as being good. If change is merely the repetition of things which have gone before, both good and bad, it is either unnecessary or undesirable. There is little to recommend the process of change itself.

This assumption of the cyclical nature of history did not have as dramatic an impact upon political thought in Western culture as you might think. The much more persuasive and pervasive notion has been the assumption that change follows a linear pattern. Quite simply, rather than assuming that change goes in a circle this idea assumes that change occurs along a straight line, never repeating but proceeding into infinity. Perhaps such an assumption was made possible by the accumulation of recorded history. With this added perspective theorists concluded that conditions do not necessarily repeat themselves and that therefore social changes would never return a society to some previous point.

We could spend a great deal of time developing the reasons why political theorists came to assume linearity rather than cyclical direction. They assumed that linearity is not so important as its impacts. The major consequence was that change became equated with good. Since change does not result in the repetition of previous conditions, society can be continually refined and perfected. Indeed, the whole thrust of change is toward perfection. Each generation makes possible the perfecting of society by the elimination of bad conditions which have existed.

Now, given these assumptions about the linearity of change, revolution makes sense. What does that mean? Once you assume that change occurs along a straight line progressing into infinity, you can envision society as being perfectible by the elimination of bad conditions and the construction of good ones. So society can be thought of as a perfectible form of social organization. In addition, the more change that occurs, the sooner that perfection will be realized. Dramatic change and high rates of change become not only acceptable but desirable—truly Utopian kinds of instruments—for the betterment of mankind. Where some earlier theorists would have seen revolution as speeding the decay of society, some political theorists of Western culture living hundreds of years later have seen revolution as the road to Utopia.

Such are the profound consequences of assuming cyclical or linear change. However, both assumptions are quite simplistic and are not the only ones that can be made. As an alternative position, perhaps a compromise, change can be viewed as a spiral. That is, conditions might tend to return, but never to exactly the same point at which they existed before. Each cycle involves some degree of return, but each return is a little further along a linear direction than the previous cycle.

Still another notion is that of differentiation. Greatly influenced by evolutionary theory in biology, this view sees societies as developing much like living organisms. That is, society changes from a simple, primitive organization to a highly complex form by a process of differentiation that is like mutation or like natural selection in biology. For example, societies develop from the primitive traditional societies described by anthropologists to highly complex industrial empires such as the United States and the Soviet Union.

This concludes the discussion of the direction of change. We must now consider the form change takes as it moves in some direction.

THE FORM OF CHANGE

You may recall that we began this chapter with a distinction between growth and progress. We spoke of growth as involving differences occurring between two points in time, not to be confused with preferred differences or progress. Now we need to examine further differences that occur as a result of growth or progress.

Logically there seem to be at least three ways that something can be altered between two points in time. They are decay, replacement, and expansion. These three forms of change have definite value connotations, but they must be thought of in neutral terms.

At first glance it is difficult to see how decay can be a form of growth. Perhaps this idea is clarified if you think of the physical changes taking place as a person grows. The early stages of human growth involve the individual becoming stronger, larger, and more capable. But as life continues, these processes tend to reverse themselves and the individual becomes weaker and less capable until finally he dies. In the same sense, societies can grow through the process of decay. In other words, conditions that were present at one time deteriorate so that they are removed.

Differences because of decay are the result of deterioration of conditions. Decay does not necessarily signal an undesirable change. As I emphasized before, decay must be thought of in neutral terms. For instance, a decay in population growth might be quite desirable.

Replacement as a form of social change results when one characteristic is substituted for another. In other words, the society may have changed because it contains a new element in place of some previous element. For example, it is possible to think of a society that changes not in size but in the kinds of life styles it allows. Rather than becoming farmers, people become industrial workers. They have substituted an industrial life style for an agrarian one. We can conceive of this taking place without increasing the number of people, although historically such substitution has taken place with an increase in numbers.

Finally then, the third form of change, expansion, is the addition of new elements that did not previously exist into the social configuration. Something changes by becoming larger. That is perhaps the most common and generally understood notion of change. Indeed, in our own society change has been equated with growth. More importantly, bigness defines goodness. We have adopted the logic—the bigger the better, and the faster we get bigger, the better we are.

It is easy to see how one can associate values, personal and social, with these three forms of change. You may believe it is either good or bad for society to decay, or subtract some element from itself over a period of time. Further, you may argue that it is either good or bad to replace elements in a society over a period of time. And finally, you may think it is either good or bad for a society to become larger over a period of time. In any case you now have a way to describe the changes occurring around you.

We have discussed the direction and the form of change. The concluding section concerns the rate of change.

THE RATE OF CHANGE

Perhaps the question of the rate of change is more a matter of perspective than of any objective characteristic. But it still remains an important question in thinking about the process of change. From a historical perspective overlooking hundreds of years, any change appears to be only a small or incremental step in the overall progression. On the other hand, from the perspective of involvement, everything that occurs seems more dramatic, more immediate, and more significant. Aside from differences in the ways change is viewed, there are also differing assumptions about the rate of change. The typical rhetoric of campus conflicts offers an insight into the distinction between the slow, incremental, and continuous process of change and the discontinuous, abrupt, and revolutionary process of change. One of the most common themes in these conflicts is the disagreement between the liberals and the radicals. So the story goes, the liberals want to work within the system, while the radicals want to destroy the entire system in order to bring about the change they desire. Tempers flare in the confrontation between those who see change as a gradual process and those for whom change must be dramatic and abrupt, complete and total. The liberals criticize the radicals for destroying the very system that will guarantee better social conditions in the long run. Meanwhile the radicals argue that the liberals are simply maintaining a decadent social structure that prevents any meaningful or real change from occurring. Liberals and radicals, both aspiring to some preferred state, find themselves on opposite ends of the pole about the best method for bringing about those changes. The liberal is saying he wants to work within the system to bring about just and equitable change while the radical is arguing to destroy that unjust system that precludes the perfection man seeks.

In my own opinion, the differences between liberals and radicals lie in the degree of confidence that they have in their Utopias. I rather suspect that most liberals lack the confidence in an ideal world that their radical counterparts can muster. The liberal is not sure he knows what the good society is. His real confidence is in procedures that will ensure a just and equitable transition from what is to whatever he may prefer. Present conditions are so intolerable for the radical and he has so much confidence in what can be that he sees no reason to maintain any part of what now exists. Indeed, maintaining even a small part of present society works against the accomplishment of the entirely new society. Thus, the two positions come to opposite conclusions about how to bring about the same kind of change in social conditions.

In any case, it is necessary to understand this distinction in a discussion or theory about social change. Some changes are procedure. They emphasize the means by which ends can be achieved. Traditionally our society has maintained that no matter how good the desirable end, it does not justify unfair or intolerable means to reach the goal. In this sense our society has had a liberal tradition and has never favored those people who have tended to view change in a more visionary way. From the radical perspective such a tradition merely perpetuates the society which must be altered. The radical's only hope is for revolution. He believes that the disruption or destruction of procedures is justified by the new society for mankind.

I want to introduce a different example to demonstrate the importance of this distinction between those people who view change as being incremental and those people who view it as being revolutionary.

This same distinction is found between the theorists who explain the growth of knowledge in science. Thomas Kuhn, for one, suggests that the growth of knowledge is not a function of building upon previously defined theories and research to some kind of gradual evolution of better understanding of the world.[11] He argues instead that scientific breakthroughs occur because older theories and views are no longer capable of explaining what is going on in that world. So science and understanding proceed not with building upon previous theories for new conclusions, but rather with the collapse of previous explanations, a fact which requires the construction of new theories.

11. Thomas S. Kuhn, *The Structure of Scientific Revolutions* (Chicago, Ill.: The University of Chicago Press, 1962).

CHAPTER 7

UNDERSTANDING CHANGING SOCIETY

In beginning this chapter I want to tell of a brief episode that in my mind captures both the magnificence and the tragedy of human change. This story really does not begin and does not end; it merely points out what to me is an extremely significant dilemma.

A young girl whom I had come to know fairly well as a student in my introductory political science class entered my office one afternoon and asked if she might have some time to talk about personal problems with her family. It was clear enough that she was deeply anguished. During that afternoon of long conversation interspersed with sobbing pauses and near hysterical laughter, I came to understand that this young girl had just come through one of the most difficult experiences for young people. The most intense moments recounted in her story had occurred the previous weekend when she had stormed out of the family home, telling her parents she would not return. Indeed her story is all too typical of young people separating from their families. One thing had led to another, and another, until the final explosion had caused her to reject most if not all of what her parents had been asking and expecting of her, much of which was not what she felt she must do with her life. In that searing kind of personal trauma comes the discovery of yourself as a unique person—not what the family might want but what you yourself are beginning to grasp as your own identity. In that stark moment she had come to the conclusion that she must separate from her family. That she must become a new person and perhaps a person quite unlike the one that her family had raised, nurtured, and loved. After all the tragedy and wonder in her story, she finally brought the conversation to its conclusion by saying, "Well I guess I am finally free—that's exciting—but I feel very lonely."

Her story is in many ways a simplified counterpart to the history of changing society. In the last chapter we talked about the theories and assumptions necessary to understand the process of social change. That was a theoretical and abstract exercise for the most part. In this chapter I want to focus upon the realities of changing societies. We will want to discuss what happens to a society when it changes from traditional to modern. We will review how political analysts have described the different kinds of societies—both traditional and industrial. Then we will turn to a well-worn argument about whether political or economic forces change the nature of societies. Here we will focus upon an understanding and evaluation of political and economic development. Finally, we will turn to the question of government in the role of bringing about policy adaptations to the problems of change. We will further analyze four hypothetical political organizations (i.e., "ideal types"), each with different kinds of systems for coping with the confrontation with change.

THE IRONY OF CHANGE

Social analysts of the nineteenth century disagreed about many things, but they found common bond in their assessment that the traditional social organization was collapsing and that some form of modern society was emerging. For many people, this trend was feared and to be prevented if possible; for other people, it was the beginning of a new hope for the liberation of mankind. Or as Robert Nisbet has said so well in his thoroughly intelligent analysis of the impact of modernization upon sociological theory:

> From precisely the same assumptions regarding the nature of historical development in modern Europe—industrialization, secularization, equality, popular

democracy, and so on—such minds as Tocqueville and Weber drew, not the conclusion of social and moral progress, but the morbid conclusion of man's alienation from man, from values, and from self; an alienation caused by the very forces that others in the century were hailing as progressive.[1]

We might be able to clarify this paradox of social change as it was viewed by theorists in the nineteenth century by letting the theorists speak for themselves about how they viewed the collapse of traditional order and the emergence of modern society. Alexis de Tocqueville, one of the most insightful of these social philosophers, observed:

> In our days men see that the constituted powers are crumbling down on every side, they see all ancient authority dying out, all ancient barriers tottering to their fall, and the judgment of the wisest is troubled at the sight; they attend only to the amazing revolution that is taking place before their eyes, and they imagine that man is about to fall into perpetual anarchy. If they look to the final consequences of this revolution their fears would perhaps assume a different shape. For myself, I confess I put no trust in the spirit of freedom which appears to animate my contemporaries. I see well enough that the nations of this age are turbulent, that I do not clearly perceive that they are liberal; and I fear lest, that the close of those perturbations which rock the base of thrones, the dominion of sovereigns may prove more powerful than it ever was.[2]

If de Tocqueville represents well the fears of the great minds in that century, Marx is perhaps the most obvious of the proponents of the theory of the breakdown of the ancient order. Marx writes the following in commenting on British rule in India:

> This loss of his old world, with no gain of a new one, imparts a particular kind of melancholy to the present misery of the Hindu, and separates Hindustan, ruled by Britain, from all its ancient traditions, and from the soul of its past history. . . . Now, sickening as it must be to human feeling to witness those myriads of industrious, patriarchal and inoffensive social organizations disorganized and dissolved into their units, thrown into a sea of woes, and their individual members losing at the same time their ancient form of civilizations and their hereditary means of subsistence, we must not forget that these idyllic village communities, inoffensive though they may appear, had always been the solid foundation of Oriental despotism, that they restrained the human mind within the smallest possible compass, making it the unresisting tool of superstition, enslaving it beneath traditional rules, depriving it of all grandeur and historical energies. . . . We must not forget that these little communities were contaminated by distinctions of caste, and by slavery, that they subjugated man to external circumstances instead of elevating man into the sovereign of cir-

1. Robert A. Nisbet, *The Sociological Tradition* (New York: Basic Books, Inc., (1966). pp. 6-7.
2. Quoted in *Ibid.*, p. 107.

cumstances, that they transformed a self-developing social state into never changing natural destiny. . . .[3]

For Marx, then, the decay of the old order was the signal for the coming of a new social, political, economic, and moral order that would allow man to grasp his own destiny, to construct a new society with purpose and hope—a society in which man and not tradition was the essence. On the other hand, de Tocqueville, looking at the same historical developments, warned prophetically that he was not so confident of man's eventual liberation. Indeed, he thought there might appear a new kind of "dominion of sovereigns" that "may prove more powerful than it ever was." That is, he predicted the totalitarian society.

Clearly then, these men saw a paradox in man's future. On one hand, man could free himself from the constraints of his past, mobilizing rationality and technological innovation to bring about a new society for the progress and liberation of mankind. On the other hand, this same freedom from tradition would allow society to become more capable of a totalitarian barbarism unknown in the history of social evils. The paradox is that man in the twentieth century finally achieved the freedom that he sought, and in the same achievement made possible the most terrible form of captivation—the tyranny of being lost and then captured by a totalitarian dictatorship.

We need to discuss how the possibility of totalitarianism could arise in the modernization process. How can it be that man is now capable of both freedom and total enslavement? I think this dilemma may be best clarified by understanding four essential phenomena—community, society, authority, power. The argument is that the transition from community and authority to society and power has made both freedom and enslavement possible.

Community we take to mean social organization that is highly cohesive because of traditions, moral myths, religious and economic patterns of behavior, and political hierarchies. Given this definition we can see that the impact of modernization brought about the freeing of man from these kinds of traditional constraints, and the consequence was a whole new notion of social organization that was non-cohesive and non-united. Indeed, it was a social organization in which individualism replaced community, in which the individual was freed of his part in the community in order to become an expression of himself. The historian of the nineteenth century, Tonnies, speaks of this distinction between community and society as the distinction between *Gemeinshaft* and *Gesellschaft*.

"The theory of *Gesellschaft* deals with the artificial construction of an aggre-

---

3. Quoted in *Ibid.*, p. 68.

gate of human beings which superficially resembles the *Gemeinschaft* in so far as the individuals live and dwell together peacefully. *However, in Gemeinschaft they remain essentially united in spite of all separating factors, whereas in Gesellschaft they are essentially separated in spite of all uniting factors.* In the *Gesellschaft*, as contrasted with the *Gemeinschaft*, we find no actions that can be derived from an *apriori* and necessarily existing unity; no actions, therefore, which manifest the will and the spirit of the unity even if performed by the individual; no actions which, insofar as they are performed by the individual, take place on behalf of those united with him. In the *Gesellschaft* such actions do not exist. On the contrary, here everybody is by himself and isolated, and there exists a condition of tension against all others.[4]

So "community," with its people bound together by tradition, became "society"—a collection of individuals free from the constraints of their community.

By "authority," we mean the institutions or individuals and the groups in the society that can control behavior of others because people extend legitimacy to what they command. In other words, they are the appropriate controllers in the society, whether they be religious leaders, kings, or aristocrats. Disintegration of such legitimized authority makes necessary power relationships that use the ultimate sanctions to control behavior. So, as the internal control of authority disintegrates, power or external control becomes the essential ingredient for holding together political relationships in the society.

Both authority and community exist only to the extent that people have internalized constraints upon their behavior. Community exists when people have developed attitudes that predispose them to act in accordance with commonly shared patterns of behavior, regardless of whether these shared behavior patterns stem from religious, economic, or social beliefs. Authority exists when people have internalized the acceptability of particular elites as being the appropriate rulers for the community. Here people have learned attitudes predisposing them to accept the appropriateness of the authorities.

As people become less controlled by these internalized constraints of community and authority, they become more free to act in ways that are not determined by widely shared behavior patterns or ruling elites. They become individuals rather than subjects of a community. But social organization requires some form of constraint upon individual action. Since internal constraints are less operative, external constraints become necessary. Power (i.e., external control over people's behavior) becomes the primary source of social cohesion.

While authority resides in the willing obedience of subjects, power derives from the use of resources (money, time, violence) that serve as

4. Quoted in *Ibid.*, pp. 75-76.

sanctions that bring about compliance rather than willing obedience. Power, unlike authority, does not require individual acceptance. Power exists whether people accept it or not. Since power is independent of individual acceptance and derives from resources, it can be collected and used to force people to behave in particular ways. Power can be collected and hoarded to such an extent that the ruling elite has literally all of the power (i.e., resources to bring about external control) in the society. Such elites may use the power to bring about vast changes in society for the good of people, but it is also clear that they can use the power to maintain their positions of wealth, status, and control. The breakdown of internalized controls of authority and community permits individuals to become free and striving individuals, but it also makes possible their total enslavement by the elite, which is able to capture the power in the society. The very elements necessary to make a better world are the same tools necessary for a totalitarian society.

Now I want to turn to the problem of describing the characteristics of traditional and modern society. I want to start with a look at how modern theorists have described traditional society.

CHARACTERISTICS OF TRADITIONAL
AND MODERN SOCIETY

Robert Redfield, in a now classic study, "The Folk Society," has described the "idealized" version of traditional society—a small, isolated, non-literate, homogeneous society with a strong sense of solidarity.[5] The ties between families and face-to-face interaction groups such as kinship groups are of crucial importance to the ways people behave in this society. Typically, there is a minimum of division of labor. That is, there are few special functions in the economy. Everyone performs the general function of providing sustenance for the immediate family. People are not divided into different service and production efforts. Because of this lack of differentiation there is little basis for social stratification. Rather than being stratified, the folk society is a homogeneous, relatively non-stratified social organization. Further, Redfield points out that its value orientations are focused upon the sacred rather than upon the secular, and that there is strict conformity to the norms of the sacred myths.

Gideon Sjoberg has found several problems in applying Redfield's folk society model as a characterization of traditional society. He has

5. Robert Redfield, "The Folk Society," *American Journal of Sociology,* 52 (1947), pp. 293-308.

developed still another idealized version, which he refers to as a feudal society.[6]

He argues that the feudal society is more resistant to change than is the folk society. He says that the feudal society and the folk society are similar in that they are relatively static and have sacred value orientations demanding high conformity, facts which make behavior patterns highly predictable and minimize conflict among members. But the two societies differ in their structural arrangements. For example, the feudal society, unlike its folk counterpart, involves large peasant populations that gain their livelihood from intensive cultivation of the soil with simple technology. This intensive use of the land for agricultural production permits some food surpluses. Such food surpluses are unknown in the folk society. Food surpluses can be used to provide the base for the formation of small communities within the feudal society. In other words, farmers have something to trade and barter for other services and commodities they might want. Because they have surpluses to use, trade services develop to provide an outlet for such exchange. These services are usually concentrated in small towns that are not isolated but that have some communication with one another. In a sense then, what Sjoberg is describing is a society in which there are multiple folk communities in communication with one another, and with enough surpluses to be able to support a class of people (e.g., the merchants) that does not have to work the land for their living.

Such a class can become the aristocracy or ruling elite of the feudal society. This class sometimes further divides into classes of rulers, priests, intellectuals, and landlords, all of whom are in large part living from the ability of the peasants to produce agricultural surpluses. Governments in such societies tend to be monarchial or theocratic, and the elites are recruited from the young in the elite class. These governments are supported by taxing the surpluses of the peasants. Education and religion in such feudal societies is largely a matter of perpetuating a myth system about the stratification of the elite from the peasant and justifying the right to rule by such notions as "divine right." This ruling elite is strengthened and perpetuated because historical records are kept and used to teach the new generations. In the folk society there is neither strata nor any establishment to breed the continuity of the stratification. It is the feudal society that has the characteristic of the stratification of an elite justified by the intellectuals, protected by the military, and provided for by the surpluses of the peasant farmers.

6. Gideon Sjoberg, "Folk and 'Feudal' Societies," *Political Development and Social Change,* eds. Jason L. Finkle and Richard W. Gable (New York: John Wiley and Sons, 1966), pp. 45-53.

Sjoberg contends that the feudal society is indeed much more resistant to change than is the folk society because of these developments in their social structure. Because it has elites that want to maintain their power and authority, and because it has elaborate myths justifying the maintenance of this power, the feudal society is more capable than is the folk society of resisting attempts to redistribute power.

Both the folk and feudal society models are of most use in our thinking about different kinds of "traditional societies" in the so-called underdeveloped nations of the world. It may be that the folk model is more applicable to particular kinds of underdeveloped nations such as those in Africa and in the Middle East. It may be more useful to think of Latin American countries and perhaps of those in Asia in terms of the feudal society model. In any case, these are two attempts to define the characteristics associated with the general classification of "underdeveloped" societies.

What do we mean by a modern society? It seems that the best way to approach this question is to make a distinction between the process of modernization and the product of that process—the modern society. In other words, we need to think in terms of a transitional phenomenon or a set of events associated with the breakdown of traditional society and the emergence of modern social conditions. The modern society can be thought of as the product of that modernization process.

We will attempt no detailed description of the modernization process in this discussion, but we will try to capture the major factors occurring with the development of society. From the many different descriptions of modernization, I have chosen to talk about five interrelated but distinguishable events that have been considered by many authors as the essential ingredients of modernization. They are (1) social mobilization; (2) industrialization; (3) urbanization; (4) the changes from subsistence to commercial production in agriculture; and (5) the application of science and technology in controlling the physical and human environment. We can discuss each of these processes in more detail before turning to the problem of describing modern society.

Karl Deutsch defines social mobilization as

the process in which major clusters of the old social, economic and psychological commitments are eroded and broken and people become available for new patterns of socialization and behavior.[7]

Deutsch goes on to say,

7. Karl Deutsch, "Social Mobilization and Political Development," *Ibid.,* pp. 205-225, particularly pp. 206-207.

Social mobilization, let us repeat, is something that happens to large numbers
of people in areas which undergo modernization (i.e. where advanced, non-
traditional practices and culture, technology, and economic life are introduced
and accepted on a considerable scale).[8]

The process that Deutsch is describing is one in which two interrelated phenomena occur. First, for whatever reasons and with whatever
consequences, people come to give up or to break away from their old
habits and commitments, and second, they become available for being
mobilized or moved into some new pattern of group membership, organization, and commitments. In other words, whether the cause is a revolution, a natural crisis, or something less dramatic occurring over a long
period of time, the result is disenchantment, disillusionment, and separation from traditional patterns of thought and behavior. It is at this point that
people become capable of being led or pushed into new and different
ways of relating to their environment.

The second major process, that of industrialization, is perhaps the
one most commonly talked about. Here we are referring to the transition
that takes place when human or animal work is replaced by machinery.
Associated with this replacement by machine power is an economy
wherein man begins to work for money rather than for his own subsistence. He does this by making products that can be exchanged for needed
goods or services that he may require for his subsistence. We may already
note that the process of industrialization usually is deeply related to the
process of social mobilization. As machinery becomes the working force
in the society, man is forced away from his traditional work role and is
thereby available to new patterns of economic involvement. Now he is
working for money in factories rather than working to grow food for his
family, and he uses the money to provide for his needs and wants. The
whole process of industrialization has also been closely related to urbanization, which is the third process in modernizing traditional society.

The term *urbanization* simply refers to rural populations moving to
urban centers. In every developed and developing country the phenomenon
is the same, peasants moving to the cities to seek employment. One could
argue that urbanization is an outgrowth of industrialization. But much of
this migration to urban centers may come about not because there are jobs
requiring workers, but because changing values in the society give people
different expectations that they go to the cities to fulfill.

The fourth process to discuss is the changing nature of agriculture in
the society. That change is from subsistence farming, typifying most of the
traditional society, to cash-crop agriculture. Whereas the peasant or farmer once grew his own food with only small surpluses, if any, in modern

8. *Ibid.,* p. 206.

times the farmer raises crops, sells them for cash, and uses the money to purchase needed goods and services. Thus the farmer becomes as dependent as the factory worker upon wages.

The final process in the sequence is the disintegration of the sacred. There is a diminishing reliance upon myth systems, sacred and otherwise, as the orientation of most people in the society is toward reliance upon science and technology. The acceptance of things the way they are changes to a willingness and belief that man can and should manipulate his physical and social environment to whatever purposes he may have created for himself. The change in behavior resulting from such a value change results in the application of technology to the problems of the society. This change from reliance upon simple technology such as wood plows and hand tools to more complex forms of technology becomes self-generating in its spiraling development. Thus man uses his new faith in science to cope with his physical and social environment in increasingly more complex ways.

In these brief descriptions we have already identified some of the characteristics of the modern society. Now, specifically, what do we mean when we say that a society is modern?

There are several different aspects of society that must necessarily be described if we are to understand what this modernity means. Whereas the value orientation in traditional society tends toward the sacred, the myth, the superstitious, in modern society the value orientation tends toward the secular, scientific, and rational. There is a rejection of those things based upon religious faith or tradition. Instead a growing emphasis is placed upon those values that are derived from individuals attempting to understand, cope with, and change their environment. The major instruments for such coping have been science and technology, which it is believed enable man to manipulate and improve his social condition.

Modern society is further characterized by economic specialization. Quite simply, individuals no longer perform general economic functions; rather they become parts, often very small parts, in the general production and consumption patterns. Whereas people once made everything for themselves, they are now part of a larger, highly complex, and specialized economic system in which they may do no more than drive the food to market, raise one type of food, or simply make the nails that go into a house. In this sense the economy of modern society is highly diffused and specialized, and therefore its parts are interdependent. The farmer cannot exist without the wholesaler and retailer, and they in turn cannot exist without the farmer and consumers working in factories, who cannot exist without entrepreneurs to create wealth by marketing new products. Economic differentiation has a definite impact upon the social structure of a society.

The social structure of modern society has a high degree of differentiation. There are many more roles in modern society than in the traditional society. Indeed, there are classes of people, webs of interdependent roles that correspond with the varying kinds of economic specialization occurring in the society. No longer is the family, for instance, an economic unit largely engaged in producing food for it to eat. Now it is a group of people existing together, perhaps working in different occupations and remaining a family for entirely different reasons than those in traditional cultures.

Associated with this social and economic differentiation is a fourth characteristic. Policymaking is concentrated and centralized in a bureaucratically differentiated elite. So the political structure of modern society, whether it is making decisions about public or private policies, tends to be characterized by a highly centralized, decision-making body that creates policy binding all the people to ways of behaving and thinking. Whether these elites are elected or assume power through revolution, the shared characteristic is that they are making the most of the decisions, although they form a very small proportion of the total population.

The phenomenon of individuality is the final characteristic. That is, the individual has assumed tremendous importance in modern society. Whether you think of individualism as a condition in which man is separated, lonely, and purposeless, or whether you think of it as a condition in which man is free, striving, and purposeful, the emphasis is upon the individual and his place in the social organization.

In the preceding discussion we have talked about the process of modernization, from traditional to modern, as well as the consequences of this process—the characteristics of the modern society. What causes this transition to occur? To a large extent, we are now focusing upon the same question that was raised in the last chapter—the question of theories of social change. Most theorists have focused upon two vital factors as bringing about modernization—economic factors and political factors. Indeed, within the ranks of analysts in this area there has been and continues to be a long standing debate about which is most important.

Some authors argue that economic development must occur before the society can modernize. Such economic determinists suggest that economic forces in history are fundamental to every other aspect of human conditions. In any case, a large part of the literature on modernization assumes that economic development, industrialization, specialization, and diversity of economy are prerequisites for any other form of development in the society. They contend that only when society is capable of producing the wealth with which to educate people, to provide for their needs, and to ensure their continuing security will such luxuries as democracy and other presumed forms of development be tolerated.

Still other scholars argue just the opposite. Economic development may or may not result in the development of other spheres in the society. They point out that it is possible to have a society that produces a great deal of wealth, which is captured by a very small elite of people and is not used for the betterment or development of the entire society. Therefore, it is not used to create an educated and secure populace enjoying wide participation in the democratically oriented politics of the country. From this point of view, economic development may be seen as a necessary condition for bringing about other forms of development, but certainly not as being sufficient to do so by itself. Political development is derived from other sources than economic growth. Unless some kind of change occurs in the policy of a society, economic development may not come about. Entrenched political elites may prevent the development of the economy if by doing so they somehow are more able to maintain their power base.

This debate is continuing and the evidence is hardly persuasive on either side of the argument. To say that political and economic development are hopelessly intertwined is the most common kind of compromise. This view suggests that both kinds of development are highly dependent upon each other, and it makes no sense to try to specify which occurs first.

Without being too superficial I would suggest that the causes of modernization are complex and involve many different forces occurring in a society. As our review of several theories of social change in the last chapter suggests, there are as many different views of what brings about change in society as there are theorists thinking about the matter. We cannot expect any theoretical closure in this assessment. To confirm that the process of modernization arises from multiple causes and is not assured by any kind of historical or inevitable sequence of events is enough, I think. Political development can occur only to be eroded by the lack of development in other spheres of social endeavor. For example, the Weimar Republic in Germany during the 1920s and 1930s might be conceived of as typifying political development. But economic crisis undermined the democracy. The democracy failed and a totalitarian system came to power, bringing about the economic development of a vast war machine. Perhaps all we can conclude is that modernization, regardless of its causes, is no guarantee of the good life for people.

In the above discussion I have attempted to bring together the highlights of various studies of traditional and modern society. As I read over what I have written, I get an overwhelming sense of smugness and perhaps even of complacency. I think this feeling is an accurate criticism of most of the theorizing about the process of modernization and national development. So before we go any further I want to add an extensive footnote to this discussion of traditional, transitional, and modern social organization. I hope these thoughts will disturb you as they do me, and that they will raise questions about the whole process we have been attempting to understand.

BEYOND MODERN: THE
POST-INDUSTRIAL SOCIETY

If you have been thinking about the kind of things we have been discussing as typifying both economic and political development, it should be clear that there are some profound assumptions involved in what has been said. One assumption is that economic productivity and the resulting material advantages for the society bring about the "good life." That democracy enhances the "good life" for people is another. As we look about us in the twentieth century, particularly in the United States, and as we look at the problems we have, the conflicts that exist, we can only wonder whether economic productivity and democracy as we know it are warranted as the only criteria of the "good life." I feel compelled to raise this question in the most vivid terms possible. There can be little doubt that our society and a handful of others have been extremely successful in developing industrial potential and productivity, thereby providing high standards of living for their people. But what has been the cost of this tremendous affluence for the few? In our own country, where only a fraction of the world's population lives, we are using a vast amount of the world's resources to sustain the production necessary for our standard of living. Not only are we devouring the world's resources, but in the process we are creating such waste and pollution and a general destruction of the environment that even our great technological and scientific establishment may be unable to reverse this trend. We are exploiting the world, its resources, and people in order to provide ourselves with these material advantages. One wonders about the rest of the world. How long will they tolerate our appetites and their sacrifices? Should they wait? How long?

In my own opinion such questions are important enough to demand careful and thoughtful consideration from every student, indeed every citizen, in this country. Perhaps it is time we re-examine the assumptions that have become almost holy writ for our society. Our equation of growth with goodness is a deadly equation, given what we can reasonably assume to be the limited resources of this world. We must begin immediately to think creatively about the construction of an economy based not upon the destruction of our environment, but upon a balanced relationship between progress and resources. There must be economies which do not require the input of vast—yes, finally all—of the world's resources for their support. Perhaps our industrial society must become some other kind of society.

What characteristics of the post-industrial society have generated the kinds of problems just described? John Kenneth Galbraith in *The New Industrial State* suggests at least one explanation of the problems of economic dynamics of the industrialized society. One of the basic themes of his book is that the process of industrialization creates its own imperatives for continuation of economic growth.

The argument follows these lines: As large industries expend vast amounts of time, talent, and capital in the development of a product for mass production, they must substantially reduce the risks of a marketplace economy in which the consumer decides what to buy and what not to buy as he calculates his own best interests. In more traditional economics, the assumption was that the producer placed a product on the market, accepting the risk that it might not sell. The profit was the inducement to take the risk. If a large corporation spends several years, thousands of engineering hours, and vast amounts of capital for resources to produce the item, the managers of the corporation are not so much interested in the maximization of profit but are much more interested in minimizing the risk of losing the tremendous investment already made. In other words, they cannot accept the uncertainties of the marketplace, with its sovereign consumer. The buying of a product must be just as carefully planned as is its production. It is essential to the continuation of the industrialization process that consumers be conditioned to spend their money on the products that industry has invested so much in developing. So industrialization requires corporations not only to be able to bring together the capital and material to make a product, but they must also be able to control the consumption of that product.

The control of the consumer is realized in many ways, such as through the use of mass media to manipulate consumer habits and expectations. Perhaps more importantly, the consumer is conditioned by cultural values to consume and to produce in this spiral of growth. So we find in post-industrial society that personal success is defined in terms of how many material goods a person can accumulate. Indeed, people are held captive to the production-consumption cycle by being led to believe that their needs are satisfied by working to produce goods, which gets them the money to buy things that define success and "meaning" in their lives. It might be pointed out that such acquisition of material goods does little to make one very happy, but most of us continue to believe that it will.

Given that the consumer is conditioned to consume by advertising and cultural values, corporations are able to plan well ahead and to expend the vast amounts of capital necessary to produce an item that will probably be purchased. What is suggested by this analysis is not a conspiracy of corporation elites to manipulate people for "fun and profit," but instead, this analysis suggests that such dynamics are necessary for the industrialization process to continue and to expand. What is described in this argument is not an evil conspiracy, but a vast industrial machine that requires these behavior traits for its operation. Growth of industry becomes a part of this spiral as corporations seek to control more and more of both the resources for production and of the markets for consumption of those products. The bigger a corporation becomes, the more control it can exert upon production and consumption of products. Corporations are thus required to grow and to expand to meet the imperatives of industrialization and mass production of goods.

If such economic processes do exist in the post-industrial society, then what kinds of results might one expect for the political, social, and economic institutions of the society? First, we might expect less differentiation between political institutions and economic ones. In more traditional views of industrial society, it is usually argued that economic institutions are out to serve private interests by gaining profits and satisfying consumer demands. Government, it is theorized, exists as a protector of the individual and representative of the public interests of all the people. So, if the economic institutions get out of line, the government can regulate and control their behavior so that it does serve the public interests and not just their profit motives. However, in this view, the government is no longer distinct from the economy. Government becomes a very important part of the technological-industrial machine and is driven by the same imperatives of industrial growth and expansion. The government may serve as a major consumer by contracting for vast amounts of military hardware, or by influencing foreign markets to become markets for consumption of our products. By using taxes to subsidize vast amounts of research for private industry, government can also act to underwrite the research and development of technology required for expansion. For instance, government contracts pay for the development of an aircraft that the government buys as a military item, but the same aircraft can be sold by the contractor to private airlines for an additional payoff for an item that the contractor took little if any risk in developing. It is always a source of some amusement to me to hear people outraged by government subsidy of the poor through welfare, but who find no problem in government subsidy of vast corporations with sums that stagger the imagination. This merger of the political and economic institutions then creates another characteristic of post-industrial society. The basic structure of such a society is no longer political or economic; it is now administrative.

If we think of society as involving conflicting interests of many different groups and people, then it makes sense to have political institutions that operate to resolve such conflicts and to regulate the rest of the society in ways that are consistent with the compromise. But in the post-industrial society we have described, there is little conflict of interests. All interests in the society are subservient to the imperatives of industrial growth and expansion. Given this consensus about the goals of the society, a political structure is no longer necessary. What is needed is an administrative structure to carry out the assignment efficiently and effectively. Such administrative structures are designed to carry out tasks, not to resolve conflicts. In fact, conflict becomes a source of inefficiency to be eliminated if at all possible. The administrative structure brings about greater efficiency by assigning roles to individuals and by organizing those roles in vast bureaucracies. In such a way, people are no longer collections of individuals with differing needs, wants, and interests; they are parts in a machine, parts that can be replaced if necessary. The individual no longer is an autonomous person but is a set of defined expectations that will get the job done. In order to assure that the job gets done efficiently, the administrative organization creates laws that can be used to protect the organizations and bureaucracy from individual deviancy. Such laws ensure that the individual will conform to his role. Laws serve to maintain the large organizations necessary to the continued growth of the society. Laws do not operate to protect the individual from society, but to protect the society from the individual.

As if the laws were not enough to guarantee the conformity of people to their roles in organizational hierarchies, there is the additional incentive of the cultural expectations that tend to define a man by his status rather than as a person. He is no longer a person, or even a significant cog, but a relationship to the organization. If he has higher status in the organization, he is more important as a person, but not indispensible. Who knows the names of the chairmen of the board for the largest corporations in this country? A man has status and meaning as an individual, not for who he is but for what position he holds in society. The very meaning of self then requires the continuation of the organization to give the status which supplies meaning for an individual.[9]

Obviously there is disagreement among theorists about whether these processes and structures are descriptive of today's post-industrial society. But it seems clear that these ideas about post-industrial society create enough doubt to invite re-examination of what we are all about as a society. We must reconsider the ways in which we can live and achieve progress without growth. We must try to understand how to preserve order without sacrificing change. What are the alternative forms of political and social organization that we must evaluate in terms of whether they achieve the "good life" for people?

---

9. The foregoing analysis is found in such sources as Jacques Ellul, *The Technological Society* (New York: Vintage Books, 1969); J. K. Galbraith, *The New Industrial State* (New York: Signet Books, 1967); Charles Reich, *The Greening of America* (New York: Random House, 1970); and Philip Slater, *The Pursuit of Loneliness* (Boston: Beacon Press, (1970).

The next section of this chapter will discuss four hypothetical models of political organization, and evaluate each in terms of its strengths and weaknesses. It will be your task to make a judgment about which, if any, of these types of social organization is most likely to bring about the "good life" in society.

FOUR TYPES OF POLITICAL ORGANIZATIONS AS PROBLEM SOLVING DEVICES

You may recall that in Chapter Two we introduced the concept of political system as a useful way of thinking about the ways people *act* in relationship to politics, and the concept of political culture to examine the ways they *think* in relationship to politics. You may want to turn back to that part of Chapter Two to review in more detail these two concepts before going on with this discussion. In any case, you should keep in mind that systems refer to the ways people behave and the interdependencies in their behavior, while culture refers to the attitudes people have about the ways they will act in the political process. With this in mind we can now proceed to develop a typology of political organizations.

This typology is simply an "idealized" or simplified description of four different kinds of political organizations. I will make no attempt to describe these organizations in detail or to give many concrete examples from real governments that might assume many of the same attributes as do these models. I will simply characterize each in terms of what I consider to be its essential components. I refer to these four types as: (1) authoritarian, (2) bureaucracy, (3) responsive democracy, and (4) creative democracy. In discussing each of the four political organizations I will describe the essential characteristic of that political system as being the way in which power is distributed. I will also characterize the essential value orientation or major shared attitude existing in the political culture. The overall argument is that particular distributions of power are maintained and accepted because people share attitudes leading them to accept the particular power arrangements. In other words, the political culture is supportive of the political system. In turn, the political system is a way of creating and maintaining the political culture. Now we can turn to a brief description of the four types and some evaluation of each as a mechanism for solving problems.

Authoritarian Political Organization

How then would I describe the distribution of power characterizing the political system of this form of organization? I think it is most accurately described as a *concentrated power distribution.* This is a political system in which most of the power is held by a small elite, an aristocracy, an economic elite, a priesthood, military or very popular leaders. But in all cases the power affecting most of the decisions made and carried out in that society is held by very few people.

If the political system is characterized by a concentration of power in the hands of a few, what kind of a political culture is supportive of such a distribution? I would argue that the central value orientation required to support such a system is one in which the emphasis is placed upon the *obedience of people* to the dictates of the power elite. How do the people come to believe that they must obey the elite? Such belief can come about through a variety of circumstances in the society. We will talk about the development of such value orientations later in the book. For now, we can say that whether such values are learned in the family or other such institutions or whether they are imposed by an elite with sanctions to enforce them, the fact remains that such a supportive culture for an authoritarian elite political system is one demanding obedience to the rulers.

What we have described to this point is a political organization in which elites make the decisions and the masses of people obey whatever the elite say they should do. Now, what are the advantages and disadvantages of such a form of political organization in coping with change-induced problems?

Evaluation: It seems to me that the strongest advantage of such an organization is its flexibility in the face of changing problems. Assuming a capable elite in this situation, we can imagine that they would be able to anticipate, plan for, and organize national resources toward the solving of major problems. Given the people's obedience, these solutions could be implemented very easily. This flexibility then could maximize the ability of the organization to respond to problems with most efficiency, since time or resources need not be spent convincing people of the changes the elite decide to make.

What are the disadvantages? There are two distinct problems that come to mind. The first has to do with the nature of the elite and the second with the nature of the masses of people in the organization. Clearly the authoritarian type operates with a high degree of flexibility and efficiency in problem solving as long as we assume that the elite is benevolent. History suggests a great deal of caution about such an assumption. Whatever the intentions or goals are, the elite have the power not only to improve the society but also to subject it to their whims and/or misunderstanding of the problems. What if the elite, even a benevolent one, lacks the capability to solve the society's problems? What if the elite visualizes only the problem of maintaining its own power rather than the real problems of helping their people? If the elite spends most of the country's resources maintaining its own power, very little remains for the development of the country.

The other major disadvantage has to do with the effects of such a political system upon the lives of people in that society. What kind of people does such a society produce? People who obey. People who live in fear of disobedience. I find this kind of political culture less likely to provide the "good life" for the members of the society. In any case, these are some of the pros and cons of an authoritarian political organization as a device for coping with the problems of change. You could undoubtedly list many more advantages and disadvantages, but this is enough to illustrate the kind of evaluation that must be made of any kind of political organization.

Bureaucratic Political Organization

The second type of political organization that I want to describe is the bureaucracy. As I described the authoritarian model as having a concentration of power characterizing the political system, bureaucratic political organization can be described as having a *functional distribution of power.* Perhaps a concentration of power is more easily conceptualized than is the notion of a functional distribution. So what do I mean by a functional distribution of power?

Here I have in mind a political organization that distributes power around the major problems that confront that organization. In other words, power is allotted to various agencies that have problems that must be solved. The bigger the problem is, the more power that is allocated to that agency. In our society, for instance, we have distributed a great deal of power to military-industrial agencies to cope with what we have seen as our major problem—defending ourselves against foreign powers. We have also distributed power to solve other kinds of problems, but we have given them a much lower priority. We do have power allocated to the functions of solving the problems of welfare, education, housing, and space programs. But in all cases the distribution of power into these other areas is of a much smaller magnitude than that given to defense.

If we can characterize a bureaucratic political organization as having a functional distribution of power, how might we describe the political culture necessary to support this system? I think the essential value orientation that must be created in this political culture is the *orientation to conform.* Here we find the assumption that man operates in the bureaucracy to solve the problems defined by the society, and that he is a replaceable unit in the problem-solving device. The criterion for his replacement becomes a question of how efficient the individual is in carrying out his part in the machine. High levels of conformity to the rules of the bureauc-

racy are required. The organization man in the bureaucracy is a conform-
ist. He is the one most likely methodically to carry out the obligations and
duties of his position.

Bureaucratic political organization has a functional distribution of
power, supported by a mass of people in the organization, who have
learned to conform to whatever prescribed behavior traits are offered by
the bureaucracy's approach to solving problems. What advantages and
disadvantages do we find associated with this model?

Evaluation: First and foremost, it strikes me that the major advantage
of such an organization is its endurance and capacity to cope with highly
complex problems. It has endurance because once it is set into operation,
it is a self-generating kind of mechanism. Once the problem is defined and
people set about the task of solving that problem, they can continue in that
capacity with little or no control. Leadership is not always necessary, since
the rules of the bureaucracy serve to define goals, actions, and even thoughts
about the problem. This system also has the capacity for dealing with many
problems at once by merely adding new elements to the bureaucracy. As
new problems arise, new agencies can be created to cope with them,
while the older problems are still being attended to by the existing agencies.

The most obvious disadvantage of such a system is its lack of flexibility. Bureaucracy creates a rigidity that in fact retards the ability of people
in the system to move resources or to change previous ways of doing
things in order to cope with different kinds of problems. There is a tendency for the bureaucracy to perpetuate itself even after the problems are
solved. There is the further tendency for bureaucrats not really to solve
problems, but to secure their jobs by extending the problems. It is almost
impossible to imagine a bureaucracy going out of business. For it to do so
would mean the loss of jobs and livelihood for many people. Unfortunate-
ly, there is also a high degree of conformity among the people in such an
organization. Somehow I find such conforming behavior no more or no
less acceptable than the obedience training received by people in the
authoritarian model. Neither obeying nor conforming seems to me to be
an essential ingredient of human development and maturation.

The third and fourth simplified types of political organizations are
often not distinguished. We usually lump these two types under the concept of democracy. I want to distinguish between what I see as responsive
political organization and creative political organization.

Responsive Democratic Political Organization

The authoritarian model has a concentrated distribution of power,
and the bureaucratic model has a functional distribution of power. The

responsive democratic model is characterized by a *varying distribution of power.* By this phrase I mean that power tends to shift to the problems that the organization confronts. Therefore, as the problems and issues vary, so does the distribution of power. In this sense the power in the system responds to the "creaking or squeaking wheel." Where the crisis occurs, power is applied. And in this sense it is a responsive political organization. What is the associated political culture?

I believe that the essential value orientation is one of individual *dependency upon material needs* such as food, clothing, housing, and security generally. What seems to be happening in this political organization is that people, through fear or insecurity and a desire for more material goods, become overly dependent upon those conditions of material well-being. As they become dependent upon this concept of well-being, they expect government to solve those problems that they feel threaten their material security. In order to exist, this kind of political organization requires people to be dependent upon heavy consumption to meet these needs. For if people were less dependent on heavy consumption to meet these needs, the system would no longer be afforded legitimacy as the mechanism required to provide for them. Perhaps the affluent society in which we live is the first real test of this kind of organization. It may well be that as a nation we are becoming less dependent upon "conspicuous consumption" simply because our society has been so successful in providing. In any case, the responsive democratic political organization is one characterized by varying distributions of power, which are allocated in response to crisis conditions in the population, and in response to the people's high degree of dependency upon conspicuous consumption to meet material needs.

Evaluation: The advantages of this model are somewhat obvious, I think. Clearly people do have material needs that require responsive governments. We do have a government in this case that is responding to the needs of people, and that is why I call it a responsive democracy.

What are the disadvantages of such organization? The most overwhelming disadvantage that I can see is that the model is responsive to the problems that people have and in turn tends to perpetuate in the minds of those people their dependency upon answering those needs. In other words, problems have to become of crisis proportions, (e.g., people must be dying, starving, out of work, fighting, or whatever, before there is a redistribution of power in the system). The model is responsive, but it does not anticipate problems. Further, I think that a culture with a dependency orientation is encouraged and perpetuated, one in which people lack purpose or direction in their lives. They tend merely to stumble along in a Pavlovian way, salivating only when they feel a material need impinging upon their security. This dependency does not appeal to most people as a desirable state of affairs. We are finally getting to a description of the fourth type of political organization, and one that I consider to be a Utopian version of society beyond the industrial state.

Creative Democratic Political Organization

I think of a truly creative political problem solving organization as one characterized not by a concentration of power, not by a functional distribution of power nor a varying distribution of power, but by an *expanding distribution of power*. That is, the amount of power is expanding and being distributed as widely as possible among people, groups, and institutions in that society. I also suspect that the kind of political culture required to support this wide distribution of power and to enable people to utilize the available power is one that is *person oriented*. In other words, in such a society people would have to learn that the major value in society is the solution of their own problems and the actualization of themselves as they solve such problems. The utilization of the expanding power available in the system is for the purpose of bringing about a better life for people and for their families. It makes possible the achievement of those purposes and goals that are intrinsic to their individual maturation.

So, my Utopian political organization is one in which there is a continually increasing amount of power available to many if not most of the people all of the time, and a political culture that teaches them to be oriented toward utilizing their power in the pursuit of their own unique and individually defined purposes.

Evaluation: The major disadvantages of such an organization, I suppose, are the same as those of any Utopian model. It is a little hard to imagine how such a wide distribution of power could continue to exist. There always seem to be aggressive and ambitious elites who are trying to caputre the power. In addition, some people appear to be willing to have the elite take that power so that they may avoid the burden of their own problems. History makes us painfully aware of the tendency for power to accrue in the hands of a few, and for the mass of people to become alienated and apathetic.

The major advantage of such an organization is its ability to anticipate problems with a high degree of flexibility. This ability should give the total organization a maximum capability for confronting, anticipating, and solving problems—not merely for responding to crisis but also for focusing its resources and energies in the most effective manner possible. This organization tends to create personalities which are autonomous, task oriented, creative and self-reliant—people not only capable of coping with their social environment but also with themselves and their own process of becoming human.

These foregoing paragraphs have attempted to describe and evaluate four simplified types of political organizations. My intent here is to enable you as a student to make intelligent evaluations of the kinds of political organization in which you are involved, whether they be national, state, local, or smaller systems such as families, churches, and schools. You will have to make your own judgments. What appears here are one man's evaluation and preferences based upon those descriptions and evaluations. I have described some alternatives, and undoubtedly no one of these simple models is completely descriptive of realities. Probably some combination of the various types would more adequately describe real political organization. With this kind of analysis in mind, it may be easier for you to make the judgments necessary about political organization in relation to problem solving. This chapter then concludes our discussion of the analysis of change. The next chapter will focus upon the general process of conflict. We will examine the creation and use of power in conflict situations.

PART IV

CONFLICT
AND THE
POLITICAL SYSTEM

CHAPTER 8

CREATING AND ORGANIZING POWER

TOWARD A CREATIVE POLITICS

It is time we seriously consider the notion of political revolution, which this chapter will examine in some depth. Without getting involved in any fancy definitions, I think that most of us think of political revolution in this manner: 1) there is a limited amount of power in a given society; 2) bad buys seem to have captured most of that power; 3) power has to be taken away from them by force, violence, or whatever means necessary; and 4) once you have taken the power, it can be used to bring about the Utopia or good society that the good guys want. Believing in this theory of revolutionary change, and it is a theory, not a law, leads to some obvious strategies.

Most of us are aware of what these strategies are. The most obvious strategy consists of making more and more people aware of just how bad the bad guys are and of how much power they have. In this way it is hoped that people will be persuaded to join the revolution and take the power away from the bad guys. Given this strategy, confrontation in the street, violent demonstrations or non-violent marches are all means of changing society. There is another way of thinking about revolution that has significant implications. My thinking about this matter has led to a different set of strategies that might serve to bring about a truly creative politics. Hopefully, this and the following chapter will be of some use to you in clarifying your own thoughts. What is the basic assumption underlying the above theory of political revolution? Most central is the premise of a limited or finite amount of power available in the society. That is, there is just so much power, and most of it is controlled by a small elite. Logically, the only way the powerless can change things is by capturing power from the elite.

You might imagine a community in which only one man has a gun, giving him a powerful weapon against his defenseless neighbors. In order to defend himself (or acquire power), another member of the community might take the first man's gun. But what happens if the members of that community realize there are many guns in the world and each member buys one? Now every member has the same power as every other member. And no one has taken any power from the man who had the first gun. In other words, no one has taken any of his power— he still has the exact same amount of power as he had previously—but now there are many more guns available. There are other examples that may be more realistic.

For instance, I think it unlikely that anyone would argue that management in American industry became less powerful as a result of the management-labor union conflicts in the 1930s. It seems to me that management is still a powerful force in this society. At the same time it is clear that unions have gained a great deal of power. Unions did not take management's power. They created their own, which made management less powerful in relation to labor.

Similarly, as long as one nation has the only atom bomb in existence, that nation is extremely powerful in relation to other nations. But once other nations create their own atom bombs, then the first nation is not nearly as powerful as it was in international affairs. We need to look at this notion of creating power in more depth.

If we assume that the amount of power in society can be expanded or contracted rather than assume that it is a constant and finite quantity, we come to different conclusions regarding strategies of social change. It is no longer a matter of taking power away from those who have it; rather it is a matter of creating new power that can be used to bring about the desired Utopia. We are no longer taking power to change society. We are now creating power to change society. Hopefully this discussion has raised some serious questions in your mind.

One such question might be—Why does anyone assume that power is limited or finite? Or—How can anyone assume that it is not limited, that it has the characteristic of expanding and of contracting rather than of being a constant quantity? The reason, I think, that many theorists, particularly elite theorists, have come to assume that power is a limited quantity is that they tend to equate power with certain kinds of resources available in the society, and most of the time these resources are limited in their nature. Some theorists argue that power derives from the ownership of property. Many of the eighteenth-century "liberal" political philosophers observed that monarchies owned most of the property in the country. The monarchies also had most of the power. So, it was assumed that the ownership of property gave that power. And since property is a limited or finite resource—there is just so much land to own—therefore power must also be limited. Marx, for example, argued that power equals control over the economy of the country, and that since control or ownership of the economic processes in society is a finite matter, power must also be finite. The way to be powerful is to gain control over the economic processes. Now, what basis do I have for assuming that power has an expanding and contracting characteristic?

I argue power is not equal to the ownership of property or to the control of economic functions. Power equals the awareness of problems. The number of problems, as anyone can tell you, is infinite, not limited by space or by the existence of other available resources.

If the number of problems is infinite and if people are continually made aware of them, the power derived from such awareness is also unlimited or expanding in nature. Such reasoning leads to some other interesting notions. If the recognition of problems creates power, we might also argue that the solution of those problems dissolves power. Now we are talking about a society in which power expands with the perception of problems and contracts as those problems are solved. In other words, when a leader is able to convince people that they have a problem, he is creating power. And when that leader is able to solve that problem or allow people to believe the problem no longer exists, he has dissolved power.

I am not suggesting anything new. E. E. Schattschneider, when he discusses the "socializing" of issues, or defining of issues in such a way as to broaden the "scope of conflict" to include the people who have previously been uninvolved, would recognize the expanding characteristic I describe.[1] He would also recognize the contracting characteristic, as he talks about the ability of elites to exploit and suppress conflicts about issues

1. E. E. Schattschneider, *The Semi-Sovereign People* (New York: Holt, Rinehart, and Winston, 1960).

in order to prevent the broadening of the conflict. Actually, many theorists in the area of political change have recognized this equation between the awareness of problems and the existence of power whether it is Schattsc- hneider talking about "mobilizing biases" and increasing the scope of conflict, or Marx talking about "class consciousness" as a prerequisite to revolution, of James C. Davies referring to the "rising expectations" of people as a precipitant of revolution.[2] All three men seem to be focusing upon the same kind of notion. As people become aware of threatening problems, they are potentially available as a power base from which to change a society.

Many theorists have already seen the relationship between the con- tracting of a political system and people's ability to care or be concerned about the problems in that society. According to many political commen- tators, apathy and alienation are the essential phenomena that reduce the possibility of a participatory democracy. Some theorists further argue that people are apathetic because they are satisfied, not because there is some- thing terribly wrong with the society. In other words, their problems have been solved, for them at least, and they are no longer aware of any threat to them or to those close to them. When people are unaware, they no longer serve as a base for power and organization to bring about change.

There is nothing very new here, but indeed this view is quite different from the common sense theory of political revolution described at the beginning of the chapter. In that theory, power is limited and has to be taken away from somebody to be used for good purposes. In this view, an expanding power base can be created by making people aware of real or imagined problems. Such as expanding power base can then be orga- nized by various elites and leaders and used to bring about change. If such leaders are effective in making these changes or adaptations and if the problems are solved, then the power base is contracted. Then there is a return to the former condition wherein power remains in the hands of a few—those who are visible and instrumental in solving the problem.

BEFORE WE CONTINUE

I think we need to relate this discussion to the general theory of conflict, consensus, and change used in this book. Where does this notion of the creation of power fit into the general framework suggested in Chap- ters Four and Five? You may recall that in those chapters we introduced the general concept that as environmental changes occur in a society,

2. James C. Davies, "Toward a Theory of Revolution," *The American Sociological Review,* Vol. 28, No. 1 (1962), pp. 5-19.

those changes alter the experiences of people and in turn their changing experiences teach them different attitudes. These include differing attitudes about the ways in which people should act in the political system. Therefore, the level of consensus in the political culture (i.e., the shared agreement about the ways to act in the political system) begins to decrease. As the level of consensus characterising the political culture begins to decrease, conflicts within that society increase. In other words, the level of conflict is defined by the perception of disagreements or problems.

Continuing with this theory, as these rising levels of conflict begin to occur it is necessary to make adaptive changes in the policy binding that society. And these adaptations have to be effective ways of dealing with the perceived problems. It is at this point that the expanding and contracting of power is relevant to the overall framework. The creation of power in the rising level of conflict and the organization and use of that power to make public policy adaptations is the focus of this and the following chapter. Chapters Ten and Eleven deal primarily with the final stages of the framework, having to do with the creation and change of consensus around the adaptive policy solutions that have been made.

With this general scheme in mind, we can return to this specific discussion of the creation of power at the point of rising levels of conflict. The next chapter deals with the use of power in making policy adaptations.

THE NATURE OF AN EXPANDING AND CONTRACTING POWER BASE

How much can the power in a society expand or contract? How is this expansion and contraction brought about? I suppose that power can expand to the extent that people can be made aware of an increasing number of problems, either real or imagined, and to the extent that they can be mobilized and organized to bring about change. We might conclude that the practical limits upon what is theoretically an infinite amount of power exist in terms of the numbers of people that can be made aware of the existence of problems. For practical purposes power can expand to the limits of the numbers of people and to the limits of their awareness of problems. As I suggested in the last chapter, it is this expanding characteristic of power that in my mind enables people to begin to cope with their own problems and to control their own circumstances in such a way as to bring about the "good life" for most people in that society.

If power continued to expand without solutions to any problems (which would contract that power), at some point in time the very problems that caused the awareness and created the power would destroy the society. We can safely assume that there are threshholds beyond which the expansion of power no longer promotes the "good life" but becomes the source of social disintegration. How far can power in the system contract?

When the "masses" do not perceive any problems and the decision-making and policy implementation lie in the hands of one man or elite, there exists the most contracted or narrowest power base. Because they have been credited with solving the problem, certain individuals have emerged as elites. In order to remain elites, they may use their power to keep people from becoming aware of new problems. Elites have at their disposal various mechanisms in society to convince people that they do not have any new problems—mechanisms such as propaganda through the media. By persuading people that everything is fine, whether or not it is, the elites can keep the power base contracted. In addition, media can be used to expose problems, real or unreal, which the elites know they can solve. Seemingly, this is one of the most common techniques to prevent the expansion of power beyond the elites' control. This point was demonstrated when our own power elites created in the minds of many people an idea of the neccessity for conquering space frontiers, with the full recognition that it was only a matter of time until man reached the moon. This creation of illusory problems with a built-in solution may have been the binding force in the United States in the 1960s.

Elites maintain power by solving problems. Problems exist to the extent people perceive threats, whether real or imagined. However, the power that accrues to an elite who solves an imagined problem is not imagined power—it is *real* power. If we are convinced that a foreign power is after us, those who prevent such an imagined conquest have gained and thereby can maintain real power. If we are convinced that going to the moon is a high priority problem, and if somebody goes to the moon, we have an example of the creation of a problem in order to gain the power that is the result of solving that problem. With the solution, the power base contracts and the elite remains powerful—not because he possesses such a great quantity of power but because others, seeing no reason to maintain it, let their power dissolve.

This expanding and contracting quality has implications for both elites and "counter-elites," or those who want to gain power. Elites are trying to define problems and issues in such a way that they can solve them and therefore maintain a contracted system. Counter-elites are attempting to create awareness of problems so that they can expand the power in order to change the system.

Any time a leader creates awareness of problems he creates power that expands the system. Often, as a result, another leader (e.g., counter-elites) creates further awareness among other groups of the problems resulting from the first leader's efforts to expand his power. This is commonly referred to as the escalation of conflict. Such escalation takes place as more and more people with differing interests are drawn into the political arena. As you can see, the expansion of power in a system by the elites is a tricky business.

The expansion of power can become an unmanageable situation for the elites in a society. As an illustration of this point, you might imagine that country X involves itself in a foreign war that seems to be destroying both its resources and its humanity. As people become aware of the problems resulting from involvement in the war, the power in that system begins to expand. As the power base expands, the elites are faced with having to contract the system by solving some problems so people will relax and withdraw from the political arena. They must persuade people that there is no problem for them to be excited about. One technique an elite might use is to convince many people in the society that the problem is not the war at all. Instead the real problem concerns the people who are trying to stop the war. Because they feel they cannot or do not want to stop the war, the elites divert attention to those in the society who do not like the war. Thus they attempt to maintain power by making people aware of a new problem—disorder and revolution. By using powers of repression such as legal sanctions, the elites convince many people in the society that they can solve this new problem of "protest." Obviously they have not solved the problem of the war that gave rise to the expanding power in the first place. Rather they have convinced many people that the real problem is the dissent over the war, a problem the elites solve, thereby contracting the system.

But such manipulation is dangerous. For when the new problem of protest is emphasized, perhaps another group is mobilized around the idea of the right to protest. As these new groups mobilize, the power expands rather than contracts. Now the expansion of power is escalating, making it nearly impossible for any one elite to regain control. The new groups—let us call them hard hats—are trying to solve the problem of protest, which in turn threatens the people who are concerned about repression. The creation of problems in order to solve problems has brought about an explosively expanding society. In attempting to expand power in order to solve a problem and maintain their power, the elites have created real and unmanageable problems. Now they are faced with the difficulty of stabilizing a society in which no one has enough power relative to the total to be able to control it. In other words, the elites must solve some problems, real or otherwise, in order to contract the system in such a way as to stabilize it, leaving them in control. This discussion assumes the elites want to maintain a status quo situation in which their power is dominant.

Conditions in society may undergo some fortuitous change. This change, although not brought about by the elite, may work to their advantage. For instance, if conditions were to change (an upswing in the economy) the system might partially contract as some problems are solved.

On the other hand, there may be no such new development, and attempts at diversion away from the real problem may fail. Having no other alternative that allows them to retain power, the elites may be faced with solving the initial problem—in this example, country $X's$ war. So indeed, the policy change may come about as the elite decides to de-escalate the war over a period of time in order to take some pressure off the system. Or the elites may have actually to end the war immediately in order to start the process of contraction in the society. At some stage in the escalation of conflict, elites are faced with having to solve problems in ways they dislike or else risk the loss of their own power, and literally, the loss of the control over the entire social organization.

In addition to what has already been discussed, there are two further aspects of creating power. The first has to do with the ways that people come to perceive problems. What are the various mechanisms in society that make people aware of problems, and thus create power? Creating power is only the beginning of policy adaptation—power has to be organized. So, what are some of the organizational characteristics necessary to use power once it has been created?

MAKING PEOPLE AWARE OF
PROBLEMS

As the preceding section has made clear, I am equating the creation of power with making people aware of problems. Once people are aware, it is also necessary to organize that power to effect policy changes. This section focuses upon individuals, agencies, and institutions in society that operate primarily as mechanisms for making the public aware of problems. The following section will continue with a look at those organizations which use power to make policy adaptations. Before we begin, I want to describe what I think is the relationship between becoming aware of problems and being activated to do something. The relationship between awareness and political activity is not as simple as it might appear.

In technical language, I suspect that the relationship between these two variables of awareness and activity is curvilinear rather than linear. What do I mean by that? In linear relationships, as one variable increases or decreases, the other variable also increases or decreases. Quite simply, if the relationship is linear, we expect people who are more aware to be more active and vice versa. But I think the relationship is not linear but curvilinear. At low levels of awareness we expect to find very little political activity or apathy among people in a group. As the extent of awareness grows among people having a common problem, the likelihood of activity in the group increases. But, I argue, activity only increases to a point. Beyond a certain threshold of awareness, the likelihood of action based on awareness begins to decrease again. To the extent that people become extremely aware of a problem, I think they tend to become immobilized or overwhelmed by such an intensely perceived threat.

Figure 7 may help you to interpret this point. You will notice that at the lowest point of awareness is the lowest level of activity expected. As the awareness increases on the Y axis, the graph indicates that there is also an increase on the X axis representing an increase in the likelihood of activity. Then there is a leveling off on the graph. The highest point on the Y axis occurs at the point of the middle values on the X axis. That is, the most activity is expected to occur at medium levels of awareness. And, as awareness continues to increase along the X axis, the likelihood of activity begins to decrease on the Y axis.

FIGURE 7

**A CURVILINEAR RELATIONSHIP BETWEEN
AWARENESS AND ACTIVITY**

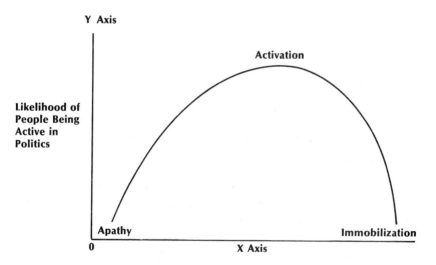

Extent of Problem Awareness in a Group of People

Here is a simple illustration. I might announce to my introductory class in political science that I am going to give two examinations during the term and that their grade will be based upon those exams. I have now made them aware of a problem. I would expect that they would become activated to do something to cope with this problem. They might perhaps even resort to reading the textbook, to attending lectures, and to taking notes. But, then, I might increase their awareness of a problem by telling them there would be weekly quizzes to make sure they are keeping up. I would expect this to activate even more strenuous efforts. It is conceivable that I might continue to introduce all kinds of devices to increase their awareness of the problem of passing the course. But, I suspect that if I told them they would be required to write five term papers, take weekly exams, and pass a two-hour final, their increasing awareness would become dysfunctional. In fact, by this time, their awareness might have become a distinct threat to their survival in college. At such high levels of perceived threat and anxiety, most students become incapable of coping with the situation any longer. They tend to be immobilized by the intensity of the threat. In the illustration above, there might be many kinds of reactions, but my guess is that few of their efforts would have anything to do with learning about introductory political science.

I do not think that people can cope with problems when the intensity of their awareness becomes too severe or extremely threatening. Some research on the behavior of people in concentration camps tends to support this notion. In environments of high anxiety and terror, individuals are immobilized and driven away from reality into a fantasy world that they create to escape such terrifying circumstances. I contend that as awareness of a political problem increases, people will attempt to cope with the problem to a point, but past that point the intensification of their awareness tends to drive them away from political activities.

Such speculation has obvious strategic implications. Perhaps the most important one is that in order to activate people politically, it is probably more useful for politicians to define problems in terms the people are able to cope with rather than in terms more severe and dramatic. Prophecies of "doomsday" about population bombs and pollution catastrophies probably have the impact of making people aware of problems, but such dire predictions also tend to incapacitate people. When people are so threatened, it is very difficult for them to take effective action toward the solution of their problems. If awareness becomes such an intimidating threat that people can no longer really imagine any way of solving the problem, they tend to disengage and withdraw from purposeful activity.

With this theoretical speculation about the relationship between awareness and political participation in mind, we can now turn to a discussion of the mechanisms in society that have the primary function of making people aware of problems and their solutions. We want to discuss the ways that power is created and dissolved by the use of such social instruments.

The Mass Media

Certainly one of the oldest rules of political elites deals with the capturing of instruments that influence public opinion. From revolutionary cadres to establishment elites, there is a clear awareness of the necessity for manipulating opinion through the available media. A printing press in the basement of the revolutionary headquarters or an international press conference called by the leader of a large world power both typify the same motive—to control the awareness of problems and solutions in the minds of as many people as possible. Certainly the stories of the lack of freedom of speech and press in dictatorial regimes are commonplace and need little emphasis here to document the point being made. Power elites, both dictators and elected representatives, know they must control and use the media in order to control the expansion and contraction of the political system. Certainly many counter-elites are just as aware of the need to develop their own instruments for influencing public opinion.

In societies in which outright manipulation of mass media is difficult or impracticable, it becomes a much more subtle operation for elites and counter-elites to gain access to the media. Ruling elites in such countries use the now common devices of calling press conferences, making major speeches that are covered by the press, or simply of having a "commission" or "committee" make available to the press its report, which serves to create a certain kind of awareness. Counter-elites are aware of the necessity of creating situations that call attention to certain problems. Demonstrations, sit-ins, and various kinds of street activities have been justified primarily as means of increasing awareness of problems existing in the society.

Not only must we consider that the elites and counter-elites are actively attempting to gain access to and control over the media, but we must also reckon with the influence of the elites who are employed in the media. Editors of newspapers and television news analysts, for instance, have a great deal of influence simply in the way they select the news to be reported, and in the way they comment upon that news. It is naive to believe that people working in the media, whether they are editors, newscasters, or owners of the media, are objective reporters of the news. Without pushing this point beyond the tolerance of people in the area of journalism, it is necessary for us to understand that their power is considerable in the sense that they are able to influence people either to be aware of problems or to believe that no problems exist.

The impact of the media upon public awareness is a highly complex situation. Elites, counter-elites, and people within the media are all involved in attempts to influence public opinion. It is no accident that the President of the United States decides to make a major public address to the nation on the same day that counter-elites are attempting to mobilize thousands of people for a "march on Washington." It is no accident that various political leaders are highly critical of the reporting of the news by the major networks while others continually praise the press. It is important for you to understand the tremendous importance of the media, but not because the media represent some kind of conspiracy attempting to rule the world. In addition to the media, there are other institutions that serve the same major function—that of increasing awareness.

The Universities

Certainly, the universities have always had and continue to have the function of making people aware of problems and solutions. Recently universities, under the impact of mass-based enrollments of large numbers of students, have become crucial institutions for making large numbers of people, not just elites, aware of problems. It is no accident that dissent and protest over government policy in many countries arises from the students and intellectuals in the universities. Whether we are talking about Latin America, Japan, the Middle-East, or our own country, it has become clear that one of the major sources of disagreement with government policy are the universities.

This source of disagreement seems to have come about for two reasons. First and most obvious, there are now more and more people attending universities. Therefore, what goes on in the educational process affects far greater numbers of people than it did previously. Since there are more people attending universities, there are more people aware of problems, a fact which tends to expand the power base in the society.

The other significant phenomenon is that governments almost have a monopoly over information and the expertise with which to influence public opinion. Literally, the only alternative source of information and expertise in society are the universities. So in a real sense, the universities compete with government in matters pertaining to expertise and information. It is university professors, researchers, and students who can in fact develop their own information independent of that provided by the government. In this way, they are competitors in the public arena, trying to convince people that there are problems they should be aware of that are sometimes different ones from those defined by government.

The United States has become most agonizingly aware of this competition for public awareness during the Vietnam conflict. I think it is clear that the protest in this country over military involvement in Indochina came primarily from our universities. Intellectuals had studied our relations with Indochina independently of the information provided by the government and they sought to make their information public. This kind of competition in the media and on the campuses between spokesmen for the government and university personnel planted the roots of the nationwide protest over foreign policy.

In any case, throughout the world institutions of higher education are assuming the task of educating people to a new awareness of problems and in some cases to possible solutions of those problems. In the United States the continuing criticism of government policy concerning not only Vietnam, but also concerning population control, pollution, and ecology have arisen largely from the universities and their intellectuals. One can only guess as to whether this will be a continuing trend. But there can be little doubt that the ruling elites, both within government and without, must begin to contend with what has become an alternative source of information and awareness about problems in the society. If one predicts anything, it is that the ruling elites will attempt to constrain in some manner the attempts by universities to influence public opinion. Certainly it is no accident that during the height of the Vietnam protest, some governmental representatives were busy devaluing and discrediting university personnel and students involved in the protest. Ruling elites must, if they are to maintain their monopoly on information, problem awareness, and therefore power, constrain alternative sources of problem awareness. In the same sense that ruling elites must manipulate the media, they must also be able to manipulate universities. To the extent that they are unsuccessful, counter-elites may create public awareness and expand a power base in the universities for their own advantage.

Just as universities are becoming an ever more obvious source of public awareness of problems, another mechanism warrants consideration —the one formed by leaders in a society.

Political Leaders

In my mind one of the most profound tragedies in modern politics has been the unwillingness of political leaders to make people aware of problems. We can explain why elites and leaders do and do not want to create more awareness of problems that mobilize power in the society. But if we have any real hope of coping with the deep and profound problems facing post-industrial society, it seems to me that we must recruit and support political leaders who set themselves above their own aspirations in order to educate people.

Perhaps the typical political leader is best characterized as believing in everything or nothing. It is almost as if political success reinforces political leaders not to educate the public about issues and problems, but forces them merely to respond with what people want to hear. There is little doubt this kind of response in a leader is preferred to a dictatorial authority that tells us what to think. At the same time, such response does avoid the duty of leaders to inform, educate, and persuade public opinion in directions necessary to solve real problems. We tend to think of this kind of leader as unusual—a statesman—rather than the normal politician. It is the unusual leader who will attempt to educate his own constituency to solve problems, or to become aware of difficult problems they do not want to consider. Often such leaders are risking their political careers to do this. If we are to have any form of democratic society, our leaders cannot simply be responsive. Leadership must be responsive and responsible for the education and involvement of people in controlling their own destiny. Over this problem our own political system has stumbled more often than not.

Political leadership, then, must involve both responding to immediate needs and desires of people and attempting to influence people toward more awareness of problems and solutions, even when such attempts may risk political defeat. In this country the tremendously influential office of the president gives him command over the media as well as prestige among many people. These resources can be used to increase awareness of problems and solutions. I can think of no more critical situation in this country than one in which all of the political leaders give up educating the public in order to preserve their political careers. Our role as followers is to expect and convince political leaders that they must be not only responsive but responsible, or future generations will inherit the disastrous consequences of our irresponsibilities.

Government Agencies

In the last few years various governmental agencies, investigatory committees, and commissions have become common means of creating public awareness. Every time a major event occurs in this society, the president or Congress forms a committee or commission to study the problem and to make a report of recommendations for action or for policy change. With the aid of the media coverage, such reports and committee sessions are useful in making people aware of problems.

Such governmental investigations have a dual function. They not only make people aware of problems, but they also make people aware of individuals who have aspirations to higher office. Candidates and potential candidates for office normally seek to head such study groups. Ruling elites and counter-elites both attempt to manipulate such vehicles to acquire an advantageous position in relation to public awareness of a particular problem. Indeed, one reason that senators have become the most likely aspirants to the presidency is that their ability to utilize such opportunities helps make them available and visible for the office.

To this point, we have focused upon the most critical agencies for creating awareness of problems. There are obviously many other mechanisms operating to create awareness and in turn to create power to change social policies. Experiences such as inflation, depression, war, and natural catastrophies, which are all widely shared among people, further act to make people aware of their own problems. All kinds of events that are beyond the control of elites or counter-elites create awareness of shared problems. Although not controllable directly, such conditions can be and usually are used by individuals to create power for their own purposes.. This strategy is so obvious that during times of natural crisis new elites are readily formed and become relatively powerful in effecting and implementing new policy adaptations.

We could spend even more time discussing these mechanisms and events, which are critical in the process of creating awareness and power in society. But what happens once the awareness of problems has created power? In the rising levels of conflict, people disagree with each other and certain interests move to achieve their own purposes by making people aware of their disagreements and problems, an awareness which in turn creates new power that must be organized to effect new public laws. The next section deals with the kinds of political organizations that typically utilize these reservoirs of power to make adaptive changes and to resolve problems.

THE ORGANIZATION OF POWER

The following discussion briefly summarizes some of the major ideas associated with one of the most developed areas of theory and research in political science. A great deal of research has involved the question of the organization of power. We cannot begin to deal with all of this literature, so we will focus upon what I consider to be the most general theory of the problem of organizing power.

The group theorists have made perhaps the most substantial contribution.[3] Indeed, they argue that group theory explains the total phenomenon of politics.. In any case, given the importance of this contribution, you should have some understanding of the basic elements of the group theory approach. What follows is a simple characterization of the group theory approach to understanding political processes.

For these theorists, the basic unit of analysis for all political processes

3. The origins of group theory in political analysis are usually associated with the work of Arthur Bentley, *Process of Government* (Evanston, Ill.: Principio Press), published in 1908. However, the more recent and still classic analysis of group theory is David B. Truman, *The Governmental Process* (New York: Alfred A. Knopf, 1951).

is the group. They define "group" in a slightly different way than the term is commonly understood. Most definitions emphasize the group as involving both shared interests and activity in pursuit of those interests. And when groups attempt to control other groups to enhance their own interests, they become political (i.e., they become interest groups or pressure groups).

Accordingly, group theorists conceptualize politics as being composed of multitudes of groups attempting to impose their particular interests upon the total social context. Obviously, such groups have conflicting interests. Also, they have different kinds and amounts of resources and organizational capabilities. Such factors make for variability in their effectiveness.

As a result, groups bargain with each other—compromise among their varied interests—to gain as much of their desired interests as is possible. They must often give in to the desires of other groups in order to get support for some part of their interests. Groups bargaining with each other are the core of analysis on which the group theorists focus their attention. The theorists focus particularly upon the characteristics that make groups more effective at influencing public law and policy.

Most of us are aware of pressure groups in American politics, and perhaps of pressure groups in other countries as well. We tend to think of groups such as the American Medical Association, AFL-CIO, and the National Association of Manufacturers as attempting to influence government policy. These groups are only part of what group theorists consider to be the basic fabric of politics. The group theorists contend that all political processes involve such groups. They conceptualize government itself as being composed of such groups. Indeed, all of politics ultimately can be reduced to varying kinds of groups.

There are different ways of classifying the various groups making up the politics of a society. From most group theorists' viewpoints, these groups are categorized according to the extent of their organization. Perhaps the most organized and therefore effective groups in society are those that are a part of the legal institutions for governing a society. That is, there are groups within society that have been given legal status to govern, to make policy. Such groups as legislatures, courts, and bureaucratic agencies are most organized (i.e., staffed by many full-time people working to achieve the interests of the particular governmental units). Congressmen, members of parliament, judges, bureaucrats, soldiers and cabinet members are all full-time operatives in a particular kind of group activity to obtain the ends defined by their organization.

Another kind of group is the associational or pressure group. It is primarily a voluntary association formed to protect the interests of its membership by influencing public policy. Some examples of this type are

labor unions, corporations, ethnic and minority associations and professional organizations. These are groups separate from the institutional
apparatus of government. But they are certainly attempting to gain access
to and control over the groups in the government that do make policy.

Still another kind of group which has impact upon policy outcomes
is that group that has a basic shared interest or characteristic but has little
formal organization to pursue those interests. Such groups as farmers, small
businessmen, ethnic groups, racial groups, religious groups, and suburban-
ites often exist without formal organization, but by their very existence
they tend to have an impact upon politicians. They are groups, whether
they are well organized or not. The group theorists argue that those in
power respond to the needs of such groups with little formal organization
simply because the elites anticipate that such groups will organize if they
are ignored. This may not be an altogether convincing argument.

A fourth kind of group is the one spontaneously formed around some
particular issue or crisis. Such a group is created around some specific issue
rather than around a continuing interest of their membership. Typical of
this type are groups formed during the early days of the Vietnam conflict
to protest American policy. Likewise, groups were formed to support such
policy. Regardless of the position taken, this kind of group is spontaneously
generated by current issues, and it often has extensive organization, but
it is unlikely to be a continuing force, in contrast to the institutional and
associational groups discussed above.

The general view of politics that begins to emerge from this conceptualization is one of a vast number of different kinds of groups competing
with one another to affect policy on particular issues. The general proposition offered by group theorists is that the groups with the most organization
and access to decision-making processes are most likely to dominate in this
competition. Given this proposition, it is clear that those groups which are
part of the actual decision-making apparatus (i.e., government) are the
ones most likely to have their interests made into law. Vast associational
groups such as labor unions and corporations, although well organized, are
at least one step removed from the actual decision-making processes. So,
they must use their organization and power to alter that process. The third
type of group, having shared interests and characteristics and with little
formal organization or access to the decision-making processes, is the least
effective in this competition. Its impact is usually gained by the efforts of
other groups within the government attempting to win its votes and its
loyalty and support by making at least some laws which are consistent with
its needs.

Finally, then, the last type of group—the group formed about a
particular issue—can have vast organizational resources while it is operative. But its continuing access to decision-making processes is usually

limited, since once it has made an impact, it typically dissolves and leaves the political arena.

We have discussed different kinds of groups and have compared the relative effectiveness of each in affecting public policy consistent with the needs of its membership. What are some of the specific shared interests which these groups have, besides wanting to affect public policy? Clearly, groups within government may have the primary interest of enacting public policy that will in turn allow them to be successful in maintaining their position in that government. So, the major shared interest of these legal political groups is the creation of policies that will gain the support of many other groups in society and will allow the institutional group to maintain its power through election or appointment as the governing body of the country.

The major shared interests of the associational groups can range as widely as do their membership's needs. It may be to make more profit for a corporation, to improve working conditions and wages, or to gain government subsidies for farming or oil resources development.

The shared interests groups having little or no formal organization can have a concern in maintaining their particular values in the society or in improving the conditions under which they have to live. The shared interests among the issue-oriented and spontaneous groups are related to their position on a specific issue.

Still another kind of interest group that we have not discussed is the type that seeks to aid in the election of officials to governmental positions. Normally, we refer to these groups as political parties. From the group theorists' viewpoint, a political party is a specific kind of group which brings together a wide assortment of people from other groups, all with the purpose of raising funds and support to elect a particular candidate to office. In other words, political parties serve to aggregate the diverse interests that exist among all the other groups in society in such a way as to elect candidates to the decision-making groups in the society. So, both politicians and parties take on the shared interest of getting elected. In so doing, they have a major impact upon the kind of compromised policy that will be binding upon all of the groups competing in the political process. Therefore, it is to the advantage of parties and politicians to serve the interests of other groups in the political process in order to have their support at election time.

What are the resources that make one group more effective than another group in this competition?

You may already be aware of the resources and tactics that groups utilize to improve their bargaining position with other groups. Perhaps a group's most obvious advantage is to be the group that actually makes the decision about the issue of controversy. Groups within government that actually make policy have the most important resource of all in the bargaining process. Another resource is the size of the group. With a large membership from which to draw financial and participation support, a group can become much more effective in determining policy. Cohesiveness of the group, that is, the intensity of its commitment and activity, can make a relatively small group much more effective than a large diverse group. The more diluted the commitment of the members, the less likely they are to give the kind of organization response necessary for the group to be effective. So, an intensely committed group of doctors can be extremely effective in preventing government from "socializing medicine," even though they are a relatively small group of professionals in the total society. If the group is geographically dispersed, it can have both positive and negative effects upon its capability. The members may be able to gain more access to government by their very dispersal, but at the same time they may tend to lose their cohesiveness and ability to perform because of the difficulty of organizing people who are geographically separated. The prestige and status of the members of a group can be a valuable resource in the bartering game. Groups whose members are doctors, lawyers, or Supreme Court justices tend to have a great deal of status in most communities. Therefore, their desires and interests may be more easily accepted as being appropriate by other groups in society. Access to the mass media is also a major resource for particular groups. Such access can be purchased with money, but it can also be gained by having members in a group who are editors or public commentators. Being a public official makes it easier to gain access to public media. We could go on to list innumerable kinds of resources. Some kinds are not so obvious as the ones mentioned. For instance, destruction, violence, and time spent in organizational activity are often major resources for groups attempting to effect public policy. But the central point is that different groups have different kinds and amounts of resources.

From this general background we can begin to see how a group theorist makes some rough predictions about the outcome of particular conflicts in the political process. He assesses what groups are involved in a particular conflict, weighs their differing resources, and then predicts the kind of outcome most likely, given the relative strengths of the groups in the conflict. Certainly, the solution will be a compromise, at least to some extent, but the most powerful group in the conflict will be the one most likely to dominate the actual form of the decision.

Now we can begin to link together the previous discussion of public awareness as a possible source of power and the actual solution of problems that cause the conflict. The group that is organized most effectively will tend to have more impact upon public policy than other groups that lack organization capability, even though the other groups' awareness may be just as strong.

Other groups, which are more interested in maintaining their own positions, may attempt to prevent newer groups from consolidating their organization into any form of continuing and well organized political group. They may do this either by solving the problems or at least by appearing to solve the problems before the new groups can begin to inject their particular interests into the bargaining process.

The fact that people become aware of their problems does not necessarily mean that any adaptive change will take place in society. An expandable power base must first be created through organization; then attempts can be made to bring about changes in social conditions. Both getting people elected to decision-making groups and using resources to influence policy are means to effect change. It seems glaringly apparent that as long as people are diverted from organizational development by spontaneous and short-lived outbursts of activity, they are playing into the hands of the ruling elites by not becoming effective agents in the bargaining process. They are acting only as a steam valve to release the power of awareness without actually having any effect upon a solution.

In this chapter I have tried to characterize politics as being an expanding and contracting power base in society. As people become aware of problems, they are available for organization of those interests by leaders. The process requires not only people's awareness to create the power, but also an organization to utilize that power to bring about the adaptive changes in public policy most consistent with the interests of those involved in the political controversy. The next chapter deals specifically with the various kinds of institutions and groups that use power and with the ways they use this power to resolve conflicts by solving problems.

CHAPTER 9

USING POWER

In this chapter we are to examine a problem that has plagued political analysis from its origins, the use of power in society. Common sense tells us that the problem of the use of power is more related to the question of who has power in society than to any other single consideration. We may begin this discussion by asking two kinds of questions that are nonetheless related.

First, the normative question—Who should use the power in society? Second, the empirical question—Who *does* use the power in society? These are really inseparable questions. The answers to the normative question are necessary to know in order to evaluate the answers to the second question. In turn, an understanding of who does use the power is necessary to develop strategies to bring about a better distribution of power, deriving from our strategies answers about who should use the power. Such questions as these have been the grist of the political theorist's mill from pre-Socratic thought to the present. This discussion in no way adequately reflects the multitudes of views about either the normative question or the empirical question. What follows is a simplification of what has been said about these questions. Hopefully such general statements will at least clarify, if not answer, both questions.

WHO SHOULD RULE THE SOCIETY?

On the one hand, there are many theorists who have argued for various reasons that elites should rule and have the power to make decisions for the society. On the other hand, there is another philosophical tradition, that the people should rule. Some textbook writers are prone to argue that conservative political thought has been commonly associated with the "elitist" position while liberal political theory has been associated with the mass or popular sovereignty notion. Somehow, for me, the discussion of conservatism and liberalism in this context does more to confuse than to clarify the different positions. So, for this discussion I prefer to talk about the distinction between elitists and populists.

What are the assumptions about man, society, and the "good life" that underlie the prescribed ways of governing the society which populace theorists advocate?

At the core of any theory that postulates that the people should have the power to rule themselves, is the notion of individual rationality. Theorists subscribing to this point of view believe that an individual is capable of defining goals for himself and is also able to select from alternatives that particular course of action most likely to achieve his goals. Quite simply, they assume that the individual is able to pursue the "good life" for himself.

Populists are optimistic about the basic nature of man. Because individuals are assumed to be rational and good, their pursuits will eventually lead to social consequences that are good for the society. This is the populists' second major assumption—that man can achieve some form of social and individual perfection in his life.

Therefore, society must be so constructed as to maximize human will, liberating the individual from social, economic, and political constraints that operate to inhibit his inherent rationality and goodness. Because rationality requires the availability of alternatives and information concerning alternatives, such theorists believe that tolerance of diverse ideas is essential. In other words, for the good society to exist, differences not only in behavior but in thought must be tolerated. It is these very differences that can increase alternatives and inform individuals as to how to calculate more rationally the pursuit of their goals.

Still another assumption associated with the populist theory is that man has certain inalienable rights. Man is a member of the human community and has certain rights simply because of the fact of his existence. These rights may be justified as deriving from an act of man's Creator or as an imperative of natural law, but in any case the rights are assumed to be an inalienable part of the human condition. To deprive man of these rights is to deprive him of his essential humanness. Given these assumptions, what are the prescriptions for the ways in which society should be organized and the ways in which decisions should be made to achieve a "good life" for most people?

Theorists of popular rule are immediately faced with two practical matters with which they must cope in order to prescribe the good political life for members of a society. It is obvious that all the people cannot make all decisions for the society. Further, it is obvious that even reasonable and benevolent people will sometimes disagree about the proper course of action. These two practical matters have been resolved with the notion of majority rule and representative government. When a majority of people decide upon a particular course of action, that decision is binding for the total community, and the majority delegates its power to a representative body. We need to discuss both ideas.

Of course, there is a major qualification to the concept of successful majority rule—the majority must be informed and educated. To be able to pursue the "good life," people must be informed about the costs and benefits of a particular decision, and they must be able to evaluate their information in order to make a good judgment about the proper course of action. There is a second qualification to the majority rule notion. The rights of the minority must be protected from violation. While the majority has the decision-making capacity for the entire community, the minority still has its inalienable rights. These rights are not to be subjected to majority manipulation. The majority cannot decide for any reason to take away the inherent rights ascribed to all people in the society. Further, by guaranteeing the rights of the minority, the majority is given the opportunity to be persuaded that their position is not preferable. In this way, the minority can become the majority. Perhaps such theorists assume that majorities will not violate minority rights because they believe that man is basically benevolent and tolerant of those who disagree with his views.

Given these prescriptions about the ways in which society should be ruled, it becomes necessary to make political structures that will permit this majority rule to occur. In most cases, the political structure most closely associated with popular sovereignty theories has been the institution of representative government—a representative, decision-making body called a parliament, a congress, a council, or a legislature. Such decision-making bodies represent the majority of the people. The political representative of the people is the one who actually makes the decision, but he does so as an advocate of his constituency's majority opinion. So, in this sense the political institution of representative government is the embodiment of the popular rule theory. The people rule through a representative body of decision makers who are required to submit themselves to continuing evaluation of their constituency concerning their actions as decision makers. Undoubtedly, many questions are raised by this discussion. Questions about the validity of any one of the number of assumptions talked about above or of the institution based on such assumptions could be raised here. But for present purposes, I simply want to characterize this conception of popular sovereignty, and the political institutions that populists argue are most likely to assure a "good life" and society. Now we need to consider the theories that argue that elites should make the decisions and have the power to control the society.

As we did with the theories of popular rule, we can examine the assumptions of elite theorists. First, elite theorists argue that although individuals and groups of individuals may be rational, they are also capable of seriously irrational action. These theorists sometimes argue that the limitations upon rationality are inherent in the human being, and sometimes they argue that such limitations are a result of social organization and conditions. But in any case, the elitists take the position that large numbers of people are not capable of making the best decisions for society. They prefer to rely upon small groups of elites that have better education, information, and capacity to make decisions. They feel that such elites are simply better qualified to see problems and alternative solutions, and therefore, more able to make good decisions for the entire society.

This elitist view that the mass of men are not capable of rational judgment is supported by another assumption they make about the basic nature of man. Most elitists are much more pessimistic about the nature of man than are the theorists of popular sovereignty. They argue that man's basic nature is either corrupt or at least corruptible. Man is basically evil, and capable of all sorts of harmful behavior toward his fellow man. For men to live peacefully with each other requires social organization, law, reliance upon tradition, and political structures that will operate to limit and prevent the inherent human condition from destroying the social order. So, populist theorists argue that man is basically good, and that the good society is one that does not inhibit or constrain that goodness, and the elitists argue just the reverse, that man is capable of evil and wrongdoing, and social constraints are necessary to limit him.

Further assumptions of the elitist viewpoint are that man and society are not perfectible and that the best we can do is to attempt to control human behavior. Community, for elitist theorists, is not a collectivity of human beings with inalienable rights. It is a fraternity of responsible human beings. The populist theorists argue that all people have natural rights as members of the human community. In contrast, the elitists believe that people must demonstrate their responsibility to the community before they can be considered members. As popular rule theorists were faced with practical difficulties in the implementation of their theory, so are the elitists.

The practical reality facing the elitists' theory is that the concentration of power in the hands of a few—the elites—can easily become a dictatorship. In a dictatorship the elites can maintain their power without responsiveness to the mass of people. The solution to this problem in theory is not to turn decision-making over to the masses, but to put checks upon the elites. In order to keep the elites from becoming corrupted, other elites in the political structure are to act as a balancing mechanism against the concentration of power in a single elite.

The elite theory of government involves one elite's being in competition with another elite in such a way as to bring about a constraint upon the actions of any one elite at any one time. Elite theorists would structure the government in such a way that no one elite has total power. Each part of the government would be given power for certain kinds of decisions. In turn, each of these elements in the political structure is to act as a guardian over the actions of the other. In our government, for instance, the Congress is given certain powers by the Constitution, the president is given other powers, and the Supreme Court is given still other powers over the actions of both. Each of these institutions for making certain decisions in society is essentially pitted against the others. Congress has powers to make decisions, which in turn are carried out by the president, who has power to veto decisions under some circumstances. Finally, the Supreme Court has power to review the decisions made by Congress and the actions taken by the president. Clearly, then, the notion of "checks and balances" in our government is a manifestation of an elitist's view of the way to prevent the concentration of power in the hands of a single elite.

I think it is clear that government in the United States is in large part a set of political structures and institutions that evolved as a compromise between popular sovereignty theory and elite theory. We have certain political institutions such as state legislatures, Congress, and elections that act to implement the populist theorists' view of the good society. We have other institutions such as the courts and the executive (e.g., president and governors) that operate to ensure that elites will make the binding decisions for the people in the society. Many have interpreted the history of our country's constitutional development as a continuing debate and compromise between politicians holding these two different viewpoints.

I now want to develop a somewhat different view of the ways in which society should be ruled. If you substitute for the notion of individual rationality or the lack thereof in the two previous theories, you can make a different assumption about the basic nature of man—that man in his natural condition is a striving, adapting organism. In coping with his problems, man demonstrates his own humanness. You should notice that I am not really talking about whether man is rational or irrational, good or bad. Rather, I am arguing that man is basically an organism striving to fulfill his potential. He is able to become more human through a process of successfully coping with the circumstances required for his survival. By solving problems arising from a changing world, he gains control over his own life and has the kind of life that is consistent with the solutions he prefers. It is in such a process that the individual can realize his potential humanness.

With this kind of perspective we are no longer focusing upon some end state or Utopia where man is perfectible or not perfectible. We are now talking about a process in which man can involve himself in the pursuit of purpose and meaningful ways of achieving this purpose. The essential characteristic of the good society is not one that either releases or constrains the individual, but one in which the individual has the opportunity to cope effectively with the circumstances and problems that he confronts daily. Man not only has to be able to think about his problems, he also must have enough power or control over his and other people's behavior to bring about solutions that are consistent with his understanding of and solutions for the problems.

If you recall our discussion in the last chapter about the expansion and contraction of power in society, it may be clear to you why I believe that the expansion of power is a prerequisite for achieving the "good life" for most individuals in the society. As long as power is held by only a few, even if the few are acting to check one another, it is not available to the individuals in the society. Powerless individuals cannot effectively cope with and adapt to the changing conditions in their lives. Expanding the amount of power in society increases the probability that individuals and groups will use some of that power to create the solutions consistent with their attempts to solve their problems. It follows that as individuals and groups effectively solve their problems, the power will contract. They will tend to be more or less satisfied with their situation until such time that changes in their environment move them once again to confront new and different problems. At that time the power begins to expand again in the society, a fact which in turn allows them once again to cope and to adapt.

The kinds of political structures that seem consistent with this notion of the "good life" and society are those institutions that prevent the accumulation of power in the hands of either public elites (e.g., government) or private elites (e.g., corporations, churches). Given this view, the prescriptions for the good political life for people are no longer limited to political institutions. Now we are talking about a life style to achieve the good society for individuals, whether they are in government or following private pursuits. According to this view, the politics of the good society must focus in human life styles rather than in political institutions.

What I am describing is a massive antidote for the most difficult problem of modern society—the alienation of people. This is the phenomenon so commonly observed in post-industrial society. People feel estranged or isolated from themselves and from their society. I believe that active involvement in directing one's own life is a prerequisite of the "good life"—whatever the "good life" may mean for the particular individual. Without this kind of effectiveness in problem solving, man cannot enjoy the "good life"—he is merely a creature of social conditions. I am not defining some kind of Utopia that man may someday achieve, but a process by which every individual in society can reach for whatever goals he believes to be good. Whatever his goal or purpose, the essential ingredient in the process is the availability of the power necessary to bring about this purpose. The good society creates opportunities and power so that individuals can develop their own potentialities and capabilities to the fullest possible extent through a process of effectively coping with personal and social problems.

The foregoing is an attempt to characterize three alternative conceptions about the ways in which power should be distributed. These ways are: (1) that the people should rule, constrained only by the institution of majority representation; (2) that elites should rule, constrained by the "checks and balances" of other elites; and (3) that individuals and groups should have enough power to solve their problems independent of elites or institutions. Each theory starts with different assumptions and reaches different conclusions. All three theories, perhaps, may be useful in your attempt to evaluate what makes for the "good life" for you and for your community. But this is only half of our proposed task. We must now turn to the second portion of the general question. Who does rule in modern societies? We move from normative inquiry to empirical inquiry.

WHO DOES RULE THE SOCIETY?

There are three major empirical theories briefly to be reviewed here. The first is commonly referred to as the power elite theory, the second is called the pluralist theory, and the third one we have previously discussed —the group or broker theory of politics.

The most startling and provocative insight for most new students of politics is the realization that all of the major political theories describing who actually does rule in a society agree upon at least one major point— that the mass of people have little if any impact upon political decision-making and the resultant public policies. An equally startling insight is that many political theorists studying the ways in which politics operates in different countries agree that the political structure of a country has little to do with how public laws are created. In other words, whether it is a parliamentary system such as Great Britain's, a presidential-federal system such as ours, or a one-party communist regime such as in the Soviet Union, the overwhelming conclusion for many theorists is that the type of government has less to do with who has the decision-making power in the society than do other factors. If neither the mass of people nor the type of government has a major impact upon public policy, then who does rule? First, we can turn to the answer that the power elite theorists give to this question.[1]

The power elitists argue that power is equated with positions in the social-economic structure of the society. In other words, those who have important status or economic positions also have a great deal of power in society. Immediately it becomes apparent that power is not confined to the government as we normally think of it. Indeed, most power may reside outside the governmental roles of elected or appointed offices. In this view, people who have status positions such as generals, judges, doctors, and lawyers, and people who have great wealth such as corporation owners, managers, businessmen, and members of wealthy families, are people having great resources of power stemming from their position in the socio-economic hierarchy. Power elitists further argue that position in the socio-economic structure and the attendant power tend to persist over time and regardless of any particular issue being debated in the political arena. In other words, those who have power because of their status or wealth tend to have that power regardless of the issues and decisions that confront the society. They tend to keep this power in order to make the decisions controlling the society in a manner consistent with their own particular interests. Of course, these theorists believe that the elite's primary interest is to preserve its power and by preserving that power to maintain its position in the socio-economic hierarchy.

Obviously it is possible for new elites to enter this socio-economic class, but the power elitists point out that only those who basically accept the same values as the existing power elite will be recruited. In this way the value system predominant among the elite is maintained regardless of which individuals actually occupy important positions. This is the kind of

---

1. Here we should cite at least the standard works relating to the power elite argument. Gaetano Mosca, *The Ruling Class* (New York: McGraw-Hill, 1939); Floyd Hunter, *Community Power Structure* (Chapel Hill: Univ. of No. Carolina Press, 1953); C. Wright Mills, *The Power Elite* (New York: Oxford University Press, 1956); Roberto Michels, *Political Parties: A Sociological Study of the Oligarchical Tendencies of Modern Democracy,* trans. Eden and Cedar Paul (New York: Dover Publications, 1959), originally published in 1915.

argument that leads to the notion of a military-industrial complex, the notion that there are groups—an elite in the business, industrial, and military institutions of the society—who basically have a common bond, that of preserving its interests and values. And the people being recruited to the elite are allowed to enter once they have demonstrated that they also share the same values and interests of the existing elite.

In this view, so-called political leaders and appointed administrators are little more than errand boys for the power elite in the society. The office holders, if they have the support of the power elite, will find the resources necessary to run their campaigns and to get elected or appointed to office. And they in turn are expected to create public laws and to support legislation that is consistent with the power elite's desires and interests.

What are we describing in this theory? Basically, a society in which there is a fairly clear distinction between the mass of people, who have little power, and the elite, who has most of the status, wealth, security, and power. The elite tends to maintain itself by recruiting new members who are acceptable to it. And the elite, regardless of the type of government or ideology they hold, determine most public policy for the total society by dominating the major institutions that make policy.

Anyone taking this position is apt to be little interested in such institutional processes as voting, getting elected, or other such behavior traits associated with political activity. His analysis of politics directs attention toward those who have the power—the elites. He expects this elite to attempt to keep this power and to utilize it, not for the public interest, but for its own private interest, preserving its position in the socio-economic hierarchy of the society. You should note that most of the research that has been used to support this kind of empirical theory has been done at the level of community studies, not at the international or national level. But it remains one of the most common theories about the way a society is ruled.

The second theory we will consider is most often referred to as the pluralist theory of politics.[2] The pluralists begin by saying that power is basically the ability to get people to act. It is a relationship among people in which some people get others to do what they might not otherwise do. Power exists in relationships among people rather than as an attribute of

2. Here again we should cite some of the leading contemporary exponents of this theory. Robert Dahl, *Who Governs?* (New Haven, Conn.: Yale University Press, 1961); Nelson Polsby, *Community Power and Political Theory* (New Haven, Conn.: Yale University Press, 1964); Arnold Rose, *The Power Structure* (New York: Oxford University Press, 1967). For perhaps the most definitive study of power structures theory, see Robert E. Agger, Daniel Goldrich, and Bert E. Swanson, *The Rulers and the Ruled* (New York: John Wiley and Sons, 1964).

some socio-economic position in the society. Pluralists further suggest that such power relationships do not necessarily persist over time, as the power elitists argue. Instead, power tends to develop around particular issues or decisions that must be made by the society. Depending upon how the issue is defined and upon whose interests are involved, elites tend to enter or to leave the political arena. Elites are activated by the definition of the issue. As the elites become interested or concerned about a particular issue, they tend to use their power to maintain their interests. So, rather than defining the politics of a society around a monolithic socio-economic elite (e.g., the military-industrial complex), pluralists argue that there are multiple elites in a society. Although different elites enter the political process at different times, depending upon the issue, it is still the elites who are making most of the decisions for the society. Elites are in fact competing or bargaining with one another about what outcomes they find most acceptable to their specific interests.

The people in the society become relevant in decision-making to the extent that they are organized, aware of issues, and able to involve themselves as an elite on particular issues of concern to them. Where the power elitists argue that it is very difficult to become a member of the elites, the pluralists argue that there is a great deal more access to the elite structure in the society than the power elitists believe. For the pluralists, elites are defined by interests, activity, and amount of resources rather than by positions in a socio-economic structure. Pluralists argue that to the extent people organize to influence a particular issue, to that extent they become a part of the competing elite structure that determines the outcome on that issue.

The pluralists and the power elitists perceive a very different kind of political process. Power elitists see little opportunity for the mass of people to influence any decisions. But pluralists, on the other hand, believe that there is a great deal of access to the decision-making process through such channels as elections, office holding, and lobbying. Thus, political office is one of many resources that can be used in the process of controlling the actions of other people in society, and winning this office is a very important kind of activity. For the power elitists, the office holder is of little consequence, since he simply carries out the wishes of the power elites. It is only fair to say that both of these theories have many advocates and some research data to support their contentions about politics.

The third major theory, which we discussed in the previous chapter, should be briefly reviewed at this point.[3] The group theory or broker theory of politics is very similar to the pluralists' argument. The major difference

3. This model was first discussed in Chapter Eight, pp. 159 ff.

I can discern is that the group theorists tend to rely upon an analysis of interest groups rather than upon a theory of multiple elites. The pluralists talk about multiple elites coming and going from the political process as their interests are involved. Group theorists talk about multitudes of groups that exist more or less continuously in the political process. The pluralists argue that elites are defined by the existing issues, while the group theorists argue that interest groups are ongoing organizations with continuing activity, competing on a day-to-day basis to define public policy consistent with their interests.

I suppose that the group model is very similar to the pluralists' model, with the exception that it tends to describe a much more stable kind of political hierarchy, one defined by the continually organized and active interests in society rather than by elites emerging around particular issues.

All of these empirical theories have their advocates among present-day political analysts. It seems to me that the power elite theory is the most pessimistic analysis, if one is evaluating the theories in terms of normative goals we discussed initially in this chapter. It is pessimistic in the sense that it sees little going on in society that reflects either the public interest or what most people think of as democratic decision-making. Power elitists say that elites exist to determine policy in their own private interests. The pluralists and group theorists have notions that incorporate the ideal of majority will in the sense that elites or organized groups from the mass of people can compete in politics to influence public policy. Unlike power elitists, pluralists and group theorists suggest that elections and influencing office holders are ways that people can influence public policy.

We do not have enough research findings at this time to evaluate these theories as either adequate or accurate descriptions of a political system, whether it is in this or in some other country. But I do think I can fairly say that these three theories represent most of the analysis that political scientists have made of contemporary politics. There can be little doubt that the theory one chooses to advocate has more to do with his basic values about politics than it does with the weight of evidence now available for making such a judgment. Perhaps further research will render a more obvious answer to the question of who does rule the society. Until such time, you are left with the task of utilizing this information to evaluate which of these different theories seems most consistent with both your own observations and your values. The implications of all of these views of politics are difficult to grasp quickly, and they require a great deal of thought.

All three theories suggest that the mass of people have little to do with important decision-making at any one particular point in time in the society. They all suggest that there is much more to politics than simply understanding who holds major political office. And they all suggest that present notions of what democracy is all about are greatly distorted.

This raises the most difficult of questions—Where are we in relationship to where we should be? The next two sections of this chapter are my attempt to answer this question partially. The first part of the answer requires us to analyze the American political scene, applying each of the theoretical perspectives we have just discussed. What are the strengths and weaknesses of our political institutions as viewed from each of the theories about how political processes actually operate? The final section suggests some of the primary problems or inadequacies that seem apparent. We need to become aware of these strengths and weaknesses in order to have the basis for evaluating and making changes.

TWO INTERPRETATIONS OF THE AMERICAN POLITICAL SCENE

I suppose the interpretation of American politics from the power elite position is the most simple and most pessimistic of the views and therefore a good place to begin. The power elitists, I believe, advance an argument like the following one about our political institutions and processes over the past three or so decades:

They see our country emerging from World War II as the most powerful nation in the world because of the tremendous technological, industrial, and military growth we were able to achieve in the course of fighting the war. The fantastic explosion of the technology of war and its related industries continued under the cold war threat of an international conspiracy on the part of communist powers to dominate international politics. Under this threat the military and corporate elites that had emerged in World War II were able to utilize the threat of a communist takeover to further their own interests of greater profits and status in our society, under the guise of "defense."

These power elite theorists argue that American foreign and domestic policy has been largely a by-product of these particular business, industrial, and military elites attempting to increase profits and status for themselves. In large part our foreign policy has been dictated by these elites in their attempt to make the United States an imperial power maintaining our economic advantage in the rest of the world. Power elitists say that we have sought to exploit the underdeveloped countries of the world, and to contain the vast expansion of communist countries in order to feed the vast machinery of our own military-industrial complex. Further, we have used the idea of a communist conspiracy to justify intervention into the affairs of a large number of countries, intervention which in turn justifies further expansion and escalation of our own military-industrial capability. In turn these countries, impoverished by this exploitation, are more actively involved in revolutionary movements. This revolutionary situation then demonstrates the "reality" of the communist threat. And in turn our country intervenes with military and diplomatic (and sometimes not so diplomatic) forces into those countries to put down the "communist revolution." Of course, such intervention also allows the military-industrial complex to entrench further its ability to exploit the situation for corporate profit and military achievement.

According to this interpretation, we are an ever expanding military-industrial power. Such a society requires the resources, energies, and skills of most of the developing world as well as of many of its allies to maintain its vast military alliances and commitments. At the same time, such exploitation generates revolutionary and unstable conditions in the rest of the world, a fact which we use to demonstrate the theory of the communist conspiracy, a theory which justifies the existence of our military and industrial might.

To continue, domestic problems are ignored because they are problems requiring a realignment of our national priorities. This realignment would entail different kinds of technology, a vast retooling of our industry for production of non–war-related goods. Naturally, there is tremendous hesitancy in the power elite to take on problems that require such a tremendous change and perhaps the sacrifice of profits. It is easier and safer to attend to the problems that increase their capacity to make profits through war, and to ignore the problems of minorities, poverty, overpopulation, pollution, transportation, communication, the cities, education, and in general the problems of creating the "good life" for people.

You should note here that this interpretation of American politics rests upon the assumption of a continuing and self-interested elite representing the military-industrial complex. That elite has made most of the decisions about the way that the society is going to conduct its affairs in both foreign and domestic matters. This elite has continued to make the decisions concerning our domestic and foreign policy regardless of who has been in political office or of whether it has been a Democratic or Republican administration. The power elitists would argue that these political structures and processes are completely irrelevant in determining the major priorities upon which this country will expend its vast wealth and energy. This elite continues to dominate our policy, regardless of what else may happen in the society.

Simplistic?—yes, and at the same time one has a great deal of difficulty dismissing the evidence that these theorists use to support their devastating analysis. They point to the vast amount of our federal budget that goes to war-related expenditures, while so little progress has been made in areas of domestic concern and crisis. In any case, their argument, which I have only briefly summarized and perhaps distorted here, is an interpretation of American politics espoused amoung many political scientists today.

Another interpretation of American politics exists among political scientists calling themselves either pluralists or group theory advocates. They argue, I think, after looking at exactly the same evidence and time period that there has been a great deal of bargaining, accommodation, and change in our society. They probably agree that there are powerful military and industrial elites dominating many of the decisions that affect the way our country carries out domestic and foreign policy. But they quickly add that there are many other elites that have also had tremendous impact upon the way we have done things during this time period.

They say that this country has been involved in at least two or three major issues. Perhaps the most important ones are the cold war, civil rights, and the problem of extremely costly military adventures into small countries of the world. They argue that around each of these major issues there has been substantial bargaining among competing elites and groups to change outcomes of decisions. They also note that indeed we have expanded our military-industrial potential and that we have been involved in several wars and near wars. But at the same time, they point out, there has been a great deal of dissent in this country over these issues, causing new elites to enter the political process. Such competition has brought about a decline in the probability of our military involvement in foreign wars. They say that there has been an increase in the amount of attention given to the problems of the poor, blacks, the cities, pollution, and over-population.

The pluralists are persuaded that the "multiple and competing elites" analysis of American politics is a relatively accurate description of the developments in the past two decades. There have been new elites created and brought into the political process. Further, pluralists point out that there are now elites among blacks, migrant labor workers, poverty cultures, native Americans, and consumers, all of which have brought about changes in the configuration of our national priorities. They predict that our society is now in the process of negotiating the differences among these new additions to the elite structure, and that eventually real changes in the distributions of benefits will occur.

Pluralists also make the point that it certainly does make a difference who is elected to office. If candidates campaigning in support of these newer priorities are elected to office, they will have major impact. They will give greater access to such groups, and they will increase the likelihood of policy consistent with the interests of many of the disadvantaged in our society. Pluralists point to the importance of the various "dove" senators in the debate over involvement in Vietnam, and suggest that without their influence and voice our involvement might have been greater than it was.

Generally, I think, the pluralists as well as the broker model theorists argue that conditions are not as gloomy as the power elitists would have us believe. Things are changing, although not as rapidly as many people might prefer. Society is in a continuing process of attempting to bargain over solutions to problems. New elites and organizations are emerging, a fact which indicates a greater probability that our society will undergo even more significant changes in the near future—not quickly but certainly.

Of course, from this view of American politics, the notion of revolution is nonsense. Change is necessarily an evolutionary process, a continuous and inevitable balancing of the demands being articulated by groups and elites in society. Revolution is merely a "justification" for the government to resist meaningful change as it focuses public attention and energy upon repressing the "revolt" rather than upon coping with the real problems. Pluralists feel that it is essential to maintain the balance among contending groups and elites in order to ensure real social change.

The power elitists' and pluralists' interpretations are greatly different. They both stem from the same evidence but are different largely because of the values held by the theorists and not because of the ultimate validity of either view. There is not enough evidence for us to accept conclusively one theory and interpretation as being clearly more correct than the other. The evidence is relatively well balanced, and it appears to conform to the explanations of either theory.

If this discussion tends to leave you a bit confused—you are not alone. How is it possible for two such different theories to explain the same set of historical developments in this country. This is probably the case any time we attempt to understand a reality—political or otherwise. Much as is true in other sciences, the same events and phenomena can be explained and described by different theories. And depending entirely upon the kind of problems, values, and strategies or goals, one theory makes more sense than another. And that is the theory you will probably select to evaluate as well as to describe the realities you confront. This book cannot put your mind to rest as to which of these theories or what other theory might most adequately describe and interpret American politics. But several points need to be considered more fully before we leave the consideration of such theories.

There are some major areas of agreement in these theories about our political system. We need to discuss these areas of agreement in order to understand and evaluate their importance. This last section is my attempt to evaluate what we do know about our own political processes and institutions in terms of perhaps the most critical problems facing our future.

RESPONSIBLE VERSUS RESPONSIVE POLITICS: A SUMMING UP AND EVALUATION

What have we actually been talking about in these interpretations of American politics just described?

In the first case, from the power elitists' viewpoint, it is clear that a monolithic elite (i.e., the military-industrial complex) is attempting to dominate and manipulate this society to further its own interests and status. In such a situation there is little chance for the public interest to be heeded, and no hope for the mass of people to be effective in controlling their own lives and society. Indeed, what we have described is an elite *responding* to its own private motives to create public policy in such a way as to maintain its position.

From the pluralist and group theory perspective, we find a different but not so dissimilar kind of operation going on in our society. In this case, we find that the political system is *responding* to issues or crises in the society, new elites are being formed, and new interests are being articulated. And these interests, through various means, all attempt to gain access to the political arena in order to create public policy.

To me, the phenomenal similarity is that in both cases we are describing a political process that is basically *responding to existing elite interests and problems.* In the first view, the response is to the private motives of the power elite. In the second view, the response is to the crisis that gives rise to the creation of new elites or interest groups. I find little in either interpretation that permits us any optimism about our future. If either the power elite viewpoint or the pluralist viewpoint is accurate, our society is doing little to anticipate or to plan for the solution of problems that are yet to have either an elite or an interest group represent them in the political arena. It seems to me that the most critical problem facing our society in the near future is that of responsibly anticipating and planning for the solutions to problems that are not yet upon us.

We must have a political system that can create responsible programs for the solutions of problems before they become of crisis proportions. There is no elite or present crisis which will focus our political processes upon the problems of world overpopulation, of environmental disintegration, and of feeding and developing the third world countries. These are the problems and crises of the future. A most disturbing question arises. Will our political system be able to develop adequate responses to such overwhelming problems if we do not react until they become crises? Or, will it be too late?

Assuming that our system is gradually evolving to a point where we will be able to tackle these problems, is it already too late? The optimists answer—"no!" We have always been able to respond to crisis, no matter how overwhelming, and in the end solve the problem. Pessimists look at the future and say that the problems on the horizon are of a different kind and of greater magnitude than those previously faced. If we wait until their full impact is upon us, it will be impossible to solve these problems.

The basic similarity in these interpretations of American politics lies in the description of our society as a responsive system rather than a responsible one. What do we want our political processes to be? I explicitly assume here that we prefer some form of democracy as the basic political organization principle of our society. What do we mean by "democracy"?

I think most would agree that democracy should have the following attributes: (1) some channels for mass participation in making decisions about the ways in which the society will be run and the ends to which it will be directed; (2) a presumption of individual dignity and that opportunities should be available for people to cope with their environment, thereby achieving their own purposes or interests; and (3) and finally, political institutions that facilitate the achievement of these conditions.

Democracy is distinguished from other forms of political organization by its emphasis upon people as individuals having the ability to bring about the "good life" for themselves. It is not difficult to imagine the alternative of an elite or totalitarian regime having complete and total control over people. Elites, rather than people in the society, dominate the making of decisions. My fear is that in failing to anticipate problems, we will inevitably move toward a totalitarian government in order to deal with the crises once they occur. My own belief is that to solve the problems efficiently and effectively, which a totalitarian government might do while ignoring the needs of individuals, is a poor solution indeed. It is not enough to plan responsibly to solve our future problems. We must also be able to engage the individuals in our society in the processes of making those plans and decisions. One-half of the solution without the other is no solution at all.

The very existence of the "good life" for people requires that they have capacity and will to anticipate, cope with, and solve their problems. Politics must become a life style for people rather than simply a political structure. The most obvious characteristic of the totalitarian regime is that most people in the society are not involved in making decisions that will allow them to pursue their own goals. They are typically following the elite's plan for the survival of the society. The totalitarian society is capable of responsible planning and solving problems, but it is not capable of engaging people in the meaningful pursuit of their own purpose and fulfillment.

I can well imagine our own responsive kinds of political institutions solving the problems of the future by resorting to more powerful elites that move in the direction of totalitarian control. In such situations, I can also imagine people being so threatened by the severity and immediacy of these problems, that they will welcome this elite domination. Such an outcome in my mind generates even more formidable problems.

If we confront problems such as overpopulation, pollution, and racism, with elite-controlled solutions, we will have solved our problems at the expense of meaning and purpose in the lives of our people. This is one way to survive and exist—but it is not the "good life."

It seems to me that our future has two perils. We must be extremely careful how we handle each peril. On the one hand, we must develop a political system that can effectively and efficiently cope with tremendously complex problems of change. On the other hand, we must also construct a political system that has the capacity to engage people in the process of solving those problems. A solution to either problem and not to both will produce less than the "good life." We must create a politics that not only responsibly plans for the solution of future problems, but solves those problems by engaging individuals in a life style of problem solving behavior that permits their pursuit of their own humanness.

GETTING IT ALL TOGETHER

It may be useful now to stand back a bit from the discussion we have been developing and to attempt to pull it together in terms of the theory introduced in Chapters Four and Five. The following is a review of where we have been and where we are going in relation to the major concepts of our theoretical framework involving change, conflict, and consensus.

Part II of this text introduced the overall framework. You may recall what the basic elements of that theory are all about. (It may be useful to refer back to Figure 6 in Chapter Five for purposes of review.) We began with an overall view of politics as involving constantly changing physical and social-psychological environments, which create a diversity of experiences for people in a society. From such experiences, people learn different and differing attitudes about what is appropriate behavior. Differing attitudes lead to a breakdown of the consensus characterizing the political culture of the society. Attitudes about the ways that politics should operate make up the political culture of a society. Consensus is the extent to which people in society agree about the ways that politics should operate. As changes in the environment create different experiences and therefore differing attitudes for people, the level of consensus in the political culture is expected to decline. In other words, more people disagree than agree about the ways that politics should operate. When these disagreements are perceived, conflict exists among individuals and groups. Conflict increases as consensus decreases.

We theorized about the ways in which power is created and used during high levels of conflict to bring about policy changes. In addition to creating, organizing, and using power to change policy, adaptations must be accepted as legitimate by the people in that society. Behavior can be manipulated and controlled externally by the use of authority and laws. But because there are not enough "watchdogs" for every person in society, people must change their values and control their own behavior. That is, people must come to believe the policy is legitimate—a law they are willing to obey.

Part III focused primarily upon the nature of change, the questions of how and why a society changes. Part IV was a discussion of conflict and the level of conflict in the political system. There we talked about the ways in which power is created, organized, and used to bring about policy changes, which are adaptations to the changes occurring in the environment. Using this theory of change, conflict, and consensus as an organizational framework, we have thus far discussed change and conflict, leaving consensus for the final section.

The subject of the following chapters is the making and changing of the attitudes underlying consensus in the political culture of a society. How do people in society come to agree upon the behavioral changes that are the necessary adaptations to a changing environment?

PART V

CONSENSUS AND THE POLITICAL CULTURE

CHAPTER 10

MAKING AND CHANGING POLITICAL ATTITUDES

We have thought about politics in this book as the ways people control and are controlled as they adapt to changing conditions in the society. We learned in the previous two chapters that the escalation of conflict among people is a source of creating and organizing power to impose external control over their behavior so that they act in ways necessary to solve problems arising from change. We also learned something about who in society should have and who does have the power to make and impose public policies. Now we are going to investigate another way that people are controlled as they adapt to changing conditions. People also adapt to change by learning different attitudes or by changing old ones so that they change their own behavior rather than being forced to change because a new law requires them to. If attitudes (i.e., internal control) change, then power and external control are less necessary to bring about adaptive behavior in the society.

The present chapter will focus upon the question of the ways that people learn and change their attitudes about politics. This area of inquiry is relatively new to the discipline of political science, and it is usually referred to as the study of political socialization. In the latter part of the chapter we will discuss the kinds of attitudes we want people to learn in a good society. What should people believe about politics? In other words, we will discuss the kinds of attitudes that seem most consistent with generating the "good life" for people.

LEARNING ATTITUDES ABOUT POLITICS: POLITICAL SOCIALIZATION

Before considering the formation of political attitudes, we need to see how individual attitudes and personalities develop. Here we will draw heavily upon psychology and social psychology as the disciplines that have done most of the research in the area of personality development. For our purposes, we need only a brief description of two major theoretical alternatives.

The first theory, largely derived from the work of Freud, is the psychoanalytic approach to personality development. Perhaps its single most important theme is that personality is formed early and remains relatively stable throughout adult life. The other theoretical approach to personality development can be referred to as the cognitive theory of human learning. It tends to emphasize the continual striving of individuals to adapt their beliefs and behaviors to changing conditions. In other words, changes in the human experience lead to changes in the human personality.[1]

Psychoanalytic theories have tended to focus upon internal kinds of processes as the primary determinants of personality, while cognitive theories have focused upon external events and conditions as the major determinants. Psychoanalytic theorists generally view human personality as a synthesis of contending internal dynamics in the person. Instinctual drives coming in conflict with social realities must be resolved in the individual's psyche, and the resolution of that conflict largely determines personality. Cognitive theorists, on the other hand, suggest that personality evolves from social interactions among people. The individual learns what he is from this interaction with other people.

---

1. This kind of distinction in approaches to socialization has been clarified by Fred I. Greenstein's "Personality and Political Socialization: The Theories of Authoritarian and Democratic Character," *The Annals of the American Academy of Political and Social Science* 361: (1965), pp. 81-95.

The importance of these two theoretical perspectives in relationship to the analysis of political socialization, I think, is most distinct in the area of determining what kinds of experiences the researcher should observe in order to understand how personality is developing and what attitudes an individual is likely to learn. From the psychoanalytic perspective, it is clear that one must focus upon the early child-rearing environment. If one assumes that early childhood experiences determine adult personality, the family is the critical institution in human development. A great deal of political socialization analysis has been an attempt to understand the impact of the father, mother, and family upon the child's early learning about life. Understanding how a child learns to cope with the realities about him makes it possible to predict how that same child as an adult will cope with, understand, and act in relation to politics.

Cognitive theorists rate the influence of the child's early learning in the family as only one and not necessarily the most important socialization mechanism. They concur the family is significant, but, they point out that later experiences are also critical to the development of human personality. Learning is a continuing process, depending not only upon the family, but also upon the schools, the work environment, and a variety of situations and experiences.[2] This combination of situations determines what the person will believe and how he will behave.

An important distinction between the two views may be the pessimism of the psychoanalytic perspective as opposed to the optimism implicit in the cognitive viewpoint. From the psychoanalytic view, once the early childhood experiences and the resultant accommodations in the psyche have taken place, the person is virtually developed, leaving only the acting out of those early learned ways of relating to reality. From the cognitive viewpoint, change becomes a more important aspect of personality development. The individual is an adaptive organism rather than a reacting organism, so he is not necessarily set for life because of any particular experience.

Regardless of the theory, the family is an extremely significant institution in forming political attitudes and is a focus for students of political socialization.

The relevance of this discussion rests upon the assumption that attitudes predispose people to behave in certain ways in the political system.

2. See particularly Herbert H. Hyman, *Political Socialization: A Study in the Psychology of Political Behavior* (New York: The Free Press of Glencoe, 1959); M. B. Smith, J. S. Bruner, and R. W. White, *Opionions and Personality* (New York: John Wiley and Sons, 1956); and Gabriel Almond and Sydney Veiba, *The Civic Culture: Political Attitudes and Democracy in Five Nations* (Princeton, N.J.: Princeton University Press, 1963).

Understanding what the attitudes are and how they were formed makes it possible to understand and predict the resulting political behavior.

In addition to the family, peer groups, school situations, work situations, reference groups, mass media, and anticipatory role socialization have been identified in socialization research as influential in forming political attitudes. Each of these factors is extremely critical in understanding the ways that individuals learn attitudes and in turn how these attitudes affect their adult behavior in the political system.

There is a distinction between those situations that involve face-to-face interaction among people and those that do not. Groups which do involve face-to-face interaction are referred to as primary groups. So, we will refer to such primary groups as being primary socialization factors. These factors include the family, school situations, and peer group influences. The second kind of socialization can be referred to as secondary socialization, and includes such factors as mass media, reference groups, and anticipatory socialization.

Primary Socialization Factors

In discussing the primary socialization factors, we are not talking about just the early socialization of the child, but about a continuing socialization from childhood through adulthood, involving a person's face-to-face interaction with others. Clearly, a child's interaction with others is largely limited to parents and close relatives. As the child moves beyond the family and enters school, his primary socialization may begin to include other adults such as teachers, and certainly it includes other peers of his own age. As he matures, primary socialization includes perhaps people in work and college situations, professors, roommates, priests, and many other adults and peers with whom he may come in contact. The point is, the primary socialization agents are those which continue to affect the person throughout his life.

Most students of socialization agree that the primary factors of socialization are the most important in determining the attitudes of an individual. Some psychologists go so far as to say that the personality itself is formed in these relationships. Our very self is defined by the relationships which we develop in these kinds of face-to-face interaction patterns. The implications of the early family environment and of primary socialization are most profound for the analysis of political behavior.

Perhaps the majority of primary socialization studies done in our discipline point out several conclusions having direct impact upon the ways we understand adult political behavior. I think the most important is that many basic attitudes, which predispose adult behavior in political situations, are established in the relationship with parents. The way children learn to relate to authority probably begins very early, as they learn to relate to their parents. Whether a child is taught to obey and respond with conformity or whether he is taught to relate to authority as being an open and communicative source of information helpful in coping with reality is largely the result of the way the child relates to his parents.[3] Some scholars suggest that the adult relates to political authority in much the same way as he learned to relate to parental authority. Research findings suggest that these attitudes are established early and are greatly resistant to change.

The implications are clear and perhaps ominous. The family is the major institution preparing people for their political life styles. Many researchers believe that this preparation is completed before the child is old enough to think and reason about the political processes and institutions in which he will be involved as an adult.

For instance, it is fairly well established that among white middle class children, party preference is made by the age of seven or eight. In this case, identification with a political party is made long before children have any information or reasonable capacity to judge which political party is most consistent with their own interests.[4]

Research findings suggest that a large number of American voters develop party identifications in the stages of early primary socialization.[5] These identifications are extremely stable, resistant to change, and continue throughout adult life. Most of you inherited the party affiliation of your parents. Choosing a political party consistent with your own interest is therefore non-existent for most of you and probably for the majority of the voting public. The party preference you inherited from your parents will most likely stay with you throughout your life. You might want to consider the implications of these research findings for democratic theory, which presupposes that an individual chooses from among the alternatives that party which is most consistent with his interests.

Research findings have demonstrated the relationship of primary

3. Studies of particular importance here include T.W. Adorno et al., *The Authoritarian Personality* (New York: Harper, Row Publishers, 1950); H. D. Lasswell, *Psychopathology and Politics* (Chicago: University of Chicago Press, 1930); Robert Lane, *Political Ideology* (Glencoe, Ill.: The Free Press, 1962); and Milton Rokeach, *The Open and Closed Mind* (New York: Basic Books, Inc., 1960).

4. For a fuller discussion see R. Lane and D. Sears, *Public Opinion* (Englewood Cliffs, N.J.: Prentice-Hall, 1964), chps. 6-9.

5. See A. Campbell, et al., *The American Voter* (New York: John Wiley and Sons, Inc., 1964), ch. 6, pp 86-96; and Lester Milbraith, *Political Participation* (Chicago: Rand McNally and Co., 1965).

socialization (family, school, peers) to the way an individual relates to the political system. Experiences that teach a person obedience, distrust of authority, and a lack of confidence in himself to control his environment, deeply affect how that person will relate to politics. He can be expected to look to political leaders to make decisions for him much as his parents, his teachers, and his boss have done.

In summary, although people learn their beliefs through experiences which are largely non-political, these experiences teach people how to relate in most social situations, including the political arena. Second, an individual has most of these experiences long before he can become familiar with, informed about, or capable of reasoning about, politics. It is not difficult to understand why many researchers conclude that as the child goes, so goes the society.

In addition to primary socialization, there are ways of learning that involve identification with some group or person and do not involve face-to-face interaction. These other ways are grouped in the classification of secondary socialization.

The Secondary Socialization Factors

Reference groups are the most obvious secondary socialization factor. A reference group is a group in the society that the individual identifies with and attempts to imitate, even though he has no face-to-face contact with its members. So, for instance, a lower class person may identify with middle class norms and values, even though he has little or no day-to-day contact with people who are in the socio-economic middle class. Or a student in college may identify with a professional group such as lawyers or doctors without having obtained membership in either profession. He may, in fact, adopt attitudes and values consistent with the reference group even though he has little contact with people having those attitudes and beliefs.

A second process closely related to secondary socialization is that of anticipatory socialization.[6] This process involves attempts by a person to anticipate adult roles that he is moving toward as he matures from adolescence to young adulthood, and to conform to the expectations that are clearly defined as a part of these roles. Students in college or high school may identify with the particular occupational roles they anticipate belonging to once they have finished their education. People might also identify with particular kinds of class roles such as those of the working

---

6. Frank Pinner, "Student Trade Unionism: Anticipatory Socialization and Role Seeking," *Sociology of Education,* 37 (1964), pp. 177-199.

class, white collar, or upper middle class. Actually, anticipatory socialization is very similar to reference group socialization, and the two may be easily discussed together. Reference group identification involves ongoing and active groups with which persons may identify even though they are unlikely ever to be a member.[7] Anticipatory socialization refers to roles (i.e., sets of social expectations about what is appropriate behavior for a particular social position) that the person anticipates acting out at some future time in his life. In both cases, the person adopts attitudes and behavior traits consistent with groups or roles with which he has no face-to-face interaction. Learning is the result of a psychological identification rather than of interpersonal contact.

Finally, mass media are assumed by many to be of tremendous importance in determining the opinions and beliefs of people. Media provide continuous exposure to information and role models outside the immediate interaction patterns of the individuals.

In my own mind, the most provocative and disturbing irony of our own society's socialization patterns is that experiences in all of the "nonpolitical" learning situations are so important in determining the ways that adults relate to the political processes. The great bulk of our learning about politics occurs in situations in which we are not given any capacity or experience in responsible problem solving or decision-making. Somehow, people are expected to be responsible human beings as adults, although having little previous experience in making intelligent and responsible decisions. All too often, experiences in the family, school, and the work situation teach people to obey and to conform rather than to confront and to solve problems. I am continually awed by people who expect the young to be responsible without allowing them to learn how to make important responsible decisions. There is little doubt that much of the so-called student unrest characterizing the 1960s and 1970s in this country stems from this dilemma. The young find themselves in a university environment, relatively free of the former social and familial constraints, with little experience in coping with such freedom and responsibility. Therefore, they make mistakes that are used as evidence of their irresponsibility.

It is difficult to imagine how to change in the structure of the family, the school, and the educational processes to bring about more responsible engagement of the young in making decisions and solving problems. Perhaps it is easier to conceptualize universities and colleges as creating situations wherein people can learn responsibility in problem solving, through participation in decision-making.

7. R. Lane and D. Sears, *Public Opinion,* chp. 4.

I would like to think this idea of a training situation might come to define higher or "liberal" education in the next decades. I can think of no more important reform in our present social structure than that of creating universities that provide as a part of liberal education courses and experiences that promote the understanding and ability to cope with complex problems. It seems to me that it does little good to consider a person as being liberally educated simply because he has taken courses in the sciences, social sciences, and humanities. Perhaps we need to think of a liberal education as the learning of attitudes and the development of a life style for coping and adapting and being able to make evaluations and judgments.

I think it is clear from our previous discussion that if one takes, as many students of socialization do, the psychoanalytic approach to socialization, one can become relatively pessimistic about the possibilities of creating a change-oriented society. Indeed, followers of the psychoanalytic approach seem to argue that the family and the early childhood experiences are so important as determinants of adult behavior that, short of manipulating the family structure, there is little that can be done to change or to construct different attitudes among adult individuals. They argue from the premise that changing society is largely a generational phenomenon. We can expect changes in individual attitudes and in social norms to occur, but only as new generations of people emerge from adolescence with significantly different childhood experiences from those their parents had. From this view, attitudinal or cultural change on the social level becomes a function of time, waiting for new generations of adults to emerge to fill roles in the society.

A somewhat different view of the possibility of attitudinal change is found in the cognitive approach to socialization. These cognitive theorists argue that it is possible to manipulate social structure in the adult's life in such a way as to create new experiences, and in turn, to create different and changing attitudes in the adult, even though he may have had contrary experiences as a child. Given this kind of perspective, I would like to discuss in the next portion of the chapter some of my own research concerning the question of the ways in which one changes individual attitudes.

CHANGING ATTITUDES

Both my own research findings and the theory to be discussed suggest there is reason for a great deal of optimism about the possibility of changing adults' attitudes, even though contrary early experiences have occurred. In other words, what basis do we have for believing that adults can change their values and behaviors, when their childhood socialization has produced attitudes contrary to those required to adapt and survive in their present context?

It may well be that our society and its many institutions virtually conspire to reinforce early childhood attitudes of non-participation, obedience, and conformity. But, we need to consider whether it is possible to change such attitudes.

My own research, which I want to introduce here, began with the question, What kinds of socialization experiences result in individuals who are oriented toward the acceptance of changing situations rather than toward the resistance of such changes? What are the ingredients of the adaptive and coping kind of personality as opposed to the resistive and status quo oriented people?

Without going into too much detail, I can set out the basic theoretical notions used and some of the results that suggest to me reason for optimism about the possibility of changing attitudes in adults. In this research, I was primarily concerned with the ways in which the individual learns to relate to authority in early and later socialization, the question of how consistent this learning is (is what he learns as a child consistent with what he learns later?) and finally, the question of the impact of these variables upon the ways that people relate to changing circumstances.

It seems to me that one learns to relate to authority in one of two ways. One can either obey the dictates of an authority, or one can relate to authority as a trustworthy source of information and experiences. Relationships to authority involving primarily the attitude of obedience, I referred to as closed socialization experiences. Open socialization experiences are those in which one relates to authority by communicating and understanding. I hypothesized that people who had learned to relate to authority in an open, trusting fashion would be more able to cope with a changing world than would people who had not. The trusting people would be more amenable to change, because they would have less fear about their ability to overcome new and perhaps difficult situations. I was also curious about the effects of mixed socialization patterns. What happens to people who have had relatively closed early socialization and later have had more open relations to authorities? Further possibilities are that they come from open childhood experiences into closed adult experiences, or that they have either continuously open or continuously closed experiences with authority throughout childhood and later life.

With these four patterns of socialization in mind, I was interested in finding out what kind of variations are related to the ability to accept change. Perhaps Figure 8 will be helpful in understanding the model of research that I employed.

The findings were far from conclusive, but here are some of the results:

Somewhat to my surprise, I found that individuals who came from closed early childhood experiences into more open socialization as young adults were most accepting of changing circumstances. The second most accepting group were those who had had consistently open socialization experiences throughout their life. The third group, which was less accepting and more resistive toward change, was that group having open early experiences but largely closed relationships with authority later in life. Most resistant to changing social and psychological circumstances were the groups who had experienced continually closed and non-communicative relationships with authority as children as well as in their present situations.

FIGURE 8

FOUR SOCIALIZATION PATTERNS IN RELATION TO THE
INDIVIDUAL'S ABILITY TO ACCEPT CHANGING CIRCUMSTANCES

Early Socialization with Authority is Open		Early Socialization with Authority is Closed	
Later Socialization with Authority is:		Later Socialization with Authority is:	
OPEN or CLOSED		OPEN or CLOSED	
OPEN	CLOSED	OPEN	CLOSED
The open-open group was second most accepting of change	The open-closed group was second most resistive to change	This closed-open group was most accepting of change	This closed-closed group was most resistive to change

You will notice the similarity in the individuals in the two groups who were most accepting of change. The similarity is that, regardless of the type of early socialization, (open or closed), those who found themselves in pre-adult experiences that were open, trusting, and communicative with authority were more likely to accept change than those with closed pre-adult experiences.

This suggests that if we can arrange social structures in our society, particularly in high schools and in universities, which invite young people into a communicative, trusting, and open relationship with their authorities, there is a real chance that we can develop people with personalities more capable of coping with, adapting to, and accepting change as part of their life style. The research findings suggest that a change in early formed attitudes is possible. And more important, the change is most likely to occur if the later socialization experiences are ones that encourage trust and communication rather than suspicion and obedience.

Now, I want to move from this report of my own research to what I consider one of the most important social-psychological theories of attitudinal change. Generally, social-psychologists have labeled this theory as the balance theory or the dissonance theory.[8] The basic elements of the theory are simple. Balance theorists argue that the individual has a basic need to make his attitudes about the world consistent. And, to the extent that his attitudes are inconsistent, he is motivated by this dissonance to change one or the other of the beliefs that is out of phase. The motivation for attitude and behavior change stems from an awareness of the inconsistency activated by a particular situation in which the person is involved. This may appear difficult to understand. An example may better explain the way this theory explains attitudinal change in a particular situation. The following is an example of a "typical" university confrontation that might have occurred between students and the university administration. I think we can come to some provocative conclusions by analyzing such a confrontation.

We can begin with some simple assumptions about the students involved in such a confrontation. You may assume that there are two types of beliefs activated in such a confrontation. First is the attitude toward authority (i.e., the university administration) and second is the attitude toward the issue that is central to the confrontation. I think we can readily imagine that some students have a positive view of authority and that others have a more negative view. We can also imagine that some students would be in favor of the issue being debated and that others would not. These two variables, thought of in this way, permit the construction of a simple typology of student behavior in a confrontation situation. Figure 9 presents the four types of students, based on these attitudes we might expect to find in the conflict.

8. There are a number of standard works on this theory. The most commonly cited are Fritz Heider, "Attitude and Cognitive Organization," *Journal of Psychology* 21 (1946), pp. 107-12; Leon Festinger, *A Theory of Cognitive Dissonance* (Evanston, Ill.: Row-Peterson, 1957); and Charles C. Osgood and Percy Tannenbaum, "The Principles of Congruity and the Prediction of Attitude Change," *Psychological Review* 62 (1958), pp. 42-55.

FIGURE 9

**FOUR TYPES OF STUDENTS AND THEIR EXPECTED BEHAVIORS
IN A TYPICAL UNIVERSITY CONFRONTATION**

Attitude Toward University Administration

	Students who like the administration	Students who dislike the administration
Students in favor of issue	Students working in student government (Cell #1)	Students involved in "militant action" (Cell #2)
Students not in favor of issue	Students in the "silent majority" (Cell #3)	Students in the "apathetic minority" (Cell #4)

Attitudes toward the confrontation issue

In cell one are students who are in favor of the issue and who also have a positive attitude toward the authority of the university administration. We can call them the "student government types." In cell two are the students who are in favor of the issue, but distrust the administration authority. These students might be called the "militant activists." In cell three are students who basically trust authority, but who oppose the issue. These students form the "silent majority." The fourth type distrusts authority and opposes the issue. We can call this type the "apathetic minority."

Assuming that these four types exist in any particular university confrontation, how does one go about analyzing the kinds of attitude and behavior change that might occur as a conflict in the university begins to escalate. The balance theorists generally use the following kind of diagram to indicate the ways in which an individual's beliefs are related to one another, and how this relationship might be expected to change in a given situation. Each of our four types of students could be diagramed as in Figure 10. You will note that the (+) on the side of the triangle indicates a favorable or positive kind of attitude while the (–) indicates an unfavorable or negative attitude.

FIGURE 10

BALANCE MODELS FOR THE FOUR TYPES OF STUDENTS

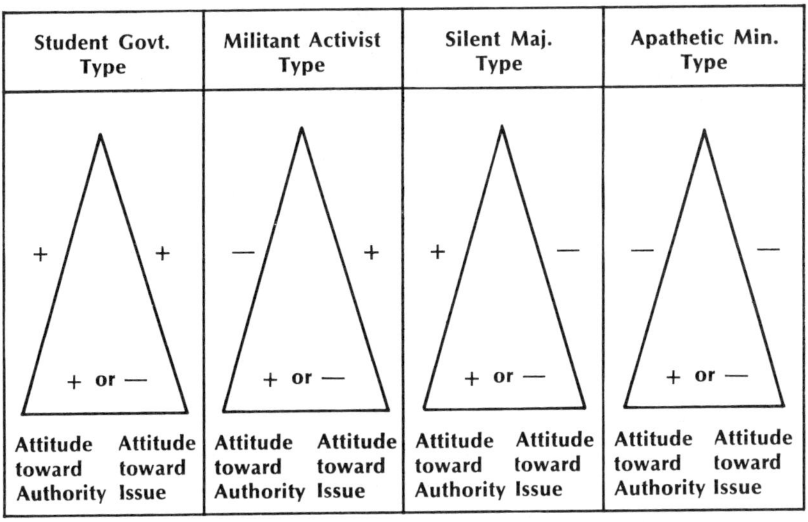

Student Govt. Type	Militant Activist Type	Silent Maj. Type	Apathetic Min. Type
+ + + or — Attitude Attitude toward toward Authority Issue	— + + or — Attitude Attitude toward toward Authority Issue	+ — + or — Attitude Attitude toward toward Authority Issue	— — + or — Attitude Attitude toward toward Authority Issue

So, for each type there are two beliefs which are connected in the conflict situation—one belief about authority and one belief about the issue itself. The two beliefs become connected when the issue is confronted and the authorities of the university make statements about the issue. It seems to me that there are logically two different statements that university authorities might make in relation to the issue. Either the authorities agree with the issue being raised or they do not.

Let us assume that the first piece of information the different types of students receive during the conflict is that the authority is not in favor of the issue. In Figure 10 at the point where the triangles are completed by a dotted line indicating the student observes that the authority has taken a position on the issue, a *(+)* indicates the student favors the issue and a *(–)* indicates the student is not in favor of the issue.

As the two attitudes—one about authority and one about the issue—are connected when the student observes the authority takes a negative position on the issue, the following results are predicted by the balance model of attitudinal change. The "student government type" experiences dissonance in this situation. That is, the student government type has a positive attitude toward authority and a favorable attitude toward the issue with which the authority takes an unfavorable position. He likes both the authority and the issue. But the authority does not like the issue. This creates in the balance model view a dissonant attitude structure. Two attitudes are connected in such a way as to be incongruent.

The dissonance theory argues that an individual in such a situation has a need to resolve the dissonance. In order to resolve it, he must change one or the other of the linked attitudes. How can the student government type resolve this dissonance? He can change his attitude about the authority, so that he still favors the issue but comes to dislike the authority. This is now a congruent belief structure that has reduced the dissonance by changing an attitude—the student changes from liking the authority to disliking the authority. In making this change in attitude toward authority, he has become a different type of student in our model. He is now a student who has a negative attitude toward authority and a positive attitude toward the issue. In other words, the student government type has become the militant activist type.

The other possibility is that the student government type changes his attitude about the issue. In this case, he retains his trust for the authority but came to dislike the issue. Thus, he becomes a part of the silent majority. Which of these outcomes actually occurs depends upon the strength of the student's attitudes about the issue and about the authority. If he is strongly committed in his trust of the authority, he will probably change his attitude toward the issue. If he is strongly in favor of the issue, he is more likely to change his attitude about the authority.

Now we can go quickly through the other three types in this same conflict situation to see how they respond when the administration acts in an unfavorable way toward the issue. The student militant does not experience any dissonance. An authority that he dislikes does not favor an issue that he does like. These attitudes are not incongruent—they fit in his mind. There is no change of attitude or behavior of the militant activist in this escalating conflict situation.

The student who trusts authority and dislikes the issue—the silent majority type—also has a congruent belief structure in this situation. He trusts the authority that dislikes an issue he dislikes. No change would be predicted for this type of student.

The "apathetic minority type" experiences dissonance because an authority that he does not like indicates dislike for an issue that he also dislikes. There might be some motivation here for the apathetic student to change his attitude toward either the authority or toward the issue. It seems probable to me that this type of student might do either. He might come to think better of the university administration or he might come to have a more sympathetic view of the issue involved in the conflict.

Assuming that most students consider issues as being more important than administrative authority, the two groups which change attitudes to resolve dissonances (i.e., student government and apathetic minority types) are moved in the direction of militancy. In other words, the model predicts that they will become "radicalized" in these conflict situations.

If we look at the same conflict situation, but with the administration taking a positive stand on the issue, we find an entirely different set of attitude and behavior changes likely to result.

Using exactly the same kind of reasoning, we can see that if the authority takes a positive position on the issues, dissonance is created for the student militant and silent majority types. Attitudinal and behavior change is more likely to occur among the militant and silent majority types than among the student government and apathetic minority types. If the administration is able to firm up its reputation among students by taking this positive stand, militants will find it hard to continue disliking the authority that is taking a position similar to theirs. We would also expect the silent majority types to decide that the issue is not as bad as they thought it was and to be more supportive of an issue that they had previously opposed. In this case, student government types and apathetic minority types are left unchanged. They continue doing their thing.

Having spelled out different expectations about the ways that people will think and act in a conflict situation based upon this model of attitudinal change, you will have to make your own evaluations of what is good and bad.

Perhaps the illustration has been useful in demonstrating the dynamics of attitudinal change from at least one theoretical perspective. I hope it has also been useful in permitting you to make judgments about the ways in which one goes about analyzing and explaining the behavior patterns and thoughts of people in conflict situations.

This section of the chapter has been an effort to examine the question of changing attitudes, given the fact that early childhood socialization has already taken place and left its mark. To this point, we have been discussing the formation and change of individual attitudes and behavior traits. The last section of this chapter I want to devote to the question of the kind of attitudes we want to form or reform in order to create a consensus supportive of society and a political system which is promoting the good life for its people.

TWO ALTERNATIVE POLITICAL
LIFE STYLES: CITIZEN AND SUBJECT

A great deal of research has been done in political science and in related disciplines upon the question of the kinds of personalities and attitudes consistent with a democratic society. This research can be organized and discussed as having two very different kinds of personalities as its focus. The classic study, *The Authoritarian Personality,* published in

1950, became the model for a great deal of subsequent analysis into attitudes which are not consistent with people's being good citizens in a democracy.[9] On the other hand, there has also been a great deal of research conducted on the type of personality which seems to be characteristic of a "good" citizen in a democratic society.

Using this analysis, the following section is my attempt to characterize the personality of the hypothetical person most likely to be a citizen in a democracy and also the personality of the one most likely to be a subject for an authoritarian regime.

In a very simple sense, the subject-oriented personality has been described as the bicycle personality. This individual bends above and kicks below. The "subject" as contrasted with the "citizen" can be grossly characterized as being someone who is submissive to authority, but at the same time can be hostile and aggressive toward people located beneath him in the same status hierarchy.

In order for us to get beyond this superficial characterization, it is necessary to describe both types around the answers to three general questions. First, what do they think about themselves? Second, what do they think about others? And third, what do they think about society as a whole? By orienting our discussion of subject and citizen personalities around these three major questions, perhaps we can develop a more accurate picture of the kind of person needed to support the good society.

The research is not easily classified. In some cases it is somewhat contradictory and in others it is ambivalent, but overall, I think the research is in agreement about the basic components of these types of personalities. We might consider first those persons who make better subjects than they do citizens.[10]

What does this hypothetical subject, the non-democratic person, think about himself? There is a great deal of agreement about one thing. The subject personality does not like himself. Sometimes this self-dislike is conceptualized as low self-esteem, sometimes as low ego strength, sometimes as lack of self-acceptance, and sometimes as weak self-identity. But in all cases, I think, analysts of the non-democratic personality concur that the subject orientation we are talking about has at its center the person who simply does not like what he knows and feels about himself.

Some researchers suggest that he thinks a great deal about himself, that he is highly introspective, but that he is unable to accept what he

9. T. W. Adorno et al., *The Authoritarian Personality.*

10. Fred I. Greenstein, discusses and lists most of the major studies relevant to this section. Other books of specific importance to this discussion include Robert Lane, *Political Ideology;* Eric Hoffer, *The True Believer* (New York: Harper and Row, 1951); Snell and Gail Putney, *The Adjusted American* (New York: Harper and Row, 1964); and Milton Rokeach, *The Open and Closed Mind.*

learns about himself. Others suggest that this person does not like to look within himself. So, he tends not to think about himself. Instead, he tends to focus upon others. But in either case, whether he is introspective or not, the conclusion is the same. This individual does not think well of himself.

Perhaps because he does not like or accept himself, the subject orientation type of person is said to project internal and often unconscious emotional feelings onto external sources. Rather than think badly of himself, he projects the bad things he feels onto individuals, groups, objects, and stereotypes. Such an example is a young man who has serious doubts about his own masculinity and sexual ability. He may have been involved in some kind of homosexual behavior or have entertained thoughts that he feels guilty about, or he may have some serious doubts about his "way with the women." Often such a young man turns this inward doubt and fear outward in such a way as to despise and be hostile and aggressive toward others in society, whom he may stereotype as queers, homos, and perverts.

Still another common tendency is to project our own uncertainties about ourselves (e.g., we think we are irresponsible, lazy, undeserving, selfish onto the poor, blacks, hippies, businessmen, and university administrators. That set of characteristics that is "dumped" upon the others is then despised and denounced. How many times have I heard someone commenting on the laziness of somebody else, when indeed it is relatively clear his concern is not with others but with himself and with his own inadequacies.

Still another example is the parent who is deeply concerned at some unconscious level about his own sexual impulses. Rather than recognize and cope with his own problems about sexual conduct he projects this fear and is deeply suspicious about the ""sexual goings-on" on the university campus or among certain groups of people—for instance, blacks in the ghetto.

This exaggerated concern with sexual activities of others and the tendency to project self-doubts about one's sexual competence onto others is still another of the attributes associated with the non-democratic personality. For the subject personality, such projection is a simple and efficient device for thinking better about himself without having to cope with his real problems. It is simpler to take what he dislikes about himself, project it upon someone else, and then despise that person rather than himself.

The answer to our first question about what the subject thinks about himself is relatively clear. Regardless of whether his view is accurate, it appears that this person is one who does not like and cannot accept himself.

Some research findings suggest that this self-hatred is often associated with high levels of anxiety and with a lack of self-discipline. In other words, this person who does not like himself often is highly anxious and incapable of controlling his own emotional or intellectual impulses. Combining this with his tendency to project internal problems upon others, we can well imagine the result—an aggressive, hostile, and often destructive tendency toward others whom the subject has come to view as his enemies.

All of these are tendencies of an individual who has real difficulty in rationally coping with his environment and in calculating how best to survive in a complex society. First, it is difficult for such a person even to imagine that he can cope with his environment since what he knows of himself leads him to conclude he is basically not capable of affecting his world, either by solving problems or by coping with difficult situations. Because he cannot conceive of doing such things, it becomes difficult for him to select among alternatives any particular one consistent with his own interests or purposes. Given his often hostile, aggressive manner and his distorted stereotypes about the world, he is almost incapable of choosing among real alternatives, even when they clearly do exist. These real choices which he might improve his conditions are so overshadowed by his own fears that he is literally incapable of self- or social control.

Now, what does this subject orientation type of person think about other people? Most of the research findings suggest that he divides the world into "we" and "they." He tends to be very accepting and submissive toward those who are defined as the "in" group, but he is aggressive and hostile toward those who are the "they,"—foreigners, strangers, or enemies. He tends to like power and toughness. He is preoccupied with dominance and submission, the strong and weak aspects of interpersonal relations. A further characteristic of the non-democratic personality is the inability to empathize with other people's problems or feelings, or to trust other people. Such a person has a great deal of difficulty in developing any meaningful relationship with other people, except when the other person is an authority figure who dictates the relationship.

So the answer to the question about the ways in which the subject thinks about others seems to be as follows: If they are people who are in his groups ("we"), and particularly if they are powerful and of higher status, he can be submissive and indeed accepting, uncritical, and trusting of whatever goes on. Toward outsiders he is distrusting, hostile, aggressive, and in real sense using such outsiders to escape his own profound lack of self-acceptance.

Finally, then, we turn to the third question, about how the hypothetical subject thinks about society in general. Here again the research findings are consistent. Since the subject does not like himself, and since he has a great deal of difficulty in relating to and liking others, he tends to dislike society also. Perhaps because of this dislike for society, he tends to separate from society (i.e., he is alienated from society). Although alienated, he still rigidly adheres to conventional norms, values, and standards of conduct that are demanded by society. Such adherence is supported by his reliance upon stereotypes to characterize others in society in simplistic black-and-white terms, with the use of superstition and myths to support such stereotypes. Finally, there is found in the subject orientation a general cynicism about human nature itself.

All in all, the picture we have sketched here in dim and often distorted lines is a pretty dismal view of a person disliking himself to such an extent that he must project these fears onto stereotypes in society and hate them rather than himself. This person is an individual who submits readily to authority in order to have some kind of socially defined self that he can accept. What he sees within is not acceptable, so he seeks a more acceptable image from some other source, such as an authority figure who says he is good, or from a social movement which gives his life real purpose and meaning. He trades his non-acceptable self-identity for a social image provided by a source of authority, whether it is a revolutionary movement or the country club set. He becomes good because some group says he is, not because he believes he is. His very self-concept is derived from rigidly conforming to the values held by those in society whom he respects as tough and powerful. The world for this person is an ugly, uncertain, and fearful jungle. Certainly we would find him among those who permit political leaders to make all big decisions because "they have better information than he does." With such a set of beliefs it is not difficult to imagine that he can find evidence in the world about him to support this view. Every man makes a world in his own likeness.

What we have just described is perhaps more caricature than characterization. But I think it is a simplified description of the personality with a subject orientation, a personality not compatible with the requirements for the maintenance of an open, democratic society.

What are the characteristics of citizens who are more compatible with an open society? Research findings suggest that such citizens are the opposites of subjects. As we described the subject orientation personality as having at its very core a distrust or self-dislike, research findings suggest that the core of the citizen orientation is a deeply felt self-confidence and self-esteem. At the very roots of an open society we find individuals who like themselves.

The citizen orientation might be characterized as involving a clearly defined self-identity, an ability to discipline and control emotional impulses and desires, and a reasonably high self-evaluation. A citizen has an accurate self-appraisal. A citizen likes what he knows of himself, and as a result he believes in his own ability to control and achieve whatever pursuits are appropriate for his own sense of purpose in life.

Whereas the subject orientation has a weak self-identity, a citizen has strong, well defined and acceptable self-image. Research findings further suggest that this self-acceptance enables the citizen to tolerate a great deal of uncertainty in events and situations around him. Because a citizen can tolerate himself, he can also tolerate, like, and trust others. Perhaps because he has the capacity to tolerate others and to tolerate uncertainties about the future the citizen is capable of pursuing long-range goals. Herein lies the answer to the second part of our inquiry into the citizen orientation. How does the citizen relate to others?

Because of his more positive assessment of self the citizen does not need to project his own internal hang-ups upon others. Therefore, he is able to relate in a more trusting and open way to other people, a fact that allows him to receive a greater amount of accurate information. So, the citizen is less likely to continue believing what his own stereotypes and fears might otherwise lead him to believe. Since he is able to receive new information, he can adjust his previous views of people and situations.

Finally, what does the citizen think about society in general? He tends to see society as he sees others and as he sees himself. As the subject-orientation personality tends to be cynical, suspicious, and pessimistic about human nature and society, the citizen-orientation personality believes that others are much like himself. In other words, the citizen is susceptible to weakness but also to strength; capable of doing poorly, but also of doing well; sometimes of being uncertain, but sometimes of having well defined purposes and goals. People can be good as well as bad, and thus society can be good as well as bad. Society is not necessarily an evil, competitive, jungle-like environment. Society provides many resources that an individual can use in the development of his own potential humanness.

To summarize briefly, the citizen-orientation personality appears to involve the following central attributes: He has an accurate self-appraisal, he accepts, and he likes himself.

Citizens trust themselves and therefore trust others. Because they trust others, citizens can receive and accurately evaluate information about people and events around them. Citizens can rely upon others without depending upon them as authority objects. Citizens have confidence in their ability to achieve the purposes which they have defined. They can set aside the need to relieve immediately anxiety and emotional impulses, a fact that permits them to gain longer term gratifications. In this sense they are more capable of calculating from the means to the ends. They can be autonomous without being isolated. Since they have a strong, well defined self-identity they have little need for any authoritatively or socially defined image to provide them with purpose and meaning. They can relate to group goals and causes without having to accept them as their own meaning for life. They can belong without losing themselves. They can imagine a society as good as themselves, and therefore, are capable of creating one.

A BRIEF SUMMARY AND AFTERTHOUGHTS

We began this chapter with a discussion of the attitudes that people have about politics (i.e., the political culture). We discussed the importance of early childhood experiences in determining the ways in which such attitudes are formed and the ways that adults behave in the political system. We noted that many students of socialization believe these childhood experiences are critical in forming the adult. Other research findings and theories suggest that attitudes can change. The human organism can adapt his attitudes, personality, and behavior to changing circumstances. Such adaptations are influenced by early childhood experiences but not necessarily determined by them. Finally, then, we discussed attitudes associated with two different life styles. One which we termed the subject orientation, incompatible with democratic society, and the other we called the citizen orientation, compatible with democratic society.

Before continuing, I want to add a few afterthoughts. The overriding theme in this book is that individuals must be able to cope with and adapt to continually arising and difficult problems. As people solve such problems, they increase their ability to cope with future situations. Such success with problem solving breeds self-confidence.

To the extent that we live in a "sick society," this sickness lies with individuals, not with the system. If institutions such as the family and the school teach obedience, conformity, and submissiveness to authority, people learn to be "subjects" who perpetuate a "sick society." If, on the other hand, our institutions teach people that they have the power and ability to control situations and solve problems, we will have the beginnings of a creative politics and a good society. I am optimistic because I believe, if we can learn to be sick, self-hating, non-trusting, dependent upon authority, and cynical, we can also learn to be well, to be liking of ourselves, trusting of others, relating openly to authority, and having a meaningful life.

CHAPTER 11

CHANGING POLITICAL CULTURE

Changing people's values is what political revolution is all about. A political revolution is successful when most people in a society change their minds. The balance of this chapter is my attempt to clarify and expand upon these statements.

First, we will discuss the advantages and disadvantages of a relatively high level of consensus in the political culture. The second section is a brief historical analysis of the variation in political culture that has occurred within our own society. The last section is an explanation of why I believe political revolution has already occurred in this country during the past two decades.

THE USE AND ABUSE OF POLITICAL CONSENSUS

As clarification, I should point out that this section is not a discussion of the function of individual attitudes or of collectively shared attitudes called social norms. Rather, it is a discussion of why it is important in a society for people to agree about the ways in which politics should operate. Our concern is with the uses of consensus in a political culture.

There are probably many functions or uses of political consensus in a society, three of which—stability, control, and "drag effect"—are most significant. Each seems to act both as an advantage and a disadvantage for society.

First, a relatively high degree of political consensus produces stability and continuity in the society. How is this stability achieved? The term *stability,* in this context, refers to the condition in which the vast majority of people have a relatively high degree of predictability about the future outcomes of their present behavior. A stable society is one in which people can predict the consequences of their present and future behavior. For instance, if they obtain a college degree now, they can be relatively certain of a good occupation and life style later. Or, if they abide by the laws of the society they are confident of a life free from coercion or physical intervention. If they work hard and save their money, they can look forward to security in their old age.

As was pointed out earlier, we assume that all people have a need for certainty in their life styles. They need to know, with some predictability, the consequences of their acts. As an individual realizes that other people agree with his prediction of future consequences, he gains confidence in what he is doing. Higher levels of political consensus (agreement among people) support the individual's certainty that what he is doing will bring about predictable consequences. Agreement in society lends support to an individual's attempts to make sense out of his world. If many others agree with an individual, or at least appear to agree, he feels more confidence in his particular view of the world and in the operation of his own lifestyle.

In this sense, consensus supports individuals in society in becoming more confident, secure, and capable of living a better life. This confidence in individuals in turn promotes greater political stability simply because there are fewer uncertainties to result in conflicts.

However, political consensus has a disadvantage—stagnation. This is the ugly side of stability, when people live in such a determined and certain kind of life style there is little individual variation. In other words, if the society is too stable, it defines individual aspirations rather than supports them. So, instead of pursuing their own goals, people are merely living out life styles defined by tradition, customs, and mores.

In a stagnant society with a high level of consensus, there is no longer room for difference; there is no longer toleration of variations in life style. Everybody knows exactly what his entire life will be like, and he sees no alternatives.

The most obvious example of such stagnation, I suppose, occurs in a primitive society. This is a society in which each generation lives identical life styles, and future generations will do the same. This sameness connotes a rigid, castelike society in which from birth to death, individuals are little more than socially defined roles. There is no room in such a well defined play for individual purpose, motivation, or aspiration.

The second function of political consensus, is that of social control. When people agree among themselves about how politics should operate, there is little need for externally imposed control. There is little need for authority or government to use coercion to bring about behavior consistent with the policies of social change. People are willing to cooperate, without police, armies, or government dictates coercing their behavior. Agreement in this sense is a way of avoiding coercion and violence in society. Because the masses are willing to conform, the elites of such a society can utilize their resources and skills for solving genuine problems.

The disadvantage of this kind of internalized control is conformity. You can well imagine a society in which people have internalized so many social expectations and constraints that they are no longer capable of defining for themselves alternative ways of doing things. Political consensus can free people from the external political control, but such consensus can also become a widely shared mass conformity that escapes coercion merely to accept enslavement. It is hard for me to distinguish between a society in which people conform out of fear of governmental sanctions and one in which they conform because they believe it is a good thing to do. Everybody is locked in, regardless of how the prison is constructed.

The third function of high political consensus is most accurately described as a "drag effect." I have emphasized throughout this book that change in society is a result of shifting consensus from one set of widely shared attitudes to another, thereby redefining the ways in which the society and politics should operate. The very existence of a consensus acts to retard any redefinitions of the ways that people in society should behave. A high level of consensus acts to screen out and to retard the rapidity with which social change can be brought about by elites in a society.

The positive side of this "drag effect" is the protection it provides against the impulsive or manipulatory efforts of elites to bring about change. On the other hand, this "drag effect" may so retard the process of social change and adaptation as to leave little chance for a society to cope with its major problems.

Higher levels of political consensus create a more or less rigid political culture that prevents elite manipulation of the mass of people; at the same time, such a culture creates an inflexible kind of social context that prevents changes necessary for the society's development.

This discussion of political consensus indicates rather clearly, I think, that high levels of consensus have both advantages and disadvantages for a society. You should keep this analysis in mind as we continue to examine the notion of changing political culture.

CHANGING POLITICAL CULTURE: WHEN DOES A SOCIETY CHANGE ITS MIND?

Large numbers of people do change their minds at the same time. But what conditions make a society ripe for such widespread change?

When consensus deteriorates, people experience conflicts with one another. Although, as we have seen, conflict makes possible creative social change, people often choose to withdraw or to escape conflict rather than take advantage of it. So, sidetracking for a moment, we may consider the means people use to avoid conflict. Mobility can be a means of escaping conflict. Daniel Lerner identifies three kinds of mobility: geographic, social, and psychic.[1]

Individuals who disagree with one another have two alternatives. They can stand and fight, or they can leave the conflict situation. Faced with growing levels of conflict and attempts to utilize power to change society, they can participate in these conflict processes to bring about policy changes, or they can withdraw to escape the conflict. People often choose to escape rather than to use conflict to bring about meaningful social changes.

One alternative to participation in the conflict is simply to move away. People can leave the area where the conflict is occurring. Another kind of mobility is that of joining a different social class. People can move by climbing a social ladder out of the social position where conflicts are most intense. Finally, people can withdraw psychically from the political conflicts that create anxiety—they may simply "tune out"—that is, become alienated. Keeping these forms of conflict avoidance in mind, we can proceed with the discussion of changing culture in American history.

Although at the individual level, attitudinal change may occur frequently, such change within a whole culture is relatively rare. The following historical description hopefully sheds some light on this. From this example we may begin to extract the elements necessary for changing our culture. One can interpret the early history of American politics as involving both geographic and social mobility, as well as social change, in

---

1. Daniel Lerner, *The Passing of Traditional Society* (New York: Free Press of Glencoe, 1958), particularly pp. 54-65.

response to conflict. Early periods of American history can be characterized as having relatively low levels of political consensus. There were vast
differences in the experiences of people located on the East Coast and
those who were part of the westward expansion. One may infer that
frontier experiences gave these people a great deal of self-confidence as
they faced the difficult problems of human survival. Because of their
experiences with European monarchies and because the new government
in Washington was so irrelevant to their lives, the frontiersmen had little
confidence or trust in governmental authority.

So a new political culture began to emerge around frontier life—a
general sense of distrust of authority, government, and officials. Although
there were pockets of agreement on how society should operate, the
country as a whole could not seem to arrive at a consensus agreeable to
both the East and the West. With such disagreements and the resulting
conflict, one would have expected some political participation to redefine
the political structure more in keeping with the new experiences, values,
and purposes. The primary reason such engagement and change were
relatively slow in coming was the availability of large, open space. Many
people chose to move away from the conflict arena rather than to resolve
their disputes.

No sooner had the frontiers been established, creating a new political
culture, than the society was shaken by the Industrial Revolution and a civil
war. Both major disturbances had a profound impact upon the individual
experiences of people.

The resolution of the Civil War did little to bring about higher levels
of consensus within the society. Again, one reason the conflict did not
result in more genuine policy adaptations was that our society had found
a new and ingenious way of escaping. The whole impact of the Industrial
Revolution caused the creation of socio-economic hierarchies of status.
Our society became obsessed with the phenomenon of social mobility,
which proved to be as effective an escape as was geographic mobility.
People could no longer run away to the frontiers, but they could and did
rise on the socio-economic ladder by getting jobs in the cities and by
improving their own particular socio-economic positions. In this way,
people were no longer locked into those social positions that desperately
needed social change. They made it on their own, without the use of
government. Many people did well, and we began to generate in our
society a large middle class—but many people did not do so well. The
Horatio Alger myth was an expression of the political consensus developing from the experiences of early industrialization. Supposedly, anyone
could make it on his own if he were competent and hard working, without
the assistance of government. Government need only to leave him alone.

In reality, there were few "captains of industry." But many people believed then and continue to believe now that they could be such successes if they wanted to work hard. Such beliefs supported a political consensus keeping government out of individual enterprises.

With the Great Depression came a third turning point in the political culture of our society. The Industrial Revolution had brought people into the large urban areas, away from farms and small towns, and they were now living amid the realities of a large and complex society. For reasons they did not understand, most people were living without the necessities for survival.

People had to create new demands and expectations about how to survive, and they had to have predictable life styles in the big cities. They turned to government. This was the beginning of a new political culture. Many people began to believe that government should have the responsibility of providing the "good life" for its people.

People living in large urban areas could not be self-sufficient. They could no longer grow their own food, build their own homes, or educate their own children. They either worked in factories or did not work at all. Government was the only organization large enough to provide for survival. Government became the focus of this expectation. As a result of the intensely felt helplessness during the depression, most people agreed that government should help provide for survival and security.

Much of the present-day political culture is still defined by the experiences of the depression period. It is still a widely shared belief that government should have the responsibility for providing a secure life style for people. In addition to protecting us from foreign aggression and to providing us with services, government should provide us with the "good life" economically, socially, and even psychologically.

I would argue that one reason these expectations fell upon government during the depression was that the previous avenues of escaping conflict and political solutions had gradually been cut off. Geographic and social mobility were no longer available means for leaving the political arena. The frontiers were gone. And the depression made it clear that very few people could climb the ladder of social mobility to escape their problems.

Now, the only escape left for most people was psychic mobility. The only alternative to participation in the conflict was and still is alienation. People escape politics by separating themselves from society. They may believe it is futile to participate in a difficult and anxiety producing conflict situation. These people feel that they are simply pawns in a game of politics over which they have little or no control.

Alienation is the present-day counterpart of the geographic and social mobility of our history. Many people find it easier to escape than to cope with the anxieties and difficulties of meaningful engagement in re-defining society.

Whether the escape is geographic, social, or psychic, withdrawal from the highly uncertain circumstances of political involvement in conflict reduces anxiety.

What can be concluded from this analysis? Under what conditions was the change in political culture made?

In each case, change was brought about by the resolution of a conflict that was of crisis proportion. The intense conflict was caused by the incompatible experiences, needs, and interests of people, whether the result of geographic expansion, the Industrial Revolution, the Civil War or the depression. When that conflict was finally faced and solved, the socie-ty had formed a new cultural consensus about the role of government. We went from considering government a threat to individual survival to con-sidering government irrelevant to survival and success, and finally to con-sidering government ultimately responsible for the survival and security of its people.

Throughout our history, people have had various means of escaping the anxieties of conflict. Sometimes, mobility postponed people's facing the conflict, but it usually added fuel to the conflict as it increased the diversity of experiences among people in the society. Life styles differed between geographic areas of the country, and between socio-economic classes. As a person sought to escape through a psychic withdrawal, he created his own unique world, which could not be shared with others.

When crisis occurs, that is, a widely felt conflict takes place, a society's survival is in the balance—will it stay together or come apart? On one side, there is a widely shared common experience during a crisis, a bond which is conducive to unity and problem solving. On the other side, because consensus on what is appropriate behavior has disintegrated, people are separated from each other by their fear, uncertainty, and differ-ences, and yet at the same time are prone to accept new values.

Although crisis is a necessary precondition, it is not enough by itself to create adaptive change and a new consensus. So, the crucial variable to be introduced here is leadership.

If emerging elites can effectively articulate alternative solutions and get people involved in solving problems, the society has a good chance of making adaptive change and of building a new culture more relevant to the needs of the present than the old one was. Since so much of the balance seems to depend upon political leadership, we need to focus upon alternative leadership styles. What are the characteristics of leadership that can steer a society through a crisis? More important, what are the qualities of political leadership conducive to solving social problems while improv-ing the quality of life?

CHARISMATIC, COERCIVE, AND
CREATIVE LEADERSHIP STYLES

Clearly, crisis and the type of political leadership that emerges in that crisis are of extreme importance in creating social change and progress. Associated with crisis in a society is a growing discontent and distrust of existing governmental institutions and processes. Many people believe a crisis to be the fault of the existing government and officials. Thus, a crisis provides additional evidence that continuing allegiance to the government is unwarranted, and that escape from the society through alienation is thoroughly justified. In other words, a crisis tends to decrease the legitimacy of the existing political processes, institutions, and officials. The leadership must articulate alternatives that will solve problems in such a way as to enable the people to accept the alternatives. This acceptance is difficult, since people generally distrust and dislike government during crisis periods. With the problem stated in this way, it seems that there are at least three alternative styles of leadership able to make this transition from old political values to newer ones. These are charismatic, coercive and what I choose to term creative leadership styles. We will discuss the strengths and weaknesses of each style.

In much of political science literature, especially the literature concerning the "underdeveloped" nations of the world, charismatic leadership is the favorite theme of many authors.[2] The notion of charisma or charismatic leadership derives from the work and writing of Max Weber.[3] Charisma is a leader's ability to use his tremendous personal attractiveness to command people regardless of their traditional attitudes, existing mores, and present life styles.[4] At a time when the offices and institutions of a country stand in poor esteem with many people, a leader with charismatic appeal can become the essential mechanism for making the required changes. In such times, people can identify with a charismatic leader and at the same time continue to believe that the present institutions are bad. The society is able to make changes through relating to the individual leader, even though the government and its institutions are thought to be faulty. As people identify with a leader, they come to accept his particular definition of issues and alternatives as a way of coping with the problems.

---

2. For an excellent and brief analysis and bibliography relevant to this discussion see Claude Ake, *A Theory of Political Integration* (Homewood, Ill.: Dorsey Press, 1967), particularly Chap. 4.

3. *Max Weber: Essays in Sociology,* ed. and trans. H. H. Gerth and C. Wright Mills (New York: Oxford University Press, 1946).

4. For an extended discussion of Weber and his thought relevant here see Robert A. Nisbet, *The Sociological Tradition* (New York: Basic Books, Inc., 1966), particularly Chaps. 4 and 6.

People can accept new ways of thinking and behaving, not because they trust the institutions of society but because they trust the personal appeal of their charismatic leader.

This option sounds very attractive, but it seems to me that there are two very profound problems with the charismatic leadership style. It is an act of faith to assume that the charismatic leader is going to be a "good guy" that is, a leader who is genuinely interested in bringing about the social development and bettering the human condition in the process. Adolf Hitler was a charismatic leader.

Still another difficulty is the problem of what happens once the charismatic leader is gone. How does the society make the transition back to some kind of acceptable institutions and processes? Both problems require a great deal of thought. I point them out here to justify the examination of alternative leadership styles.

Another style—coercive leadership—is, perhaps, the most probable to occur at least from the viewpoint of historical evidence. In my mind, it is also the least acceptable of the three possibilities. Coercive leadership is one response to a crisis in which the government is distrusted by many people. Elites can use coercion to effect change in political consensus consistent with their public policies and programs.

This coercion is the beginning of a totalitarian state. Because there are no obvious alternatives, people accept repression and coercion of existing elites as a way of solving their problems. Some students of politics today seriously consider this repression an acceptable alternative if there is no other way to make the transition to new values to solve the problems.

I find this dubious reasoning at best. Perhaps, because of my own prejudices, I have serious reservations, beyond the obvious fear of coercion and authorized violence. People learn, from coercion and manipulation, not only a further distrust of government, but also they learn further withdrawal and alienation as a means of survival. People do not learn to solve problems and develop their own potential under such coercion. They learn to obey or to get out of the way of those solutions imposed by the elites.

It is conceivable that the elites may succeed in solving those problems giving rise to a crisis. However, it is unlikely they will engage people in meaningful and purposeful lives in the process. There is also the further problem of deciding where coercion ends and where genuine social acceptance of the changes begins. In other words, where does compliance come back into the picture for a society that has given itself to a coercive elite? After the passing of time—perhaps a generation or so—younger generations might accept the new definitions of society without question and in so doing be capable of living relatively good lives. But such a transition requires that a large number of people give up their "freedoms," asking present society to give up its "good life" in order to make better conditions for future generations. This seems to be the most optimistic argument one can make in defense of coercive leadership style.

If leadership based on charisma and coercion were the only alternatives, I suppose I would hope for the charismatic leader. But, I think, there is another alternative—creative leadership.

Three prime characteristics are associated with the notion of creative leadership. It is responsive, responsible, and facilitative. By responsive, I mean that it is capable of understanding and reacting to the expectations of the people. By responsible, I mean that it is able to anticipate and to plan for the solution of problems that have not yet reached crisis proportions and that people in the society have not yet clearly understood. By facilitative, I mean the ability to engage people in decision-making required to solve problems. But even if creative leadership were available in a society—how would it be able to make the transition from traditional political culture to the new definitions of consensus required to cope with the problems without using either charisma or coercion?

This transition can be achieved by involving people in the processes of solving the problems that caused the crisis. Once people are engaged in problem solving, they become autonomous, and leadership itself becomes less critical to the transition.

This involvement is not accomplished by simply telling people to solve their problems. Creative leadership identifies and articulates alternative programs and further utilizes its position in society to educate people to accept new and different ways of thinking and acting. Such leadership serves to make people aware of what problems they have and of what problems they might anticipate, while at the same time providing people with resources and encouragement. In general creative leadership facilitates the engagement of large numbers of people in meaningful adaptation and in making political decisions about adaptation for the development of the society.

My own feeling is that a large number of people in this society are more capable of accepting change and new ways than are the leaders. It appears that the mass of people are more progressive and attuned to social change than are the existing elites, both those within and without the government. However, it appears to me, that we now have a unique opportunity for making dramatic social change in this country. Because of the continuing crisis experienced by many people in our society, and because of their genuine feeling that the crisis must be solved, many individuals want to be a part of that solution.

The result of creative leadership is the channeling and focusing of the vast energies, talents, and skills of a large number of people in society toward the solution of common problems. This mass involvement not only produces more alternatives, it also produces a greater likelihood that people within the society will accept the alternatives that are made available. Furthermore, it occurs to me that the very process of engaging people in thinking about and acting toward the solution of problems is the only way society can teach its members to become more significant, self-confident human beings.

Creative leadership seems conducive to the society that facilitates not only effective solutions to problems but also the creation of human life styles in which people learn how to cope with problems. I see creative political leadership as an antidote not only to change-generated problems, but also to the most profound problems of post-industrial society—alienation of individuals from a feeling of communal trust and purpose.

With this discussion of three alternative leadership styles more or less completed, we can now turn to an even more speculative portion of the chapter. I think that a social revolution has already occurred in our country in the last two decades.

THE REVOLUTION IS OVER—AND NOW WHAT?

When I start a discussion with a heading as intentionally provocative as the notion that revolution has already occurrred in America in the last two decades, I had better clarify rather carefully what is meant. I am not using the term revolution as it is normally used. Normally the term is associated with the violent overthrow of an existing political regime. I am using the word in the broader sense, and I think in a more meaningful one.

I mean by revolution that the central premises and goals of the political consensus of a society have changed. Most people in society during the last two decades have changed their minds about how their society is going to develop and about what it is going to achieve as its national purposes.

Normally, the point of a violent overthrow of an existing regime is to install new elites, who attempt through propaganda, reorganization of institutions, and coercion to bring about a change in the minds of many people. Typically, after a period of total coercion and manipulation, a new generation of people grows up accepting the revolutionary definitions of society, and in time, the society comes to change its values and goals.

In my mind what has occurred in this country is an entirely different phenomenon, perhaps an unprecedented one. I think that this society has already changed its mind. After teaching and living among young people in a university situation, it is obvious to me that they have a much different world view, expectations, purposes and goals for this society than did their immediate predecessors in American universities. What are these differences and how have they come about? Obviously, what follows is speculation, but it may provoke some thought.

Perhaps the security of an affluent society has provided the fertile soil for the growth of these new values and purposes. Because a generation of parents were able to provide a relatively wealthy and at least financially secure life for their children, a generation of young adults have learned different values than those of their parents. Security breeds an openness to new ideas and values. The spread of many of these values is greatly intensified by the strong peer pressures of a generation of young people who have come to distrust the traditional authority of adults, government, and history. Such peer pressure to accept the new values is of course most likely to occur in the universities and high schools.

Our educational system has become the breeding ground for change and a new social ethos not by intent but largely because it was unable to provide legitimate and authoritative responses to the many questions of a critical and even antagonistic generation of young people. Perhaps, we are now reaping the rewards (or punishments) of an educational process that has taught children to be critical, idealistic, and aggressive in their confrontations with problems. Whether by accident or by intention, it seems clear to most of us who teach this nation's young people that these future elites are different from previous generations.

We might also speculate that this counter-culture has arisen in response to the common experience of young people with mass media. They have all been brought up on a common if sometimes tasteless diet of mass media influence. Without belaboring whether the media comprise a liberal or conspiratorial mechanism in our society, there is little controversy over the fact that the media have provided a common experience that is influential in the development of value orientations.

Young people have seen war, poverty, pollution, and expressions of racism enough that these experiences form an integral part of their early life, in association with their earliest experiences in the family. Experiences of others as seen on television, whether real or not, have left impressions. These have become "facts" with which each young person must cope in understanding his world. In a real sense, young people are in search of a theory to make reality meaningful. Their search sometimes leads them to the classroom for that theory. If education ignores their needs, young people will provide each other with such explanations. Although these theories are often not comprehensible to parents, the young people who seek community and communion in their participation in the counter-culture readily understand.

Still another continuing and profound experience shared among young people in this society has been an immoral and incomprehensible war. The Vietnam conflict has taught young people many lessons that the classrooms and authorities cannot counteract. What are these lessons? Authority (government) often is not able to solve many problems. Government will lie to protect its national purposes, whatever they may be. A little nation can stand off the terrible power of our military might (even when the little nation is communistic). Government itself is not to be trusted as a source of information about the world or as credible leadership for that world.

Placing all of these common experiences in the educational processes along with the effects of the mass media and of the continuing cold and hot wars, many of today's young people anticipate a future involving a struggle for survival. Whether adults or governments believe it, many young people, particularly the brightest ones (and the future elites of our society), believe that the continued existence of life on this planet can no longer be assumed. The fact of continued existence has become a question to be answered. And the answer is by no means obvious or even likely in the minds of many young people. Existence itself has become a question in the light of growing evidence of overpopulation, the degradation of the environment, and the continuing insanity of our social priorities and policy.

Perhaps the profundity and the immensity of these shared crises and experiences have forged the adaptations in values, attitudes, and behaviors often referred to as the counter–culture, and of which the older generation has become begrudgingly aware.

No revolutionary cadre has seized power, defined or coerced social progress. Presently, it appears that political elites little understand the changes in the attitudes of many young people. Instead we have a mass of people, perhaps even a majority, who are maturing into the adult roles of our social system and are bringing with them a very different set of attitudes than previously existed. In other words, this society is changing its mind, not by an act of political violence or by the overthrow of existing regimes, but by the maturation of its young people. The "invasion" of our culture and territory is not the horizontal attack of a foreign aggressor, but the vertical attack of our children upon our social and political culture.

It would be naive indeed to believe that this vertical invasion will not be greatly coerced and compromised by the existing and resisting culture. But the invasion will produce a society with a very different definition of itself than now exists. The only way I can describe this difference is to say that the revolution is over and that we are now waiting for the new society to grow up.[5]

5. For similar and expanded arguments see Philip Slater, *The Pursuit of Loneliness* (Boston: Beacon Press, 1970) and Charles Reich, *The Greening of America* (New York: Random House, 1970).

If the revolution has already occurred, what are the attitudes and values which have changed? It is difficult to assess what the new political consensus will be. But I can share some of my thoughts on the nature of these attitudes.

I think in its essence, the emerging counter-culture is both a religious and a political event. Religion here means man's search for purpose, and politics means the ways that people go about constructing a society more consistent with purpose. The life style of the young people's culture is a mixture of that of a priest and that of a politician. To understand it as either, rather than as both, is to misunderstand it completely. What appears curious from a distance is often fairly simple once you get close enough to see well. What are some of the elements of this life style, which, I think, is composed of both a seeking for religion and for politics?

Perhaps the most central element is the valuing of humanness and acting accordingly rather than behaving in a way that will be judged by society or authority as permitting admission into the human community.

Being human involves the most profound and deeply felt experience of self in relation to others. The trust which can be created in such an intense experience permits not only self-awareness and confidence, but also a greater ability to rely upon and relate meaningfully to other people. A trust so generated can be projected upon social institutions. A person who can trust himself and others is more likely to trust processes and institutions that encourage his confidence in being human. Responsible action can flow from such an alliance between individuals and their society. It can be responsible action because individuals will act to promote the common purposes and needs of a society that values its individual members.

This strong emphasis upon humanness and its consequent action is different from the present culture's emphasis upon evaluating a person as good only when he behaves in a way consistent with certain values and goals. The acceptance of the person in this latter case is conditional. But many young people believe that trust and humanness emerge from the assumption of worth, not from its demonstration. To trust oneself and then to act is a far different thing than to trust oneself as a consequence of one's acts. The former notion involves an unconditional acceptance of self, while the latter permits the possibility of failure and consequent separation from one's community.

An emphasis upon trust as the essential requisite of the human condition leads to a much different criterion for evaluating social conduct than now exists. The demonstration of success through financial adventures and achievement is of little consequence, but the willingness to accept others is a critical component in judging institutions, processes, and people. A government that provides material advantages and opportunities while neglecting the need to be open and available to people, thus encouraging their trust, is not a legitimate government, given these values. To be trustworthy is more important than to be efficient. Indeed, being trustworthy is a pre-condition to achieving efficiency.

The authority of experience, history, expertise, or tradition is suspect because it requires externally imposed conditions for the acceptance of self. Such authority is irrelevant to one who is in search of a human relationship. Morality is evaluated by evidence of human concern with other humans rather than by obedience to law or other such imperatives, whether they be socially or intellectually derived. Being loved and accepted is more important than being liked or approved of. There must be a communion of objects into a subjective whole in which no part is apart. One cannot know such communion through the observation of parts. Such wholeness precludes observation and manipulation. It must be experienced, not seen and directed. The most elemental component of existence becomes self, and the trust of others becomes the agent for the achievement of social meaning, purpose, and change.

We have discussed at some length now the reasons and results of a revolution in our social consciousness—what more need be said? Perhaps we had better return to the realities that confront us.

What I am arguing here is not all that much. I am saying that social change is often thought to involve the imposition of change by the dictates of new elites gaining power in the society. What is now occurring is perhaps the reverse of this "normal progression." The young people have already accepted a new view of their society and of their condition. They have a view that is still not articulated or defined by any existing elite. They have a view of the "good life" and of society. They want only the accomplishment of that view in the real world. They have a world view; they seek a world.

All of this discussion assumes that it is as much an act of revolution to change one's mind or the mind of someone else as it is to overthrow the regime of a country.

If all that has gone before in this book is of any use in calculating strategy in our political world, it suggests, I think, that there are two major points of access for bringing about meaningful social change. The first is the creation, organization, and use of power to change political elites and the public policy binding the behavior of people in a society. The second point of access into this spiral of political processes we have described is the bringing about of change in the ways that people think. To change the character of consensus by elite manipulation is only one way of doing it. Consensus can also change as a consequence of common experiences with continuing crisis. No elite need tell us we must survive. Our very existence is our guide.

Genuine social change can occur as the result of power as well as the result of value changes. One does not necessarily follow the other. The process is reversible. Cultural values can change, a fact which in turn changes the policy adaptations made in a society. Just as easily, policy adaptations can change the existing cultural values. These themes introduced here are the major ones in the last chapter of this book. What are the ingredients of a creative politics—a creative politics that involves the confrontation with problems, and the bringing about of solutions to those problems by the engagement of large numbers of people in problem solving and in decision-making processes. To solve problems is not enough. People must be involved in the solutions. By such participation they can derive a sense of worth, dignity, competence, and ability to cope with the complex environment in which each individual must survive.

PART VI

TOWARD A CREATIVE POLITICS

CHAPTER 12

POLITICS, PROBLEMS, AND PROPOSALS

We shall end as we began, by discussing politics as the ways people in society confront and solve change-generated problems. I see this chapter as the bridge between the foregoing analysis of politics and the action strategies required to bring about a creative politics more likely to adapt to change.

We began this book by focusing upon a basic contradiction between the individual pursuit of valued goals and the collective survival of the society. Now, I want to return to that basic problem and attempt to establish criteria for the evaluation of a good society, a society that fosters the creation of political life styles facilitating an individual's pursuit and achievement of his essential humanity, and at the same time that promotes the collective good of the people in that society. After examining criteria for the good society and the politics by which such a society can be created, we need then to focus upon the major avenues suggested by the previous analysis for bringing about such social progress. Finally, I want to discuss some proposals to put the theory and analysis into practice.

THE GOOD SOCIETY

The saddest, indeed the most despairing, commentary leveled at contemporary political analysis deals with our inability or unwillingness to deal intellectually with the problem of designing a good society in the context of post-industrial mass society. Whether it is because we do not think we have the answer to such a question or, more likely, because we know we do not have answers to such grave questions, we have failed in our obligation to inform and educate our society about the nature of the "good life" and about the politics necessary to achieve the good society. This obligation to both student and citizen is clear, and the time is late.

As we peruse the history of what other minds in other times have thought as they grappled with the problem of defining the good society, we find many different answers.

Some thinkers have urged that the good society is one in which the knowledgeable people, the thoughtful ones, and the philosophers of society become the ruling elite. Such an elite could guide the society and its people in directions and toward goals that the mass can little understand, but goals from which they would greatly benefit. The crucial social choices would be made by people with the competence, skill, and expertise to make such decisions, as well as to impose them. Such an elite could anticipate social problems and channel the energy, resources, and talents of that society toward the progress and development necessary to overcome them. The "good life" would be defined and brought about by men of reason and expertise, but its benefits would be shared by all people.

Others theorists, less confident in the virtues of man's reason, have argued that society should place primary reliance upon established authority, the mores developed over generations of experience, and the well defined— coercive, if necessary—political institutions that will guide and impose the "good life" upon an undeserving, often unwilling, mass of selfish people.

The single most important change in this history of political thought was the notion that the mass of people had both the right and capability to control their own destiny. This notion of the mass of people governing their own social development is largely derived from the liberal political philosophers of the eighteenth century. It became the criterion for evaluating the "good life" and society. But even with this profound change, a recurring theme is found in the practice of democracy, if not in the theory. Even though people's right and capability to rule themselves was assured, the mechanism for bringing about these rights was a contract with a government. Democracy helped to delegate decision–making to a representative body that could be evaluated on the criterion of its being more or less responsive to the needs of the people. Again, the choices made by individuals were not choices about their own purposes and goals for their society so much as they were choices about who would best represent those interests and make decisions in the collective interests of the society. Thus, the notion of representative democracy became another answer to the question of defining the "good life" for people.

Perhaps the next critical point in this history of thought attempting to establish criteria for the "good life" was the profound recognition by Karl Marx that the "good life" was to be achieved not through political institutions, representative or otherwise, but through the fulfillment of man's need to have control over his own circumstances and future. Such control, in the Marxian view, was to be accomplished by distributing the control of economic functions in the society to all people. This distribution in turn would give people the power to bring about the implementation of their choices.

Marx envisioned the good society as one in which the collective pursuits and productivity of all individuals are commonly shared, leading to the meaningful engagement of every man in a social context that will be productive of necessities as well as of the opportunity for self-government. The collective good, Marx felt, is to be achieved through individual productivity that at the same time assures individual involvement in the society. Marx clearly saw the consequence of industrial society as the separation of man from control over his life and purpose. He sought a cure for such alienation in the notion that all men share in the meaning to be derived from the collective pursuits of their society.

If Marx was a visionary, Max Weber was a prophet of our social condition in the industrial society. For Weber, the "good life" was to be achieved through the rationalization of social processes and institutions by way of bureaucracy.

The good society in this view is one that analyzes, rationally defines its problems, and creates organizational hierarchies of roles to solve problems. For Weber, a good society was a bureaucracy, which is to promote the collective good through primary reliance upon the accumulated expertise and rationality of men performing roles it defines. Weber felt that it assures the "good life" for an individual by placing him where the rational calculation of means to ends is the operative condition, rather than a reliance upon tradition, mores, or myths.

Beyond these views that we have briefly discussed here, there have been few serious attempts among contemporary social theorists to do more toward the design of the good society. Modern social scientists have offered some fragments toward such a design, but as yet there is no well defined blueprint of a good society in the post-industrial context.

Perhaps one of the most widely discussed contemporary Utopias has been that of B. F. Skinner in his book *Walden Two*.[1] This was his attempt to define the good society in terms of the basic postulates of behavioral psychology. The good society in this "Utopia" is one in which the individual is assumed to be a responsive mechanism and one who will respond to good social conditions and stimuli.

The good society is a social configuration so designed that individuals receive stimuli that promote the values that have been accepted in the construction of that society. The Utopia is constructed so that the values many people agree upon such as knowledge, tolerance, and the ability to relate to others, are taught to the individual through his experiences in the controlled community.

The society is a stimulus and the individual responds to that stimulus. Once again, we find a good society in which individuals are not meaningfully engaged in making the decisions concerning their own lives and futures. The people are conditioned by their response to social stimuli, regardless of how good or valuable such stimuli may be.

Still another fragment in contemporary social science, and in my mind perhaps the most significant contribution to a definition of the "good life," is that concept offered by the humanist psychologists.[2] Typically, such psychologists have argued that the central attribute for becoming a good person is the engagement of the individual in a process of meaningful choice. In other words, the "good life" is one of purposive action toward self-defined goals and one of making choices rather than of being conditioned by a response to some social or authoritatively defined context.

Such theorists argue that the individual realizes his potential as a human through the making of choices about his own purposes and through acting out the consequences of such choices. The emphasis here is not upon the end state either of society or of the individual but upon the process of life itself. The "good life" is not so much something to be achieved as it is a way of getting there.

These theorists have not spoken to the problem of how such individual lives can be pursued in a context in which the constraints of

1. B. F. Skinner, *Walden Two* (New York: Macmillan, 1962).

2. See any or all of the following books, which advocate similar notions. Carl Rogers, *On Becoming a Person* (Boston: Houghton-Mifflin, 1961); Rollo May, *Man's Search for Himself* (N.Y.: New American Libraries, 1967); Ashley Montagu, *On Being Human* (New York: Hawthorne Books, 1966); Gordon W. Allport, *Becoming* (New Haven: Yale University Press, 1955); and Abraham Maslow, *Eupsychian Management* (New York: Richard Irwin, 1965).

economic, social, and political origin prevent the individual from meaningful choice making. If the society and the roles which society requires of the person are in large part already defined, then where is there room to pursue one's own choice without the complete rejection of society itself? The pursuit of the "good life" for these theorists appears to me basically to be the pursuit of an individual Utopia and not a design for social reformation and progress.

We have to this point been sketching with broad strokes in order to give perspective to our discussion of the criteria of the good society. We can now turn to the finer detail in order to clarify the criteria which seem to have emerged from the foregoing analysis. What emerges from all of this for me are the following criteria that might be utilized to evaluate social conditions to judge whether a society is promoting the "good life" for its people.

The good society must be able effectively to anticipate, cope with, and solve the problems of human survival. The good society must facilitate and perpetuate the ability of the individual to have control over his personal and his social circumstances. The good society must be one in which the political elites are responsible for the articulation of alternative paths of social development, and also are responsive to the needs of the individuals in the society. The final, and perhaps the most significant, criterion of the good society is the one in which the individual through his making of choices affecting his own circumstances and future can promote the collective good of the society as a whole.

The final criterion is one that has been recognized by many social philosophers and most clearly articulated by Adam Smith. Smith in *The Wealth of Nations* argued that the good society is one in which individual avarice and seeking after wealth work to the collective advantage of the whole society. As individuals become wealthy, there is more wealth to be shared in the total society.

Whereas Smith's conception of the laissez–faire society was premised upon the assumption that human nature essentially seeks pleasure through profits, we have more recently found through the efforts of cultural anthropologists that such universal assumptions about man and society are unwarranted. Indeed, seeking after wealth is not an attribute of human nature so much as it is a product of a particular culture pattern in which most of Western civilization has participated. This fact points out the necessity for examining the value premises that are engrained in a society and for analyzing the ways that those values determine the possibilities for defining the "good life" and society. In other words, the "good life" can be defined only with some attention to the kinds of values that are widely shared in a particular society.

Still another provocative notion in this attempt to define the good society is the one developed by Ruth Benedict.[3] She introduced the concept of "synergy" in her attempts to define "patterns of good culture." In her terminology, a "high synergy" social configuration is one in which the acts or skills that prove to be advantageous to the individual, are, at the same time, advantageous to the social collectivity.

Rather than assuming, as did Adam Smith, that all individuals pursue wealth and that wealth is a universal criterion for evaluating the "good life," Benedict points out that the particular value premises existing in the society largely define the kind of good society that is possible. From this perspective, it is conceivable that values other than wealth can be pursued by individuals and that such pursuits are good to the extent that they also work to the advantage of all the people in the society. Indeed, material wealth may be one value which cannot be pursued by individuals without the exploitation of the collectivity.

You may recall the example of the "tragedy of the commons" with which we began this book. The problem was that the pursuit of individual good defined in terms of material wealth (i.e., the profits accrued from selling the cattle) had the ironic and tragic collective impact of bringing about an exploitation and the final destruction of the collective good of the society (i.e., the use of the common pastures). As individuals pursued, rationally, their own profits, the common pasture was eventually exhausted from the large numbers of cattle grazing there. Without the common pastures, the community was without a way of economic survival.

Can we derive from this kind of analysis some attribute that assures a synergy relationship between the individual and the collectivity? What values can individuals pursue without exploiting other people? What values tend to promote relations wherein the person's pursuits are compatible with the collective good?

As I reflect upon these questions, it seems to me that the essential distinction between societies in which individual purposes do promote collective good and those in which they do not is that between values of an infinite nature and values of a finite nature.

This may sound a little hard to understand. It is really a fairly simple notion. As long as those symbols and materials that are valued most are finite or limited in nature, then necessarily some individuals get more of whatever is valued, at the expense of others. However, to the extent that the objects and symbols valued by people are infinitely available, all persons can acquire those objects and symbols to their maximum potential

3. Ruth Benedict, "Synergy—Patterns of Good Culture," *Psychology Today* 4 (1970): pp. 53-55.

while at the same time not reducing the amount of valuables available to others in the collectivity. If there is only so much of something to be had, then someone is necessarily going to have more than others. But if there is an unlimited supply, then everybody can have as much of the valuables as can be achieved.

Where is all of this taking us? It seems to me that what this points out is the necessity for evaluating the good society in terms of the availability of what is valued. In the good society the highest priorities and values should be of an infinite nature. What are such values? Dignity, trust, self-confidence, competence, and the ability to solve problems are values that can be infinite or unlimited in nature. There is no limitation upon the amount of dignity, self-esteem, and individual competence that can be accrued by individual members of a community.

On the other hand, there are clearly values in our present society's norm structure that are finite or limited in nature, and therefore, do require the exploitation of some people for the advantage of others, the values of wealth and status being the two most obvious examples. To the extent that certain individuals in our society value and achieve material wealth and social status, other people will have less material wealth and social status.

Using this discussion as background, we can attempt to bring together the criteria for evaluating the "good life" and society for people. What kinds of things do we want to be characteristics of a good society?

I think we want a society capable of anticipating and effectively responding to its problems by focusing the energies, creativity, and talents of individuals in such a way as to bring about solutions to the problems of survival. At the same time, we want a society that meaningfully engages people in a process of making choices about their own circumstances and future, a society that encourages individuals to reach their full potential as human beings. We want a society that gives priority to values that have the characteristic of being infinitely available to all, rather than priority to objects and symbols that require the exploitation of some people for the advantage of others. This is, in essence, a process of human thought and action toward purposes and goals rather than some form of static social Utopia. And, at its very core, this process is political, and it engages the people of the society in making decisions and choices in their attempts to cope with personal and social problems, a fact which in turn permits them to achieve their own humanness through the solution and effective adaptation to these problems.

It seems that a synergistic political process exists to the extent that individuals are task oriented and involved in problem solving activities. But such orientations and behavior patterns are of little consequence for the betterment of a society unless individuals have the power to control their

circumstances, and to direct them toward the kinds of solutions and purposes they desire. This process of engagement in a politics in which people
create, organize, and use power to achieve their purposes results in greater
personal feelings of worth and dignity, while also making social survival
more likely. Pursuit of these values and feelings of self-competence does
not necessitate the degradation or exploitation of the same qualities in
others.

We began by defining politics as the ways that people control and
are controlled in the process of adapting to change-induced problems. In
my mind, this becomes the core of a definition of the good society—a
society and politics that engages people in reaching their potential. A
society in which people create, organize, and use power to control their
lives and circumstances in such a way as to anticipate and to solve the
problems of survival, which threaten the existence of the collectivity.

With these thoughts about the good society in mind, we can now
turn the discussion to the problems and action strategies necessary to begin
the socio-political processes we have been describing.

CREATIVE POLITICS: TOWARD THE
SOLUTION OF THE PROBLEMS OF
POST-INDUSTRIAL SOCIETY

We will solve the problems of post-industrial society as we are able
to convert functional roles in bureaucratic and institutional processes of
problem solving into creative and purposeful political life styles. The
phrase "a political life style" is my attempt to describe the way that people
must think and act in making and influencing choices necessary to solve
the problems. I am not merely talking about "better citizenship." Creative
political life styles are not merely attempts by people to understand issues,
to support candidates, and to vote. The creative political life style requires
a continuing involvement in individual choice making and collective decision–making. Such involvement requires a clear understanding of self-
needs and political dynamics in order for individual and collective decisions to result in the solution of both personal and social problems. For a
final time, then, I need to summarize the analysis of political dynamics
used in this book to explain what is going on in this society. We need to
clarify this theory in order to identify the major points of access into the
political process, the points where political life styles can be most effectively acted out.

Our overall framework of analysis in this book argues that as historical and social conditions change the experiences of people in society, this
fact tends to decrease their shared agreement about how their society

should operate. These disagreements become the materials of conflict that must be effectively resolved by policy adaptations. Such political adaptations or policies, then, must be engrained into the beliefs of individuals in that society. Adaptive changes must be made legitimate in the minds of people in the society. The decline in consensus that promotes the conflict and then is resolved must be again increased by the overall acceptance of new policy by people in the society. Once such policy changes have been accepted by people, legitimate stability is gained and the cycle begins again. Thus the spiral of politics progresses.

In this type of analysis, it becomes clear, I think, that there are points of access to this overall process which are easier than other points for people to affect. First, people can work for the creation and organization of power to influence elites in determining the public policy of the society. Second, people can engage themselves in the process of changing the attitudes of people toward the kind of cultural consensus required to support a political system that is adequately anticipating and coping with the problems of survival.

These two separate strategies emerge from this analysis. They are not incompatible, but do involve different goals and tactics. We need to clarify the basic problems before we discuss strategies for survival.

What are some of the major problems confronting our society presently and in the near future? The list is long, but I think most of these problems can be classified under three major headings—changing individuals, changing socio-economic structures, and changing international relations among the countries of the world. We need to discuss each of these major problems in terms of the kinds of elite orientations, policy adaptations, and individual value changes that will be required to cope with and to solve them.

The notion of individual survival in our post-industrial society no longer carries the implication of physical security. Perhaps the most serious and profound problem that we have today as a result of affluence and of our own ability to survive materially is that we have lost purpose—both national and individual purpose. We have lost the individual realization of our own worth as humans.

Some people have referred to this problem as alienation, others have called it boredom, and still others have thought of it as the absurdity of existence in this time. By whatever name, the problem can be identified as individuals lacking purpose and meaning.

It is as if the kinds of values and attitudes that have been required in our historical development as a materialistically successful and productive society, now conspire to destroy individual dignity and sense of worth. Our society has defined life styles that were synergistic in the previous episodes of our history. People have been required by society to be productive and materially oriented, and success has meant the accumulation of individual wealth that has made us a wealthy nation.

Such values and life styles have been central to the development of our present affluence and power. However, I think the essential consequence in this post-industrial era has been people trained to conform to roles that have little meaning for them, beyond satisfying the economic requirements of productivity, efficiency, and the accumulation of wealth. How is it that we find so many people, particularly among the younger generation, who have played the game according to the socially defined rules of success—being achievement oriented, success oriented, college degree oriented—and who still do not feel good about themselves? They believe and do all of these things in order to have the valuables that our society uses to elicit individual effort. At the same time, we find many of those individuals most successful in this game still find little to give them purpose and meaning.

I believe that as long as social roles rather than individuals define objectives and goals, we are dependent upon external criteria for our own worth, and because of this dependency upon these social roles and expectations, we are lost. Individual purpose must replace social expectations. Such purpose derives from our ability to cope with, understand, and make choices about the ways that we should live in a post-industrial, mass, and anomic social context.

The second class of problem includes problems of ecology, overpopulation, pollution, and the problem of a non-expanding economic process. Again, by whatever name, it becomes apparent to many of us that a socio-economic system constructed to be productive and efficient to the exclusion of conservation and the preservation of its natural and human environment, is no longer an acceptable definition of what should be the socio-economic structure of a society.

Economic growth and bigness are no longer satisfactory criteria for judging a society. Quality of life rather than quantity of material goods must become the criterion for judging socio-economic structures. The notion that we must have some kind of a giant economic structure turning out products that are to be wasted and consumed infinitely has been the source of the continuing exploitation of natural resources. The consequence has been that we are continually dumping "junk" into the world and charging people for it. We must begin to design and to think about social and economic programs that will promote economic processes that are no longer primarily exploitative. We must create an economy that enhances the environment in the process of rendering a progressive outcome. What does all of this mean?

The difference between an industrial social context in which productivity of goods and their consumption is central, and a stable state economy that returns resources to the environment in order to get resources from it, might be the beginning of such thought and design. Such an economy produces that which is needed for survival while at the same time preserving the environment. Perhaps this is a simple, too simple, example of the kind of socio-economic restructuring that must be done, but it appears to illustrate the kind of change that may facilitate our survival.

It is entirely conceivable that there are countries that have greater potential than other countries for being able to produce foodstuffs and the products necessary to clothe and house the world's population. It is also possible that other societies are more capable of producing the goods, tools, and industrial products necessary for human survival. Simply stated, we should maximize the kinds of economic capabilities of the various countries of our world rather than assuming that each country must produce and survive on its own. We need to take advantage of the economic strengths of various countries that have capability, while at the same time providing for those countries which cannot presently produce the technology required for world development. We need to think of ourselves as a world community facing ultimate destruction unless we begin to construct and to distribute economic and social priorities in such a way as to take advantage of existing economic and social capabilities throughout the world. We are not, nor can we be, isolated from the problems of the world. Our human needs for survival are interdependent, whether nations are or not.

We must begin to develop social and political programs that, rather than subsidizing the construction of military hardware and technology, encourage the production of goods required for international survival. We must change the value system in our society that equates goodness with bigness, and begin to think in terms of life styles and values that promote individual problem solving through non-exploitative social and economic programs. Progress must be equated with the quality of life rather than with the quantity of material produced.

Finally, we can turn to the third major problem—international relations in our present and future world. I do not think that a great deal of reflection is required to say that the continuation of our international relations around the premise that we must defend ourselves rather than promote cooperation toward human survival must be changed. We must begin to detach ourselves from the political ideologies that have previously dominated our foreign policy. We must see ourselves no longer as some kind of superior political Utopia to be imposed upon a "backward" and often unwilling world. We must understand that we are a part of a vast and totally interdependent structure. Such realization will bring about an ideology of survival rather than an ever escalating balance of terror. To conduct our international relations upon the assumption that we must constrain our enemies, and that we must be able to destroy the rest of the world in order to survive, invites the very consequences that such a policy seeks to avoid. Our fears, real or not, only encourage such fears in others— whether we speak of people or of nations.

We must understand that our survival is not dependent upon our ability to defend ourselves against other powers, but upon our ability to encourage and solicit the cooperation of those powers for the mutual survival of all. It is difficult to imagine individuals in society having purposeful lives when the vast majority of their experiences with their own government are associated with either the destruction or preparation for the destruction of people and environment. Such defensive policies breed personal alienation from society and its problems. What good does it do for individuals to solve their own difficult problems when the overwhelming problems of international warfare, world starvation, and planetary destruction loom to overshadow and to prevent such efforts?

It is such a cycle that prevents us from accomplishing any major social or individual changes. The ways in which each of these three major problems interrelate may now become all the more clear. The frustration and meaninglessness of the international scene work to further the same feelings about the possibilities for doing anything about our domestic socio-economic structure, a fact that makes individual changes less conceivable and less likely. How can one seriously consider committing his life and talent to the solutions of smaller problems when he is constantly overwhelmed by the realization that the world about him may collapse? An absurd international and national situation is a contribution to the absurd individual life style.

Now we can summarize where we have been, and then we may discuss some proposals for change in individual values and public policy. We have identified three major problems in post-industrial society. The first problem is the alienation of the individual from himself and his society. The second problem is the socio-economic structure oriented toward an expanding production-consumption cycle. The third problem is the competition of nations with one another to gain their own national interests. The solutions to these problems are clearly interdependent, but can be discussed separately.

To solve the problem of individual alienation from self and from society, we need to substitute purposeful life styles for bureaucratic roles. That is, we need to substitute life styles in which people are making choices and have enough power to bring about desired consequences in their lives rather than being dependent upon the conformity to role expectations for individual meaning. Alienation stems from the dependence upon social expectations for meaningful lives. To reduce these feelings of alienation, people must have the sense of competence and significance that derives from being able to make meaningful choices and from being able to act out the consequences of these choices. If people can come to accept themselves for what they are and can become rather than because they perform successfully the expectations of society, then they can reduce their reliance upon others and upon institutions as sources of meaning. To reduce this dependence is to become autonomous and whole, that is, less alienated.

If individuals become less dependent upon social and economic role expectations as the source of purpose in their lives, then we can expect to change such structures without threatening the meaning of individual lives in the society. In other words, to the extent that people are less dependent upon bureaucracies and large organizations for their "success" in life, they will be more likely to accept change.

To solve the problem of an expanding socio-economic cycle built upon ever increasing production and consumption will require that we construct an economy that is more oriented toward non-expansion, that is, a stable state economy. In other words, we must have an economy that is no longer evaluated by its ability to produce and consume efficiently, but that is evaluated by its ability to meet human needs while not exploiting the environment. We need an economy that meets individual needs rather than produces material goods that act as false gratifications of human needs. People consume and produce in order to gain status and more material goods, which are indicators of status. People do not need status—they need acceptance. As long as they seek status, they cannot gain acceptance. We must have an economy and social structure that gratifies human needs rather than uses people to serve the requirements of an expanding economy.

The solution to the problem of an international arena permeated by conflicting national interests lies in nations being able to conceptualize themselves as interdependent human need structures rather than as independent national interests competing for survival. We must see that it is in our mutual interest to cooperate for survival rather than to compete for national interests. Success in the competition for national interests can no longer be a criterion for a nation's foreign policy. Foreign policy must begin to facilitate the mutual cooperation of countries, regardless of their historical or ideological differences. We must have the cooperation of other nations in order to bring about our own survival. Our problems of survival are based in the interdependency of needs of all people in the world. We cannot solve our own problems without other nations solving them with us. Overpopulation, ecological disintegration, and arms races are not problems that one nation can solve. The solutions and the mechanisms to bring about solutions must be based on international cooperation or they will not be successful. We cannot solve our overpopulation problem as long as the rest of the world ignores their contribution to the problem.

If these are the problems and some alternative goals for solving them, then how do we get from where we are to where we should be? We have said that politics is the way that people control and are controlled as they solve problems such as we have just discussed. Further, we recognized that, given the model of politics presented in this book, there are two major points of access to the politics of the society to bring about change. First, we must be able to create, organize, and use power to affect political elites in such a way that they are more likely to bring about the proper solutions. Second, we must begin to change individual values in this society so that people are more likely to accept the kinds of changes required for our survival. The final question is, What kinds of proposals should we be trying to influence political elites and people in society to accept? This last section is my attempt at least to illustrate the kinds of proposals that may bring about the necessary changes for social survival.

SOME PROPOSALS FOR ADAPTIVE CHANGE IN POST-INDUSTRIAL SOCIETY

My purpose here is not to describe any particular proposal for social change, but instead, to illustrate the kind of thinking that seems necessary if we are to have personal and public adaptations to solve the problem.

We can begin by thinking about the institution of the family in our society. It seems to me that we have to reconceptualize the notion of the family so that it no longer means an institution for raising children, nor does it mean an institution to provide economic security, nor even does it mean an institution for inculcating social expectations and values. The family is going to have to become a type of relationship among people in which they can gain self-acceptance and support for experimenting with what they are and want to be. The family cannot be something that disintegrates when the child reaches adulthood. The family must be a continuing series of human relationships that the person has available from birth to death, a series of situational relationships in which the person can have the acceptance of others for what he is and not for what he does. It must be a series of relationships that permit the individual to be accepted and supported, regardless of his success in performing up to social expectations. We must learn that such supportive families need not be confined to the family that we come from or the one that we marry into and form. But there may be many different "families" developed in a variety of situations that the individual confronts throughout his life. In this mobile society, it does not make sense to think of the family as something that one leaves behind. The family must be a set of relationships that we are immediately and continually involved in. Such a series of families that the individual may have are not permanent institutions but are situational relationships that he enters and leaves as his wants and needs change. The commitment in these families is to accepting and helping others grow, and growth often means that the individual must leave the family. Relationships must not be measured in terms of the length of commitment, but in terms of the kind of relationship that exists, no matter how long it exists.

We also need to rethink the educational process. We have thought of education in our society as being basically training to perform a role in the occupational structure. We must change this value. We must begin to educate people not for productive jobs, but for life styles that involve responsible action to solve personal and social problems. It seems to me that the consequence of teaching young people the personal value of being able to cope adequately and competently with complex personal and social problems is a higher value than merely being able to produce for social rewards or for financial gain.

Schools, colleges, and universities must be reconceptualized as involving situations in which people are given responsibility to act out choices. Such choices may result in both successes and failures for the student. Education must be a process of experimenting to find oneself and a compatible life style. Such experimentation cannot be evaluated by others, since its impact is upon the individual, and not upon producing an individual who meets certain social expectations.

Since our educational process is deeply engrained in this society, change is most likely to come about by the creation of alternative educational processes rather than by changing existing ones. Such proposals as the voucher system, in which students are subsidized by government so that they can choose a particular kind of educational experience, may be a step in this direction. If we cannot change existing institutions, we must create and expand alternatives so that we are no longer dependent upon existing institutions.

We must begin to understand our economy as one that not only provides material goods for our survival, but as one that also is expected to provide human services for human needs. It may be feasible to continue our mass production and consumption patterns for those material goods required for survival. But it is also feasible to begin to decentralize that part of our economy that has to do with providing for other human needs such as public health, human welfare, and education. Those material goods that are most efficiently produced by centralized and extremely large corporations will continue, and hopefully will be used to help supply material needs for other people in the world. But we must not have an economy totally dependent upon such material productivity. We should move toward a more balanced economy, one which provides material goods by continually centralizing the production of such goods into a larger corporation structure, but one which moves to decentralize and to create an ever larger portion of the economy that is community based and that serves human needs other than material. Such human services could be located at the local level rather than becoming a vast impersonal bureaucracy.

We also need to consider the problem of converting our present socio-economic structure to different forms. Perhaps here we need to consider government subsidy of people in order for them to make the individual changes in their life styles required to convert our total economy. We should have a program financed in much the same way as social security is presently funded, a program to provide each individual at least four years in his working life as paid time off from his normal occupational role. People could use this time off to return to the colleges and universities to be re-educated, to experiment with different life styles and to change their values, interests, and vocation. People should have this opportunity to change without being penalized by financial insecurity and loss of status.

Finally, we need to reconceptualize our foreign policy so that we are no longer evaluating our success in terms of national alliances that allow us to defend against our enemies. We must have policy evaluated in terms of how successful we are in gaining the mutual cooperation of nations in the solution of the interdependent problem of world survival. The problems of overpopulation and a spoiled environment are not confined to national boundaries, nor are the solutions to such problems. We should distribute our foreign aid to countries on the basis of their contributions to the solution of such problems, and on the basis of their agreement for mutual cooperation rather than the basis of their hypocritical acceptance of our particular ideological beliefs. We must promote mutual cooperation rather than promote our national interests.

These proposals are not the final answers. Perhaps they will provoke in you the kind of criticism and thought that will lead eventually to more realistic proposals for change. The time is short. The problems are immense. We must begin now.